SO-BEZ-469

The Complete Guide to Passing Your Real Estate Sales License Exam On the First Attempt

Everything You Need to Know Explained Simply

Revised 2nd Edition

Ken Lambert

Updated and Revised by Michael C. Cavallaro

THE COMPLETE GUIDE TO PASSING YOUR REAL ESTATE SALES LICENSE EXAM ON THE FIRST ATTEMPT: EVERYTHING YOU NEED TO KNOW EXPLAINED SIMPLY REVISED 2ND EDITION

Copyright © 2016 Atlantic Publishing Group, Inc.
1405 SW 6th Avenue • Ocala, Florida 34471 • Phone 800-814-1132 • Fax 352-622-1875
Web site: www.atlantic-pub.com • E-mail: sales@atlantic-pub.com
SAN Number: 268-1250

Library of Congress Cataloging-in-Publication Data

Names: Cavallaro, Michael J., author. I Lambert, Ken, 1974- The complete
  guide to passing your real estate sales license exam on the first attempt.
Title: The complete guide to passing your real estate sales license exam on
  the first attempt : everything you need to know explained simply revised /
  by Michael J. Cavallaro.
Description: Revised 2nd Edition. I Ocala : Atlantic Publishing Group, Inc.,
  2016. I Revised edition of The complete guide to passing your real estate
  sales license exam on the first attempt, 2009. I Includes bibliographical references.
Identifiers: LCCN 2016005670 (print) I LCCN 2016007078 (ebook) I ISBN
  9781620230619 (alk. paper) I ISBN 1620230615 (alk. paper) I ISBN
  9781620230770 ()
Subjects: LCSH: Real estate agents--Licenses--United States--Examinations,
  questions, etc. I Real estate business--Licenses--United
  States--Examinations, questions, etc. I Real property--United
  States--Examinations, questions, etc.
Classification: LCC HD278 .C38 2016 (print) I LCC HD278 (ebook) I DDC
  333.33076--dc23
LC record available at http://lccn.loc.gov/2016005670

Printed on Recycled Paper

Printed in the United States

Reduce. Reuse.
RECYCLE.

A decade ago, Atlantic Publishing signed the Green Press Initiative. These guidelines promote environmentally friendly practices, such as using recycled stock and vegetable-based inks, avoiding waste, choosing energy-efficient resources, and promoting a no-pulping policy. We now use 100-percent recycled stock on all our books. The results: in one year, switching to post-consumer recycled stock saved 24 mature trees, 5,000 gallons of water, the equivalent of the total energy used for one home in a year, and the equivalent of the greenhouse gases from one car driven for a year.

Over the years, we have adopted a number of dogs from rescues and shelters. First there was Bear and after he passed, Ginger and Scout. Now, we have Kira, another rescue. They have brought immense joy and love not just into our lives, but into the lives of all who met them.

We want you to know a portion of the profits of this book will be donated in Bear, Ginger and Scout's memory to local animal shelters, parks, conservation organizations, and other individuals and nonprofit organizations in need of assistance.

– Douglas & Sherri Brown,
President & Vice-President of Atlantic Publishing

Disclaimer

The material in this book is provided for informational purposes and as a general guide to passing the real estate sales license exam. Basic definitions of laws are provided according to the status of the laws at the time of printing; be sure to check for a change or update in laws.

Table of Contents

Preface **11**

History Behind Licensing 11

A profession is born *12*

Chapter 1: Preparing for Your Exam **15**

Understanding Licensing Requirements 15

Examinations 16

State Questions 17

Testing Formats 18

Real Estate Agent vs. Broker 19

What Is a REALTOR®? 20

What to Take to Your Exam 20

Preparing for the Exam 21

Tips to Manage Test Anxiety 22

Test-Taking Strategies 23

Arriving at the Exam 24

Mastering the Real Estate Exam 25

Food and water *25*

Follow directions *25*

Read every word *25*

Keep moving *26*

Use scrap paper to its full advantage *26*

Do not rush *26*

Learn the process of elimination *26*

Avoid overanalyzing..*27*

Change answers..*27*

Be prepared for math questions..*27*

Cramming...*27*

Case Study: Distractions..28

Chapter 2: Real Estate Practices and Principles............................ 29

Real vs. Personal Property...29

Real property's physical characteristics...............................*32*

Real property's economic characteristics.............................*32*

Property (or legal) rights..*33*

Land descriptions..*34*

Contracts and Deeds...35

General contract classifications and elements.....................*36*

Unenforceable contracts, termination of offer, and valid contracts...........*38*

Purchase and sale agreements..*39*

Miscellaneous P&S Agreement concepts and terms...............*53*

Deeds..54

Types of deeds...*54*

Key elements of a deed...*57*

Other important deed and title terms................................*58*

Leases and Property Management..................................60

Freehold and non-freehold estates......................................*60*

Types of leasehold estates (or "tenancies").........................*61*

Types of leases...*61*

Obligations of the lessor and lessee....................................*62*

Lease options...*63*

Assignment vs. sublease..*64*

Other lease terms and considerations.................................*64*

Property management basics...*65*

Real Estate Brokerage...66

Broker-related terms and types of agencies........................*66*

Agent's professional responsibilities and strategies............*69*

The Multiple Listing Service (MLS)...................................*70*

Marketing strategies and basics..*70*

Land development and building construction *72*

Property income analysis.. *73*

Case Study: Being Licensed in Multiple States 74

Case Study: Taking the Exam Seriously 75

Chapter 3: Real Estate Law.. **77**

Real Estate Law and Regulations by State 77

Basics of License Law... 79

Licensing requirements.. *80*

Typical laws and statutes *80*

Contracts and Legal Documents.. 82

Destruction of property between P&S Agreement signing and closing...... *86*

Federal Fair Housing Law 87

Key provisions of the FHA *87*

Housing not covered by the FHA... *88*

Enforcement and fines of the FHA *89*

Truth In Lending Act ("Regulation Z") 89

Early and final Regulation Z disclosure requirements.................... *90*

Disclosure requirements for ARM loans *91*

Right of rescission.. *92*

Advertising disclosure requirements *92*

Property Disclosures and Transferring Ownership....................... 93

Chapter 4: Real Estate Finance (Mortgages)...................................... **97**

Mortgage Terminology.. 99

Taxes.. 109

Real Estate Settlement and Procedures Act (RESPA)................. 110

Controlled Business Arrangement (CBA)..................................... *110*

Computerized Loan Origination (CLO) *111*

HUD-1 — RESPA Uniform Settlement Statement...................... *112*

The Loan Process... 116

Step one: find out how much you can borrow *116*

Step two: select the right loan program *118*

Step three: apply for a loan *119*

Step four: begin loan processing.. *121*

Step five: close your loan *121*

Mortgage application checklist *121*

Conventional mortgage information & techniques *124*

Prime *124*

Subprime *124*

Nonprime *125*

The secondary market *126*

Special Financing Agreements 126

Condominiums *126*

Condotels *127*

Half-share and quarter-share mortgage *127*

Real Estate Investment Trusts (REITs) *127*

Credit Unions *127*

USDA Rural Housing Service *128*

Mobile homes/manufactured homes *128*

Private lending ("hard money") *128*

Bridge (or blanket) loan *129*

Land contracts *129*

Case Study: Dealing with Referral Partners 129

Case Study: Real Estate & Affordable Housing Law 131

Chapter 5: Real Estate Appraisal **135**

When an Appraisal is Needed 138

Loans/mortgages *138*

Real estate taxes *138*

Insurance *138*

Estate settlement *138*

Condemnation *139*

Business acquisition *139*

Exchanges *139*

Value Elements 139

Influences and Variables to Value 140

The Appraisal Process 142

Market approach *143*

Income approach *144*

Cost approach..*145*

Case Study: Being Cautious About Home Valuations 146

Chapter 6: Math Review for the Real Estate Professional 149

Decimals..149

Addition of decimals *150*

Subtraction of decimals *150*

Multiplication of decimals...*150*

Division of decimals..*151*

Fractions..152

Addition of fractions *152*

Subtraction of fractions *153*

Multiplication of fractions...*154*

Division of fractions..*155*

Percentages 155

Percent to decimal..*156*

Decimal to percent...*156*

Percent to fraction..*157*

Fraction to percent...*157*

Decimal to fraction...*157*

Fraction to decimal...*158*

Measurement of Distance, Area, and Volume 158

Area..*159*

Acreage *162*

Volume *162*

Perimeter *165*

Formulas and Formula Aids...166

Other Math Notes and Useful Terms 168

Interest...*168*

Amortization...*168*

Profit & Loss *169*

Investment *169*

Rate of Return *169*

Net Income...*169*

Taxation *170*

Proration & Settlement *171*

Depreciation.. *176*

Answer Key: 177

Chapter 7: Practice Tests and Answer Keys **179**

National Practice Exam #1 179

National Practice Exam #2 204

Answer Key for Practice Exam #1 230

Answer Key for Practice Exam #2 235

Case Study: Pre-Exam and Course Options 241

Case Study: The Exam & Niche Real Estate 242

Chapter 8: Decreasing Anxiety and Maintaining Positive Attitude **243**

Practical Advice on Being and Staying Positive: 244

Words of Wisdom 245

Case Study: Dealing with Emotions Before the Exam 248

Conclusion **253**

Glossary **255**

Appendix A: Pre-Approval Letter **369**

Appendix B: State-by-State Guidelines for the Real Estate Agent Exam **371**

Appendix C: State Real Estate Commissions & Bureaus **373**

Appendix D: Uniform Appraisal Report **381**

Appendix E: Sample Good Faith Estimate **389**

Appendix F: Acronyms **393**

Bibliography **397**

Index **399**

ou have made the decision to become a licensed real estate professional. Congratulations! Real estate is an exciting and rewarding career choice; preparing for the licensing exam is your first step toward reaching your goals.

All 50 states and the District of Columbia require that salespersons obtain their license before practicing. The most important fact to understand is that a real estate license is governed by your individual state's laws and regulations.

History Behind Licensing

When the colonists from England settled in America, many experienced a less-restrictive version of the feudal system in which the English monarchy owned all of the land. The king divided it into parcels known as feuds, and he gave this land to the lords who remained in the monarchy's service. In turn, these lords subleased parts of the land to their own subjects; thus the term "landlord" was born. Over time, the monarchy loosened its grip on the rights to property, but it still remained restrictive.

By the time of the Revolutionary War, the colonists shook off the feudal system and instead pursued the allodial system, which allowed individuals to own the land. Thus, the "American Dream" was born. The United States Constitution and subsequent Bill of Rights further solidified the individual's right to own property. These important documents became the foundation of later licensing laws and regulations that govern today's real estate profession.

A profession is born

Early in our nation's history, people lived in small communities and people knew when property was transferred. Even when pioneers moved to new and unexplored regions, they became owners of the property by living and working on it. By the late 1800s, American society had changed enormously — the population had grown considerably and people moved to find new opportunities. As a result, more real estate was bought and sold, but now the buyers and sellers did not know one another, so they needed a person they could trust to handle the transaction. They relied on a trusted agent, usually a lawyer or other professional, who also knew the property. Eventually, a distinct real estate profession emerged.

In the United States, modern real estate law took shape as the country expanded westward in the late nineteenth century, starting in 1862 with the Homestead Act. This allowed private ownership of U.S. land in exchange for improving and developing the land for at least five years. The U.S. government distributed more than 300 million acres of public property to private landowners through the Homestead Act, creating the basis for the real estate market.

As the United States began to develop the protection of property against the state, the Federal level responded with the passage of the Fourteenth Amendment in 1868, which prohibited any state from depriving citizen property without due process of law. Licensing only began in the early 1900s, which is a relatively short time period when taken from a historical perspective.

How did the real estate profession and licensing of its agents begin? Well, it all started before the colonists came to America. In other words, it started in England. Our way of practicing real estate heralds back to English law and the king's ways.

In 1908, the National Association of REALTORS® (NAR), a trade group of the real estate industry, was founded to help set standards of conduct and to increase public confidence in the profession. By 1963, all 50 states and the District of Columbia required salespeople and brokers to be licensed, lending further credibility to the vocation. *(By 1940, all states at that time required licensing; Alaska and Hawaii were not yet states.)*

Although the real estate market took a severe downturn in the mid-2000s, the market has since rebounded. In 2014, real estate construction alone contributed to nearly $1.1 trillion, more than 6.1 percent to the nation's economic output as measured by Gross Domestic Product.

Although this is a brief history, it will help you realize that you are embarking on a noble and rewarding profession. Remember: a real estate license is based on the laws of the United States Constitution, the Bill of Rights, subsequent federal laws, and your state's individual laws and regulations.

Now that you know a portion of real estate history, you can begin the first step in your career by learning how to prepare for your examination.

Preparing for Your Exam

he latest findings show that less than half (44 percent) of those who take the real estate licensing examination pass the test the first time. Do not let those statistics alarm you. You are already heading in the right direction by purchasing this book and beginning the process of preparing.

How do you prepare for your real estate licensing test? The first step is to find out what your home state's licensing requirements are, because every state is different. Listed at the end of this book within the Appendix are the governing agencies for all 50 states.

Understanding Licensing Requirements

All states require that real estate salespeople are licensed to practice. Each state is governed by its own real estate law to award licenses. Every state has its own education requirements, methods of examination, test versions, age requirements, citizenship, application procedures, and criminal background checks. For example, some states will require you to have pre-licensing courses and some states will allow you to take the examination after you register — no pre-licensing courses required.

Examinations

Every state has its own version of the examination. States either create their own tests or contract with one of the four standardized testing services. The services are:

- Applied Measurement Professionals
- Prometric
- Pearson Vue
- Psychological Services, Inc.

Contact these agencies directly if your state uses one of these companies to obtain an information packet on the exam. Below is the contact information for these companies.

Applied Measurement Professionals
18000 W. 105th Street
Olathe, KS 66061-7543
www.goamp.com

Prometric
Canton Crossing
1501 South Clinton Street
Baltimore, MD 21224
866-PROMETRIC (776-6387)
443-455-8000
www.prometric.com

Pearson Vue
Three Bala Plaza West, Suite 300
Bala Cynwyd, PA 19004
http://home.pearsonvue.com

Psychological Services, Inc.

3210 East Tropicana

Las Vegas, NV 89121

800-733-9267

https://candidate.psiexams.com

Regardless of whether your state contracts with a testing service or creates its own examination, the real estate topics and information you need to study are basically the same. The difference among the tests is how many questions are given for each topic. Keep in mind that you will also need to know your state's specific real estate laws to successfully pass your licensing examination.

Depending on your state, the questions might be interspersed throughout your examination or on the second portion of the examination. Get in contact with your state to find out what type of test you are required to take. If your state is contracted with one of these testing companies, call them to receive their information. That way you are sure to have the latest up-to-date materials.

Keep in mind that if you live in a state where you are required to take a pre-licensing course, your instructors will most likely know this information and will be able to guide you. Still be sure to call your state to fill in any information your instructors do not have.

State Questions

When you contact your state, here is a set of questions for you to ask to make sure you receive all information pertinent to passing your state-specific examination:

- What are the requirements to become a licensed real estate agent in my state?
- Which exam is given in my state?
- What topics are covered on the exam?
- How much does the test cost?

- How do I register for the exam?
- How much time am I given to take the exam?
- How is the exam scored?
- What is the passing score?
- Am I penalized for wrong answers?
- Is the exam on a computer or is it handwritten?
- What am I allowed to bring with me when I take the test?
- How do I make arrangements for special needs? (for example, handicapped accessibility or medical needs)
- Where and when is the exam given?
- If allowed, what type of calculator may I use?
- When do I receive my score?
- What are the state-specific topics covered on the exam?
- What is the format of the test? Multiple-choice? True/False? Fill-in-the blank? Essay?
- Is there anything else I need to know?

Testing Formats

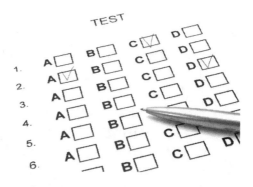

There are significant differences in the states' licensing exams. Some states have long examinations and some states have short ones, but the purpose behind all examinations remains the same: to test your knowledge and measure your understanding of real estate principles. The test is broken into two parts: the first section is general in nature and the second part is state-specific, covering your state's license laws.

The examination can have a variety of formats including multiple-choice, true or false, fill-in-the-blank, and short-answer questions. However, most states administer the multiple-choice exams exclusively.

All tests are timed. The time allotment is determined by the state, which can run anywhere between three to five hours. Do not let the timing alarm you. Later, you will learn how to master the time on your examination.

Another variation among the states is what constitutes as a passing score. Also, some states may penalize you for a wrong answer. If not, then it will become important for you to guess at the answer. In these cases, a blank answer is always a wrong answer. Later, we will discuss test-taking strategies such as how to guess through the process of elimination.

As you can see, every state has different examinations and processes. However, the key to passing your real estate examination will be to study the materials and master them in order to pass whichever type of test you are required to take.

Real Estate Agent vs. Broker

All states have at least two license levels: one for the real estate agent (salesperson) and one for the broker. The difference between these two designations is based on a legal definition, which varies by state law.

The difference between a real estate agent and a broker is contingent upon level of experience and education. For example, most states require you to become a licensed salesperson first and practice in this area before you are allowed to become a broker. Most states also require a broker to have additional educational and professional development courses before he or she can sit for the broker license.

Some real estate agents may add a consultant or associate title to their name, or they might refer to themselves as sub-agents. Although brokers typically have more education and training than agents, some states consider a broker's license an entry-level position in a real estate career. But in most cases, brokers can either work for themselves or hire agents to work for them.

An associate broker is someone who works for a brokerage firm and has the advantage of access to a vaster real estate network. However, an associate broker has to pay a fee to join the brokerage firm or earn commission on their transactions.

What Is a REALTOR®?

A REALTOR® is a professional designation bestowed on the licensed agent by the NAR for membership in the group. A REALTOR® must abide by a strict code of ethics and is committed to the real estate profession through treating all parties in the transaction honestly and fairly and by maintaining high education standards.

Not all licensed agents are REALTORS®, but every REALTOR® is a licensed agent. This is not to say that if you are not a member of the NAR that you do not have ethics, because all licensed agents must abide by certain standards. However, this designation is over and above the existing requirements, and some sponsoring brokers require their agents to become a member of this professional trade group. For additional information about this designation, visit **www.realtor.org**. To find out more information on your state's licensing requirements, go to the list of state bureaus and commissions in the appendix or visit a portal like the one offered by Mortgage Daily News (**www.mortgagenewsdaily.com/real_estate_license**).

What to Take to Your Exam

Once you know your state requirements, have diligently studied the information in this book, and know your individual state laws, it will be time to register for the exam. Procedures vary from state to state on how to register, so make sure you read and follow them carefully. For example, some states require a broker to sign your application form. Generally, you must send in an application and a fee to take the test. Your state will then send back an entry permit into the examination. The information will include where and when you will be taking the exam. If there is an error, make sure you contact your state agency immediately. The same holds true if you have any additional questions.

Verify with your state agency what is allowed into your test-taking area. Find out all procedures so you are as well prepared as possible, and also remember to find out if you are allowed to use a calculator in the exam. If so, find out what type of calculator is permitted. Graphing calculators, smartphones, and tablets are often restricted. Verify this information with your state agency. Also, check to see if you can bring additional batteries with you, or better yet, put new ones in before the exam.

Preparing for the Exam

The best way to prepare for the exam is to study. You cannot go into a real estate exam, even with taking the pre-licensing courses, and expect to pass the exam without spending some earnest time studying. The tests are too difficult, and some questions are designed to confuse you. The examinations are to see how well you understand the many facets of the real estate profession. You must prepare, study hard and master the material.

The best way to start studying is to make a plan. It is a good idea to think about how much time you actually need to study before registering for the exam. Allowing too much time can be detrimental, because you might not devote enough effort if you think you have plenty of time. You may start cramming for the exam just to meet your test date. On the other hand, not allowing enough study time will result in rushing and cramming. Do you need 30 days, 45 days, or can you master the materials in 10 days? Determining how much time you may need is a personal choice.

One of the keys to successfully passing your real estate test will be to take the exam when you are at your peak knowledge performance. In other words, when you know as much as you can know about all the topics and feel confident in your ability, take the exam. If you do not take the test soon after reaching this peak, you may start forgetting the information.

When you find out the dates and times the exam is given, make a plan on how you are going to fit study time into your daily calendar. Most experts agree that you should study every day for at least 20 minutes to avoid feeling overwhelmed.

Tips to Manage Test Anxiety

The number one tip to manage test anxiety is to be prepared. Knowing your subject will help you feel confident and in control of the situation. Also, taking the practice exams in this book will help you to know what to expect from the test. When you know your information and what to expect, you will feel empowered, and this will help you to pass the exam.

Managing how you think and feel internally is another component of being successful on the real estate examination. Having a positive attitude really does make a difference and is a great way to manage test anxiety. Pay attention to your self-talk and do not let negative thoughts take control of your mind. Also, do not let others scare or discourage you by telling you how hard the examination is. Yes, the test is difficult, but you must believe in yourself and your ability to pass. Say, "I will pass this test." You can do it — and on your first try.

Being confident in your ability is related to a positive attitude. However, it remains a little different because self-confidence also comes from knowing your material and being prepared for the exam. In other words, you are self-confident because you have mastered the subject. Picture yourself in your future real estate career — speaking at listing presentations, showing homes, and making sales. Practicing future success in your mind will help boost your self-confidence and keep you motivated to study.

Studies show that physical activity helps focus your mind and increases certain chemicals in the brain known to improve your mood. It also has a relaxing effect, which is important with the additional stress associated with preparing for your test. If you are currently on an exercise schedule, do not quit now; keep it up. If you are new to exercising or have not been doing it, now is a good time to add some physical activity to your day. Start out slowly, with just 10 minutes of walking per day. Gradually increase your time until you reach 30 minutes per day. It may help you lose those extra five pounds, as well as help you pass your real estate licensing test.

It is natural to be nervous about the upcoming test. Use that nervousness to your advantage by focusing your mind and remaining vigilant.

If you are extremely intimidated by the test and feel it is impairing your performance, consider seeking professional help to overcome your fears. There are many psychologists, career coaches, and life coaches who should be able to assist you.

Test-Taking Strategies

A few days before the exam, make a trial run to the location of the examination. If there are traffic delays or construction projects that interfere with your drive, you will want to know about those challenges before the examination day. If possible, make the drive at the exact time you will on test day, so you will know what it will be like. If you need to make changes to your directions, make them before test day. If you have Bluetooth, a smartphone, or a tablet, consider using an app to get traffic conditions ahead of time.

Try not to study the day or night before the exam. By this time, you should have adequately prepared so that you do not need another full day of studying. Instead, relax, see a movie, or take a bike ride with your family or friends. Try to do something that you enjoy to take your mind off of the exam. If you must study, review your weak areas or trouble spots to help you gain additional confidence.

The night before the exam, make sure you set out all materials that you need to take with you the next day. You will need the following items, including anything else your state agency instructs you to bring:

- Registration/Entrance ticket to the exam
- Calculator
- Photo ID (you may need two forms)
- No. 2 pencils
- Watch
- Sweater or jacket (you never know the temperature in the exam room)

You should also get plenty of sleep the night before the exam. A well-rested mind and body will boost your stamina for the test. Allow enough time in the morning for a good breakfast of both carbohydrates and proteins. Studies show that this improves your brain performance. Your mom was right — eat your breakfast!

Arriving at the Exam

You will want to arrive to your test site at least 30 minutes in advance of the exam. Arriving early assures that you will have adequate time to use the restroom, compose yourself, and get to know and understand the building set-up. Take some deep breaths, tell yourself that you will pass, and head into the examination room.

Make sure you understand all procedures for the examination. If you are taking the exam on a computer, you will probably be given a practice session first to make sure you understand how to operate everything. If you have any questions, ask the test facilitator.

Mastering the Real Estate Exam

The key to mastering the licensing test is time management. In order to complete all questions in the allotted time, you should be through 50 percent of the questions when half of the time has expired. If you are behind, pick up the pace. Remember, a skipped question is a wrong answer and will affect your overall grade.

Here are other important tips for successfully passing the licensing exam.

Food and water

To prepare for a lengthy exam like the real estate license exam, you should be nourished. In order to produce mentally, you need to fuel the brain. Being aware of the helpful and the hurtful foods will be beneficial in making menu choices. The following foods are natural concentration enhancers for the brain: dark chocolate, blueberries, salmon, green tea, beats, bananas, spinach, and eggs (**www.health.com**). Also, be sure to drink plenty of water, and, if allowed, bring a water bottle into the testing room. Continuous hydration is advantageous while taking a lengthy exam. This preparation step is easily overlooked but will pay off in the long run, because having a grumbling stomach is not the way to get through an exam.

Follow directions

It sounds simple, but you want to read over all the directions in each section to make sure that you understand them. If you skip over the directions or read them too quickly, you stand the chance of picking the wrong answers. Watch out for trick questions.

Read every word

Make sure you read every word in every question and answer, but read them quickly. It is extremely important that you keep the correct pace but not at the expense of missing key elements of the questions. Pay attention to what you are reading so you can pick the correct answer.

Keep moving

If you do not know the answer to a question, skip it and come back to it later. Make sure that you note which question you skipped so you know which question to return to. If you are allowed scrap paper, mark the question number on it. If you are taking the test on a computer, follow the directions on how to come back to skipped questions.

Use scrap paper to its full advantage

If you are allowed scrap paper, quickly jot down definitions and math formulas on it. When difficult questions or math problems come your way, you will be able to calmly work through them while referring to your notes.

Do not rush

Rushing leads to panic. Instead, work at a steady pace so you can remain calm throughout the test.

Learn the process of elimination

When you come to a question, and you are not sure of the answer, begin the process of elimination. Mark off the one or two answers that you know are wrong. Then, think through the answers that are left to choose the one that you feel answers the question best. If you cannot come to a conclusion, you have two options: skip the question and come back to it, or go ahead and guess (especially if you are pressed for time and there is no penalty for guessing). Your odds of guessing the correct answer improve when you have eliminated incorrect answers. You can also try this two-step strategy:

Step 1: Eliminate the most implausible answers first. Test makers usually built at least one obviously wrong answer into every multiple choice question, so look for that one first and eliminate it from consideration. Doing so will increase your odds of choosing the right answer every time. Some implausible answers may appear silly or don't relate to the question.

Step 2: Use your gut feeling to make a quick guess. Losing time on the test can cost you points if you don't finish on time and have left some easy questions unanswered. So in order to avoid dwelling too long on a difficult question, rely on your gut feeling.

Avoid overanalyzing

Generally, the first answer that comes to you is the correct one. Do not think too much about the question. Be comfortable with your ability. Part of the problem with overanalyzing is that you begin second-guessing yourself. Most instructors caution against second-guessing. When grading exams, more often than not, instructors see the correct answer erased and the wrong one filled in. Avoid the urge to overanalyze and second-guess. If you are well prepared, you will tend to recognize the correct answer immediately.

Change answers

This might seem like a contradiction to the last tip, but it is not. There will be times when it makes sense to change your answers. As you proceed through the test, one question might jog your memory or help clarify an earlier question. It is a good idea to go back and change your answer if you realize you made a mistake on a previous question.

Be prepared for math questions

Approximately 10 percent of the real estate exam is related to mathematics. Test-takers must master skills in arithmetic, geometry, algebra, and word problems. Chapter 6 will focus on how to solve sample math problems covered on the licensing exam.

Cramming

"Cramming" is when one vigorously studies immediately preceding the day of testing. This is not a suggested method of preparation. The day before, you should primarily be focused on preparing materials for the test and being sure you have enough gas in your car. These kinds of tasks should be done rather than spending numerous hours studying. However, skimming through and reviewing the more difficult concepts is time well spent. One should study in increments. The studying process should be planned in plenty of time and allow for unexpected occurrences.

You will be surprised at how much you know when taking the exam, so work through all questions at a steady and even pace. Skip questions you do not know or that will take more time to figure out, and come back to them after you have completed the easier questions. Just make sure that you do not incorrectly mark an answer because you skipped its corresponding question. Periodically check to make sure your question numbers and answer numbers are aligned properly.

CASE STUDY: DISTRACTIONS

Tamsyn C.
Public School Teacher, 12 years

It is important to avoid becoming distracted, which has happened to me while taking an exam. The seat I was assigned to was the last desk in the first row. The room had an adjoining door immediately to my left, and, unfortunately, I could hear the audio recording from the next exam room. A portion of this exam required test-takers to listen to a prerecorded paragraph and spell, punctuate and capitalize the excerpt correctly. The adjoining room began the recording about eight seconds after the class in which I was seated. This distraction nearly kept me from passing the four-hour exam.

Chapter 2

Real Estate Practices and Principles

*I*n order to pass the real estate license exam, be sure to read and master all of the chapters in this book. This chapter will cover the typical real estate practices and principles that are most important in succeeding as a real estate sales agent. The information presented herein is critical and should be used as a reference as you begin your new career journey.

Real vs. Personal Property

Real property is defined as the land plus all buildings and improvements (whatever is affixed) to the land — including all rights and benefits applicable. These rights will include *subsurface rights* (as in potential landowner, water rights, mining/mineral rights, or oil rights), but may or may not include *air rights*. Air rights would be described as the area directly above the property lines up into the atmosphere — such as where a plane would fly. Improvements would include all buildings and structures as well as utilities and other site and landscape improvements that make the property more appealing and useable. Note that the buildings do not have to be living space. Garages and sheds are also improvements.

Real property is further broken down into *corporeal* and *incorporeal.* Corporeal refers to all of the tangible rights such as building or utility improvements (items that you can touch and feel). Incorporeal property would be considered intangible and includes things like rights of way or easements.

For use throughout this book (and in the field), the words *real estate, real property,* and *realty* will be understood as synonymous.

Personal property is anything that is *not* real property, as listed above. This is also referred to as "personalty" or "chattel" and can include any moveable items such as lawnmowers, furniture, clothing, televisions, and the like. Personal property is anything that is not attached to or affixed to the real property (not being attached to the land itself or the buildings on the land). In a property transaction, items such as plumbing fixtures, cabinets, and doors are considered real property, as they are indeed attached to the home/property.

In some cases, there are discrepancies on what is truly real property, and any such clarification should be listed in writing within the Purchase and Sale Agreement. Items that are often argued about between buyers and sellers can be window treatments (drapes, curtains), chandeliers and refrigerators. Appliances such as washing machines and dryers can also be confusing and lead to problems during the transaction. Items such as stoves/ranges and dishwashers are nearly always considered real property as they are permanently piped, drained, and/or wired to the building (not merely plugged in like a refrigerator). A key aspect to determine whether an item is personal or real property is its portability.

Emblements (or *fructus industriales*) are also considered personal property. These are crops grown on a property by the physical efforts of the person living at the property.

Fixtures are one group of items that consistently become a matter of interpretation. Personal property that over time becomes real property is called a "fixture." A new owner buys a roll of carpet at a store. This is called personal property. But once that carpet is nailed in place in a wall-to-wall installation, that same carpet becomes part of the property, and is thus part of the real property. The manner of an item changing from real to personal property is called *severance*. An owner could do this by cutting down a tree in order to sell the firewood or bark mulch. More often than not, an item is changed from personal property to real property, as in the carpet example. Another example would be an owner buying a dishwasher and then installing the dishwasher in their kitchen.

In order to determine whether an item is a fixture or not, you must consider the following:

1. **Intent of the parties:** In the case of a 30-unit apartment building, one would expect the window air-conditioning units to remain with the property, but not in a single-family home.

2. **Method of annexation:** Can the fixture be easily removed, without a skilled professional/contractor, and without a large amount of time and effort?

3. **Agreement of the parties:** This should always be in writing, and should be listed and initialed as part of the Purchase and Sale Agreement.

A *trade fixture* is normally personal property that does not remain with the real estate during a transaction, because said fixture is specifically used for the tenant's (or former owner's) business purposes. An example would be display cases in a jewelry store. They are not affixed to the building, but they are used in a business manner. Trade fixtures are normally part of a commercial real estate transaction.

Real property's physical characteristics

Land is immobile: One cannot relocate a piece of land.

Land is indestructible: One can alter the surface or destroy the buildings upon the land, but the property or parcel itself will never go away.

Land is unique: When all factors are considered, absolutely no two parcels of land are identical. This is important when considering valuation of said property.

Real property's economic characteristics

Improvements: The things that are added to increase or change the use of the land, such as roads, utilities, or buildings.

Scarcity: Also known as typical supply and demand. As a specific type of property becomes less available, its value goes up. For instance, if a buyer is looking to purchase a four-family apartment building in a town that only has one such property, the fact that there is less direct competition in that town will mean that the value of the one four-family will be higher than normal.

Long-term investment: Real estate is considered a "fixed" entity or investment, because in many cases a property holding will be for decades. This is a key factor — especially in regard to financing and interest charges. The investor knows that after the entire mortgage debt is paid off (which could be 20 to 30 years), they will then own a property outright, which will have a concrete value at a later time. Historically, if a borrower achieved *equity of redemption,* it meant he or she has the right to reclaim his or her property once the debt secured by the mortgage has been discharged. The equity of redemption was the right to petition the courts of equity to compel the lender to transfer the property back to the borrower.

Location: Or, as the old real estate saying goes, "location, location, location." Of all the characteristics mentioned, it is clear that a property's exact location is the most important in determining value. Location can have the following attributes to consider: proximity to public transportation, zoning, school district, scenery, tax base and rate, community services, and scenery.

Property (or legal) rights

There are five key categories of legal rights that private ownership entails:

1. *Exclusion:* to limit others from entry as you choose
2. *Disposition:* to sell, transfer, or will as you desire
3. *Enjoyment:* to use without others infringing on your property rights
4. *Possession:* to hold and use or not use as granted by a lease
5. *Control:* to use at your own discretion (within the law)

However, there are the following limits to these legal rights. These generally include the *Rights of Other Persons*, as well as *Government Limits to Rights*.

Rights of Other Persons generally refers to the fact that one's neighbors have a right to *quiet enjoyment* of their own property. An example would be if you turned your stereo system up as loud as it could go, whether it be at 2 p.m. or 2 a.m., most likely that would infringe upon your neighbor's rights — and you would be in the wrong, legally. To know these rights, you might have to do some research on the area's noise ordinance.

The government also limits your property rights via the following five avenues:

1. *Escheat:* This is relatively uncommon, but if an owner dies without a will and without any known survivors to inherit the property, the state can then accept ownership. Under law, this is called *intestate succession.*

2. *Taxation:* Cities, towns, and counties finance their operations mostly through property taxes on residential properties. If an owner does not pay their taxes, it is possible for the town to seize the property. The city or town has the right to tax the property owner via "Ad Valorem Taxation."

3. *Building Code:* Any structures built on the land must be constructed in accordance with the applicable local or state building code. This code ensures that the building is built safely and is structurally sound. Many older buildings and homes were built before there were any building codes, and as such, their use to be occupied and used is called "grandfathered" use. However, if an addition or new work was to be done on said home, including plumbing and electrical work, all new work must be done in accordance with local building codes. The health code (involving water and sewage) is often part of the building department.

4. *Zoning Ordinance:* Also called zoning, this is a form and method of master community planning that is common in most regions. A town as a whole would not want a strip mall built in the middle of a 30-house residential subdivision, so a buyer would not be able to build this if it is in contradiction to the current zoning bylaws and district maps.

5. *Police Power:* Used to enforce the laws of the community, often based on a willful denial of a building code or zoning violation as described above.

Land descriptions

Especially pertaining to buildable, empty lots — listings of land and lots/parcels will often be described according to their characteristics, such as rolling, wooded (heavily, sparsely), steep-grade, flat, wetland, well-draining, pastureland, or farmland. Anything defined as a place where something exists or originates as a right to be held and located in law is called *a situs*.

Appraisers, as well as developers and real estate investors, will often need to analyze the specific attributes of the land parcel in order to obtain a relevant true market value. Often, a potential buyer will ask you, the real estate agent, the following questions:

- Has a perc (percolation) test been done?
- Is there an approved septic design?
- Is the lot on town water and/or sewer service?
- Is there a private well on site? Drilled or dug well?
- Have soil borings been completed?
- Have test pits been dug?
- Have wetlands onsite been marked and delineated?
- Is there ledge at or just below the surfaces?

These and other questions may come up, and if you do not know the specific answers, it is best to contact your broker or the seller directly. Do not guess or assume in any of these matters. It could result in legal ramifications for you.

Contracts and Deeds

Contracts: A contract is merely an agreement between two parties to do something. If one of the parties does not fulfill their end of the contract, legal action can be brought against them. A real estate Purchase and Sale Agreement or an Offer to Purchase form is a type of written contract and is a key to becoming a knowledgeable REALTOR®. Some examples and brief definitions in the real estate arena are:

Listing Agreement: A contract between a seller and a real estate firm to sell a property.

Purchase and Sale Agreement: A contract between a buyer and a seller to purchase a piece of property for some consideration (normally money).

Buyer Agency Agreement: A contract between a buyer and a real estate firm to assist the buyer in purchasing a property.

Lease: A contract between a landlord and a tenant agreeing to rent a property for a specified amount of money and time, under specific guidelines and restrictions.

Deed: A contract between grantor and grantee conveying title to property for some consideration — also referred to as a title deed.

Mortgage Note and Mortgage Deed: These two instruments will be needed any time there is financing that is required to purchase real estate. The mortgage note is a promissory note to pay, and the mortgage deed is a contract that transfers interest in the real estate to the bank or lender subject to the mortgagor repaying the loan in full.

Option: An agreement between two parties where one party has the right or option to do or not do something within a specified time.

Right of First Refusal: Similar to an option, but here a price is normally not specified. An example would be a tenant who has a right of first refusal to match any bona fide offer if the landlord plans to sell the property.

General contract classifications and elements

Note that it is not anticipated that you will master all contract terms or be able to draft tedious contracts or agreements. That is better left to the real estate attorneys that you will be working for. However, you should be versed in these generalities.

Expressed vs. Implied: An expressed contract is one that is very specific and usually in writing. A real estate contract must be an expressed contract. An implied contract is one where the specifics of each party's responsibilities are not noted, in writing or verbally.

Bilateral vs. Unilateral: Bilateral refers to the fact that each party must do something for the sake or gain of the other party. A purchase and sale agreement is a bilateral contract. A unilateral contract is one where one party agrees to do something if the other party does something, but the other party is under no obligation to perform said action. For example, if you post a $100 reward in the newspaper for lost property, the reward you offer is a unilateral contract because you are the only person who has taken any action in this contract and no other party is specifically responsible or obligated to find your lost property.

Executed vs. Executory: An executed contract is one where both parties have finished everything that each has agreed to do. In addition, an executed contract must be signed by both parties in compliance with standard legal practices. This is as opposed to an executory contract, where some or all of the items from one or both parties have not been completed at all or in full.

It is still a binding contract (assuming it has been properly signed by both parties), but there are terms which have not yet been met.

Consideration: There will be something of value exchanged for something of value. This does not always have to be in the form of cash/money, but it does usually take the form of a tangible item. Sometimes it could be a trade for another piece of real estate or a tangible asset like a sailboat or yacht. This can also be done in a manner in which the item given is not done at this exact contract time. For example, a buyer may state that he will pay the full listing price over the course of 10 years (an example of seller financing), or the buyer will let the seller have complete use of his Aruba timeshare for the next three years.

Offer and Acceptance: There must be complete agreement on all items, terms and pricing for a contract to be valid. The party making the offer (which is not always the buyer) is the *offeror*, and the person receiving the offer is the *offeree*. The accepted offer must be communicated back to the offeror in order for it to be a binding contract.

Competency: Both parties must be competent to enter into a legal agreement. Competency is a matter of age, mental status, ability, and emotional condition. In cases of the elderly who may be senile, often a guardian and/ or a power of attorney will be the one signing the documents on behalf of the actual party.

Consent: Consent, or agreement to the contract, must be under no duress or extreme measures to either party. It must be the party's free act out of their own free will.

Unenforceable contracts, termination of offer, and valid contracts

A contract is unenforceable in the following circumstances:

Statute of Limitations: There is a legal and specific time limit on most contracts, and all actions must be completed by that time frame or else the contract is null and void.

Laches: Similar to the statute of limitations, but here the time limit is not set specifically within the contract but is instead more general and is enforced upon a "reasonable" period of time.

Estoppel: If it was later determined to be a bill or charge established by error, the new owner cannot be held accountable for paying said written debt.

In real estate, many offers for a property will be presented and then will consequently not be accepted or the time limit may run out. Here are some other reasons for an offer to be terminated legally:

Death of Offeror: If the offeror dies before the offer is accepted and communicated back to him/her, the offer ceases.

Time Limit: As stated elsewhere herein, time is always of the essence in a real estate transaction.

Offer Revoked Prior to Acceptance: Remember that an offer is only valid when it is accepted (approved and signed by the seller) and this acceptance is communicated either verbally or in writing (usually via the real estate agent) back to the buyer. At any time during this time frame, which may be two or three days, the offeror/buyer can rescind his offer for any reason.

Acceptance: Once an offer is accepted fully and the offeror is made aware of this, the offer legally becomes a contract and is no longer an offer.

Counteroffer: Frequently in real estate there are negotiations, and the seller will often present a counteroffer. This new counteroffer will void any previous offers. Neither party is obligated to accept the terms of this new counteroffer.

We also must understand the difference between a valid contract and a void contract.

A *valid contract* is one that has a binding force on both parties, where all legal requirements have been met. A majority of contracts you will deal with are valid contracts.

However, *a void contract* is one where the terms cannot be binding due to a key technicality or circumstance. For instance, Mr. Jones may accept an offer on a property, but if Mr. Jones is not the legal owner of this property, this would then be deemed a void contract.

In addition, there is something called a *voidable contract*. This is when one party has the option to fully void the contract if he or she wishes.

Purchase and sale agreements

Probably the most important document you will encounter and work with is the Purchase and Sale Agreement. Please review the following terms and the sample P&S Agreement shown on the following pages. Note that our sample is from the State of New Hampshire, and your specific P&S form will vary slightly. However, all regions have the same basic information needed on their Purchase and Sale forms.

Sample "AS IS" Residential Contract For Sale and Purchase

"AS IS" Residential Contract For Sale And Purchase
THIS FORM HAS BEEN APPROVED BY THE FLORIDA REALTORS AND THE FLORIDA BAR

FloridaRealtors®

1* PARTIES:_____ ("Seller"),
2* and _____ ("Buyer"),
3 agree that Seller shall sell and Buyer shall buy the following described Real Property and Personal Property
4 (collectively "Property") pursuant to the terms and conditions of this AS IS Residential Contract For Sale And Purchase and
5 any riders and addenda ("Contract"):
6 **1. PROPERTY DESCRIPTION:**
7*   (a) Street address, city, zip:_____
8*   (b) Property is located in: _____ County, Florida. Real Property Tax ID No.:_____
9*   (c) Real Property: The legal description is_____
10
11
12   together with all existing improvements and fixtures, including built-in appliances, built-in furnishings and attached
13   wall-to-wall carpeting and flooring ("Real Property") unless specifically excluded in Paragraph 1(e) or by other terms
14   of this Contract.
15   (d) Personal Property: Unless excluded in Paragraph 1(e) or by other terms of this Contract, the following items which
16   are owned by Seller and existing on the Property as of the date of the initial offer are included in the purchase:
17   range(s)/oven(s), refrigerator(s), dishwasher(s), disposal, ceiling fan(s), intercom, light fixture(s), drapery rods and
18   draperies, blinds, window treatments, smoke detector(s), garage door opener(s), security gate and other access
19   devices, and storm shutters/panels ("Personal Property").
20*   Other Personal Property items included in this purchase are:_____
21
22   Personal Property is included in the Purchase Price, has no contributory value, and shall be left for the Buyer.
23*   (e) The following items are excluded from the purchase:_____
24

25   **PURCHASE PRICE AND CLOSING**
26* **2. PURCHASE PRICE** (U.S. currency):..$_____121500.00_____
27*   (a) Initial deposit to be held in escrow in the amount of **(checks subject to COLLECTION)** ....$____500.00____
28   The initial deposit made payable and delivered to "Escrow Agent" named below
29*   **(CHECK ONE):** (i) ☐ accompanies offer or (ii) ☒ is to be made within _____ (if left blank,
30   then 3) days after Effective Date. IF NEITHER BOX IS CHECKED, THEN OPTION (ii)
31   SHALL BE DEEMED SELECTED.
32*   Escrow Agent Information: Name: _____
33*   Address: _____
34*   Phone: _____ E-mail:_____ Fax:_____
35*   (b) Additional deposit to be delivered to Escrow Agent within _____ (if left blank, then 10)
36*   days after Effective Date..$_____
37   (All deposits paid or agreed to be paid, are collectively referred to as the "Deposit")
38*   (c) Financing: Express as a dollar amount or percentage ("Loan Amount") see Paragraph 8.............$____121500.00____
39*   (d) Other:_____.............$_____
40   (e) Balance to close (not including Buyer's closing costs, prepaids and prorations) by wire
41*   transfer or other **COLLECTED** funds..$_____0_____
42   **NOTE: For the definition of "COLLECTION" or "COLLECTED" see STANDARD S.**
43 **3. TIME FOR ACCEPTANCE OF OFFER AND COUNTER-OFFERS; EFFECTIVE DATE:**
44*   (a) If not signed by Buyer and Seller, and an executed copy delivered to all parties on or before _____
45*   _____, this offer shall be deemed withdrawn and the Deposit, if any, shall be returned to
46   Buyer. Unless otherwise stated, time for acceptance of any counter-offers shall be within 2 days after the day the
47   counter-offer is delivered.
48   (b) The effective date of this Contract shall be the date when the last one of the Buyer and Seller has signed or initialed
49   and delivered this offer or final counter-offer ("Effective Date").
50 **4. CLOSING DATE:** Unless modified by other provisions of this Contract, the closing of this transaction shall occur and
51   the closing documents required to be furnished by each party pursuant to this Contract shall be delivered ("Closing") on
52*   _____ ("Closing Date"), at the time established by the Closing Agent.
53 **5. EXTENSION OF CLOSING DATE:**
54   (a) If Closing funds from Buyer's lender(s) are not available at time of Closing due to Truth In Lending Act (TILA) notice
55   requirements, Closing shall be extended for such period necessary to satisfy TILA notice requirements, not to
56   exceed 7 days.

Buyer's Initials _____ _____   Page 1 of 11   Seller's Initials _____ _____
FloridaRealtors/FloridaBar-ASIS-2 Rev.8/13 © 2013 Florida Realtors® and The Florida Bar. All rights reserved.
Serial#: 079445-600140-1810218

forms simplicity

Sample "AS IS" Residential Contract For Sale and Purchase

57   (b) If extreme weather or other condition or event constituting "Force Majeure" (see STANDARD G) causes: (i)
58   disruption of utilities or other services essential for Closing or (ii) Hazard, Wind, Flood or Homeowners' insurance,
59   to become unavailable prior to Closing, Closing shall be extended a reasonable time up to 3 days after restoration
60   of utilities and other services essential to Closing and availability of applicable Hazard, Wind, Flood or
61   Homeowners' insurance. If restoration of such utilities or services and availability of insurance has not occurred
62*   within _____ (if left blank, then 14) days after Closing Date, then either party may terminate this Contract by
63   delivering written notice to the other party, and Buyer shall be refunded the Deposit, thereby releasing Buyer and
64   Seller from all further obligations under this Contract.

65 **6. OCCUPANCY AND POSSESSION:**
66   (a) Unless the box in Paragraph 6(b) is checked, Seller shall, at Closing, deliver occupancy and possession of the
67   Property to Buyer free of tenants, occupants and future tenancies. Also, at Closing, Seller shall have removed all
68   personal items and trash from the Property and shall deliver all keys, garage door openers, access devices and
69   codes, as applicable, to Buyer. If occupancy is to be delivered before Closing, Buyer assumes all risks of loss to the
70   Property from date of occupancy, shall be responsible and liable for maintenance from that date, and shall be
71   deemed to have accepted the Property in its existing condition as of time of taking occupancy.
72*   (b) ☐ **CHECK IF PROPERTY IS SUBJECT TO LEASE(S) OR OCCUPANCY AFTER CLOSING.** If Property is
73   subject to a lease(s) after Closing or is intended to be rented or occupied by third parties beyond Closing, the facts
74   and terms thereof shall be disclosed in writing by Seller to Buyer and copies of the written lease(s) shall be
75   delivered to Buyer, all within 5 days after Effective Date. If Buyer determines, in Buyer's sole discretion, that the
76   lease(s) or terms of occupancy are not acceptable to Buyer, Buyer may terminate this Contract by delivery of
77   written notice of such election to Seller within 5 days after receipt of the above items from Seller, and Buyer shall be
78   refunded the Deposit thereby releasing Buyer and Seller from all further obligations under this Contract. Estoppel
79   Letter(s) and Seller's affidavit shall be provided pursuant to STANDARD D. If Property is intended to be occupied
80   by Seller after Closing, see Rider U. POST-CLOSING OCCUPANCY BY SELLER.
81* **7. ASSIGNABILITY: (CHECK ONE):** Buyer ☐ may assign and thereby be released from any further liability under this
82*   Contract; ☐ may assign but not be released from liability under this Contract; or ☒ may not assign this Contract.

83 **FINANCING**

84 **8. FINANCING:**
85*   ☐ (a) Buyer will pay cash or may obtain a loan for the purchase of the Property. There is no financing contingency to
86   Buyer's obligation to close .
87*   ☒ (b) This Contract is contingent upon Buyer obtaining a written loan commitment for a ☐ conventional ☐ FHA ☐ VA
88*   or ☒ other ___USDA___ (describe) loan on the following terms within _____ (if left blank, then 30) days after
89*   Effective Date ("Loan Commitment Date") for **(CHECK ONE):** ☒ fixed, ☐ adjustable, ☐ fixed or adjustable rate loan in
90*   the Loan Amount (See Paragraph 2(c)), at an initial interest rate not to exceed _____ % (if left blank, then prevailing
91*   rate based upon Buyer's creditworthiness), and for a term of ___30___ (if left blank, then 30) years ("Financing").

92*   Buyer shall make mortgage loan application for the Financing within _____ (if left blank, then 5) days after Effective
93   Date and use good faith and diligent effort to obtain a written loan commitment for the Financing ("Loan Commitment")
94   and thereafter to close this Contract. Buyer shall keep Seller and Broker fully informed about the status of mortgage
95   loan application and Loan Commitment and authorizes Buyer's mortgage broker and Buyer's lender to disclose such
96   status and progress to Seller and Broker.

97
98   Upon Buyer's receipt of Loan Commitment, Buyer shall provide written notice of same to Seller. If Buyer does not
99   receive Loan Commitment by Loan Commitment Date, then thereafter either party may cancel this Contract up to the
100   **earlier of:**
101   (i.) Buyer's delivery of written notice to Seller that Buyer has either received Loan Commitment or elected to
102   waive the financing contingency of this Contract; or
103   (ii.) 7 days prior to Closing Date.

104   If either party timely cancels this Contract pursuant to this Paragraph 8 and Buyer is not in default under the terms of
105   this Contract, Buyer shall be refunded the Deposit thereby releasing Buyer and Seller from all further obligations under
106   this Contract. If neither party has timely canceled this Contract pursuant to this Paragraph 8, then this financing
107   contingency shall be deemed waived by Buyer.

108   If Buyer delivers written notice of receipt of Loan Commitment to Seller and this Contract does not thereafter close, the
109   Deposit shall be paid to Seller unless failure to close is due to: (1) Seller's default; (2) Property related conditions of the
110   Loan Commitment have not been met (except when such conditions are waived by other provisions of this Contract); (3)
111   appraisal of the Property obtained by Buyer's lender is insufficient to meet terms of the Loan Commitment; or (4) the
112   loan is not funded due to financial failure of Buyer's lender, in which event(s) the Deposit shall be returned to Buyer,
113   thereby releasing Buyer and Seller from all further obligations under this Contract.

Sample "AS IS" Residential Contract For Sale and Purchase

114*   ☐ (c) Assumption of existing mortgage (see rider for terms).

115*   ☐ (d) Purchase money note and mortgage to Seller (see riders; addenda; or special clauses for terms).

116   **CLOSING COSTS, FEES AND CHARGES**

117   **9.**   **CLOSING COSTS; TITLE INSURANCE; SURVEY; HOME WARRANTY; SPECIAL ASSESSMENTS:**

118   (a) **COSTS TO BE PAID BY SELLER:**

119   • Documentary stamp taxes and surtax on deed, if any   • HOA/Condominium Association estoppel fees

120   • Owner's Policy and Charges (if Paragraph 9(c) (i) is checked)   • Recording and other fees needed to cure title

121   • Title search charges (if Paragraph 9(c) (iii) is checked)   • Seller's attorneys' fees

122*   • Other:_____

123   If, prior to Closing, Seller is unable to meet the AS IS Maintenance Requirement as required by Paragraph 11 a

124   sum equal to 125% of estimated costs to meet the AS IS Maintenance Requirement shall be escrowed at Closing. If

125   actual costs to meet the AS IS Maintenance Requirement exceed escrowed amount, Seller shall pay such actual

126   costs. Any unused portion of escrowed amount(s) shall be returned to Seller.

127   (b) **COSTS TO BE PAID BY BUYER:**

128   • Taxes and recording fees on notes and mortgages   • Loan expenses

129   • Recording fees for deed and financing statements   • Appraisal fees

130   • Owner's Policy and Charges (if Paragraph 9(c)(ii) is checked)   • Buyer's Inspections

131   • Survey (and elevation certification, if required)   • Buyer's attorneys' fees

132   • Lender's title policy and endorsements   • All property related insurance

133   • HOA/Condominium Association application/transfer fees   • Owner's Policy Premium (if Paragraph

134   9 (c) (iii) is checked.)

135*   • Other:_____

136*   (c) **TITLE EVIDENCE AND INSURANCE:** At least _____ (if left blank, then 5) days prior to Closing Date, a title

137   insurance commitment issued by a Florida licensed title insurer, with legible copies of instruments listed as

138   exceptions attached thereto ("Title Commitment") and, after Closing, an owner's policy of title insurance (see

139   STANDARD A for terms) shall be obtained and delivered to Buyer. If Seller has an owner's policy of title insurance

140   covering the Real Property, a copy shall be furnished to Buyer and Closing Agent within 5 days after Effective Date.

141   The owner's title policy premium, title search, municipal lien search and closing services (collectively, "Owner's

142   Policy and Charges") shall be paid, as set forth below

143   **(CHECK ONE):**

144*   ☒ (i) Seller shall designate Closing Agent and pay for Owner's Policy and Charges (but not including charges for

145   closing services related to Buyer's lender's policy and endorsements and loan closing, which amounts shall be paid

146   by Buyer to Closing Agent or such other provider(s) as Buyer may select); or

147*   ☐ (ii) Buyer shall designate Closing Agent and pay for Owner's Policy and Charges and charges for closing

148   services related to Buyer's lender's policy, endorsements, and loan closing; or

149*   ☐ (iii) **[MIAMI-DADE/BROWARD REGIONAL PROVISION]:** Seller shall furnish a copy of a prior owner's policy of

150   title insurance or other evidence of title and pay fees for: (A) a continuation or update of such title evidence, which

151   is acceptable to Buyer's title insurance underwriter for reissue of coverage; (B) tax search; and (C) municipal lien

152   search. Buyer shall obtain and pay for post-Closing continuation and premium for Buyer's owner's policy, and if

153*   applicable, Buyer's lender's policy. Seller shall not be obligated to pay more than $ _____ (if left blank,

154   then $200.00) for abstract continuation or title search ordered or performed by Closing Agent.

155   (d) **SURVEY:** At least 5 days prior to Closing, Buyer may, at Buyer's expense, have the Real Property surveyed and

156   certified by a registered Florida surveyor ("Survey"). If Seller has a survey covering the Real Property, a copy shall

157   be furnished to Buyer and Closing Agent within 5 days after Effective Date.

158*   (e) **HOME WARRANTY:** At Closing, ☐ Buyer ☐ Seller ☒ N/A shall pay for a home warranty plan issued by

159*   _____ at a cost not to exceed $_____. A home

160   warranty plan provides for repair or replacement of many of a home's mechanical systems and major built-in

161   appliances in the event of breakdown due to normal wear and tear during the agreement's warranty period.

162   (f) **SPECIAL ASSESSMENTS:** At Closing, Seller shall pay: (i) the full amount of liens imposed by a public body

163   ("public body" does not include a Condominium or Homeowner's Association) that are certified, confirmed and

164   ratified before Closing; and (ii) the amount of the public body's most recent estimate or assessment for an

165   improvement which is substantially complete as of Effective Date, but that has not resulted in a lien being imposed

166   on the Property before Closing. Buyer shall pay all other assessments. If special assessments may be paid in

167   installments **(CHECK ONE):**

168*   ☒ (a) Seller shall pay installments due prior to Closing and Buyer shall pay installments due after Closing.

169   Installments prepaid or due for the year of Closing shall be prorated.

170*   ☐ (b) Seller shall pay the assessment(s) in full prior to or at the time of Closing.

171   IF NEITHER BOX IS CHECKED, THEN OPTION (a) SHALL BE DEEMED SELECTED.

Buyer's Initials _____ _____   Page 3 of 11   Seller's Initials _____ _____

formsimplicity

Sample "AS IS" Residential Contract For Sale and Purchase

172 This Paragraph 9(f) shall not apply to a special benefit tax lien imposed by a community development district (CDD)
173 pursuant to Chapter 190, F.S., which lien shall be prorated pursuant to STANDARD K.

174 DISCLOSURES

175 **10. DISCLOSURES:**

176 (a) **RADON GAS:** Radon is a naturally occurring radioactive gas that, when it is accumulated in a building in sufficient
177 quantities, may present health risks to persons who are exposed to it over time. Levels of radon that exceed federal
178 and state guidelines have been found in buildings in Florida. Additional information regarding radon and radon
179 testing may be obtained from your county health department.

180 (b) **PERMITS DISCLOSURE:** Except as may have been disclosed by Seller to Buyer in a written disclosure, Seller
181 does not know of any improvements made to the Property which were made without required permits or made
182 pursuant to permits which have not been properly closed.

183 (c) **MOLD:** Mold is naturally occurring and may cause health risks or damage to property. If Buyer is concerned or
184 desires additional information regarding mold, Buyer should contact an appropriate professional.

185 (d) **FLOOD ZONE; ELEVATION CERTIFICATION:** Buyer is advised to verify by elevation certificate which flood zone
186 the Property is in, whether flood insurance is required by Buyer's lender, and what restrictions apply to improving
187 the Property and rebuilding in the event of casualty. If Property is in a "Special Flood Hazard Area" or "Coastal
188 Barrier Resources Act" designated area or otherwise protected area identified by the U.S. Fish and Wildlife Service
189 under the Coastal Barrier Resources Act and the lowest floor elevation for the building(s) and /or flood insurance
190 rating purposes is below minimum flood elevation or is ineligible for flood insurance through the National Flood
191* Insurance Program, Buyer may terminate this Contract by delivering written notice to Seller within _____ (if left
192 blank, then 20) days after Effective Date, and Buyer shall be refunded the Deposit thereby releasing Buyer and
193 Seller from all further obligations under this Contract, failing which Buyer accepts existing elevation of buildings and
194 flood zone designation of Property. The National Flood Insurance Reform Act of 2012 (referred to as Biggert-
195 Waters 2012) may phase in actuarial rating of pre-Flood Insurance Rate Map (pre-FIRM) non-primary structures
196 (residential structures in which the insured or spouse does not reside for at least 80% of the year) and an elevation
197 certificate may be required for actuarial rating.

198 (e) **ENERGY BROCHURE:** Buyer acknowledges receipt of Florida Energy-Efficiency Rating Information Brochure
199 required by Section 553.996, F.S.

200 (f) **LEAD-BASED PAINT:** If Property includes pre-1978 residential housing, a lead-based paint disclosure is
201 mandatory.

202 (g) **HOMEOWNERS' ASSOCIATION/COMMUNITY DISCLOSURE: BUYER SHOULD NOT EXECUTE THIS
203 CONTRACT UNTIL BUYER HAS RECEIVED AND READ THE HOMEOWNERS' ASSOCIATION/COMMUNITY
204 DISCLOSURE, IF APPLICABLE.**

205 (h) **PROPERTY TAX DISCLOSURE SUMMARY: BUYER SHOULD NOT RELY ON THE SELLER'S CURRENT
206 PROPERTY TAXES AS THE AMOUNT OF PROPERTY TAXES THAT THE BUYER MAY BE OBLIGATED TO
207 PAY IN THE YEAR SUBSEQUENT TO PURCHASE. A CHANGE OF OWNERSHIP OR PROPERTY
208 IMPROVEMENTS TRIGGERS REASSESSMENTS OF THE PROPERTY THAT COULD RESULT IN HIGHER
209 PROPERTY TAXES. IF YOU HAVE ANY QUESTIONS CONCERNING VALUATION, CONTACT THE COUNTY
210 PROPERTY APPRAISER'S OFFICE FOR INFORMATION.**

211 (i) **FIRPTA TAX WITHHOLDING:** Seller shall inform Buyer in writing if Seller is a "foreign person" as defined by the
212 Foreign Investment in Real Property Tax Act ("FIRPTA"). Buyer and Seller shall comply with FIRPTA, which may
213 require Seller to provide additional cash at Closing. If Seller is not a "foreign person", Seller can provide Buyer, at or
214 prior to Closing, a certification of non-foreign status, under penalties of perjury, to inform Buyer and Closing Agent
215 that no withholding is required. See STANDARD V for further information pertaining to FIRPTA. Buyer and Seller
216 are advised to seek legal counsel and tax advice regarding their respective rights, obligations, reporting and
217 withholding requirements pursuant to FIRPTA.

218 (j) **SELLER DISCLOSURE:** Seller knows of no facts materially affecting the value of the Real Property which are not
219 readily observable and which have not been disclosed to Buyer. Except as provided for in the preceding sentence,
220 Seller extends and intends no warranty and makes no representation of any type, either express or implied, as to
221 the physical condition or history of the Property. Except as otherwise disclosed in writing Seller has received no
222 written or verbal notice from any governmental entity or agency as to a currently uncorrected building,
223 environmental or safety code violation.

224 PROPERTY MAINTENANCE, CONDITION, INSPECTIONS AND EXAMINATIONS

225 **11. PROPERTY MAINTENANCE:** Except for ordinary wear and tear and Casualty Loss, Seller shall maintain the Property,
226 including, but not limited to, lawn, shrubbery, and pool, in the condition existing as of Effective Date ("AS IS
227 Maintenance Requirement").

Buyer's Initials _____   Page 4 of 11   Seller's Initials _____ _____
FloridaRealtors/FloridaBar-ASIS-2   Rev.8/13 © 2013 Florida Realtors® and The Florida Bar. All rights reserved.
Serial#: 079445-800140-1810218

formsimplicity

Sample "AS IS" Residential Contract For Sale and Purchase

228 **12. PROPERTY INSPECTION; RIGHT TO CANCEL:**

229* (a) *PROPERTY INSPECTIONS AND RIGHT TO CANCEL: Buyer shall have ___7___ (if left blank, then 15) days*
230 *after Effective Date ("Inspection Period") within which to have such inspections of the Property performed*
231 *as Buyer shall desire during the Inspection Period. If Buyer determines, in Buyer's sole discretion, that the*
232 *Property is not acceptable to Buyer, Buyer may terminate this Contract by delivering written notice of such*
233 *election to Seller prior to expiration of Inspection Period. If Buyer timely terminates this Contract, the*
234 *Deposit paid shall be returned to Buyer, thereupon, Buyer and Seller shall be released of all further*
235 *obligations under this Contract; however, Buyer shall be responsible for prompt payment for such*
236 *inspections, for repair of damage to, and restoration of, the Property resulting from such inspections, and*
237 *shall provide Seller with paid receipts for all work done on the Property (the preceding provision shall*
238 *survive termination of this Contract). Unless Buyer exercises the right to terminate granted herein, Buyer*
239 *accepts the physical condition of the Property and any violation of governmental, building, environmental,*
240 *and safety codes, restrictions, or requirements, but subject to Seller's continuing AS IS Maintenance*
241 *Requirement, and Buyer shall be responsible for any and all repairs and improvements required by Buyer's*
242 *lender.*

243 (b) **WALK-THROUGH INSPECTION/RE-INSPECTION:** On the day prior to Closing Date, or on Closing Date prior to
244 time of Closing, as specified by Buyer, Buyer or Buyer's representative may perform a walk-through (and follow-up
245 walk-through, if necessary) inspection of the Property solely to confirm that all items of Personal Property are on the
246 Property and to verify that Seller has maintained the Property as required by the AS IS Maintenance Requirement
247 and has met all other contractual obligations.

248 (c) **SELLER ASSISTANCE AND COOPERATION IN CLOSE-OUT OF BUILDING PERMITS:** If Buyer's inspection of
249 the Property identifies open or needed building permits, then Seller shall promptly deliver to Buyer all plans, written
250 documentation or other information in Seller's possession, knowledge, or control relating to improvements to the
251 Property which are the subject of such open or needed Permits, and shall promptly cooperate in good faith with
252 Buyer's efforts to obtain estimates of repairs or other work necessary to resolve such Permit issues. Seller's
253 obligation to cooperate shall include Seller's execution of necessary authorizations, consents, or other documents
254 necessary for Buyer to conduct inspections and have estimates of such repairs or work prepared, but in fulfilling
255 such obligation, Seller shall not be required to expend, or become obligated to expend, any money.

256 (d) **ASSIGNMENT OF REPAIR AND TREATMENT CONTRACTS AND WARRANTIES:** At Buyer's option and cost,
257 Seller will, at Closing, assign all assignable repair, treatment and maintenance contracts and warranties to Buyer.

258 **ESCROW AGENT AND BROKER**

259 **13. ESCROW AGENT:** Any Closing Agent or Escrow Agent (collectively "Agent") receiving the Deposit, other funds and
260 other items is authorized, and agrees by acceptance of them, to deposit them promptly, hold same in escrow within the
261 State of Florida and, subject to **COLLECTION**, disburse them in accordance with terms and conditions of this Contract.
262 Failure of funds to become **COLLECTED** shall not excuse Buyer's performance. When conflicting demands for the
263 Deposit are received, or Agent has a good faith doubt as to entitlement to the Deposit, Agent may take such actions
264 permitted by this Paragraph 13, as Agent deems advisable. If in doubt as to Agent's duties or liabilities under this
265 Contract, Agent may, at Agent's option, continue to hold the subject matter of the escrow until the parties agree to its
266 disbursement or until a final judgment of a court of competent jurisdiction shall determine the rights of the parties, or
267 Agent may deposit same with the clerk of the circuit court having jurisdiction of the dispute. An attorney who represents
268 a party and also acts as Agent may represent such party in such action. Upon notifying all parties concerned of such
269 action, all liability on the part of Agent shall fully terminate, except to the extent of accounting for any items previously
270 delivered out of escrow. If a licensed real estate broker, Agent will comply with provisions of Chapter 475, F.S., as
271 amended and FREC rules to timely resolve escrow disputes through mediation, arbitration, interpleader or an escrow
272 disbursement order.

273 Any proceeding between Buyer and Seller wherein Agent is made a party because of acting as Agent hereunder, or in
274 any proceeding where Agent interpleads the subject matter of the escrow, Agent shall recover reasonable attorney's
275 fees and costs incurred, to be paid pursuant to court order out of the escrowed funds or equivalent. Agent shall not be
276 liable to any party or person for mis-delivery of any escrowed items, unless such mis-delivery is due to Agent's willful
277 breach of this Contract or Agent's gross negligence. This Paragraph 13 shall survive Closing or termination of this
278 Contract.

279 **14. PROFESSIONAL ADVICE; BROKER LIABILITY:** Broker advises Buyer and Seller to verify Property condition, square
280 footage, and all other facts and representations made pursuant to this Contract and to consult appropriate professionals
281 for legal, tax, environmental, and other specialized advice concerning matters affecting the Property and the transaction
282 contemplated by this Contract. Broker represents to Buyer that Broker does not reside on the Property and that all
283 representations (oral, written or otherwise) by Broker are based on Seller representations or public records. **BUYER**
284 **AGREES TO RELY SOLELY ON SELLER, PROFESSIONAL INSPECTORS AND GOVERNMENTAL AGENCIES**
285 **FOR VERIFICATION OF PROPERTY CONDITION, SQUARE FOOTAGE AND FACTS THAT MATERIALLY AFFECT**
286 **PROPERTY VALUE AND NOT ON THE REPRESENTATIONS (ORAL, WRITTEN OR OTHERWISE) OF BROKER.**

Buyer's Initials _____   Page 5 of 11   Seller's Initials _____ _____
FloridaRealtors/FloridaBar-ASIS-2   Rev.8/13 © 2013 Florida Realtors® and The Florida Bar. All rights reserved.
Serial#: 079445-600140-1810216

formsimplicity

Sample "AS IS" Residential Contract For Sale and Purchase

Buyer and Seller (individually, the "Indemnifying Party") each individually indemnifies, holds harmless, and releases Broker and Broker's officers, directors, agents and employees from all liability for loss or damage, including all costs and expenses, and reasonable attorney's fees at all levels, suffered or incurred by Broker and Broker's officers, directors, agents and employees in connection with or arising from claims, demands or causes of action instituted by Buyer or Seller based on: (i) inaccuracy of information provided by the Indemnifying Party or from public records; (ii) Indemnifying Party's misstatement(s) or failure to perform contractual obligations; (iii) Broker's performance, at Indemnifying Party's request, of any task beyond the scope of services regulated by Chapter 475, F.S., as amended, including Broker's referral, recommendation or retention of any vendor for, or on behalf of Indemnifying Party; (iv) products or services provided by any such vendor for, or on behalf of, Indemnifying Party; and (v) expenses incurred by any such vendor. Buyer and Seller each assumes full responsibility for selecting and compensating their respective vendors and paying their other costs under this Contract whether or not this transaction closes. This Paragraph 14 will not relieve Broker of statutory obligations under Chapter 475, F.S., as amended. For purposes of this Paragraph 14, Broker will be treated as a party to this Contract. This Paragraph 14 shall survive Closing or termination of this Contract.

DEFAULT AND DISPUTE RESOLUTION

15. DEFAULT:

(a) **BUYER DEFAULT:** If Buyer fails, neglects or refuses to perform Buyer's obligations under this Contract, including payment of the Deposit, within the time(s) specified, Seller may elect to recover and retain the Deposit for the account of Seller as agreed upon liquidated damages, consideration for execution of this Contract, and in full settlement of any claims, whereupon Buyer and Seller shall be relieved from all further obligations under this Contract, or Seller, at Seller's option, may, pursuant to Paragraph 16, proceed in equity to enforce Seller's rights under this Contract. The portion of the Deposit, if any, paid to Listing Broker upon default by Buyer, shall be split equally between Listing Broker and Cooperating Broker; provided however, Cooperating Broker's share shall not be greater than the commission amount Listing Broker had agreed to pay to Cooperating Broker.

(b) **SELLER DEFAULT:** If for any reason other than failure of Seller to make Seller's title marketable after reasonable diligent effort, Seller fails, neglects or refuses to perform Seller's obligations under this Contract, Buyer may elect to receive return of Buyer's Deposit without thereby waiving any action for damages resulting from Seller's breach, and, pursuant to Paragraph 16, may seek to recover such damages or seek specific performance.

This Paragraph 15 shall survive Closing or termination of this Contract.

16. DISPUTE RESOLUTION: Unresolved controversies, claims and other matters in question between Buyer and Seller arising out of, or relating to, this Contract or its breach, enforcement or interpretation ("Dispute") will be settled as follows:

(a) Buyer and Seller will have 10 days after the date conflicting demands for the Deposit are made to attempt to resolve such Dispute, failing which, Buyer and Seller shall submit such Dispute to mediation under Paragraph 16(b).

(b) Buyer and Seller shall attempt to settle Disputes in an amicable manner through mediation pursuant to Florida Rules for Certified and Court-Appointed Mediators and Chapter 44, F.S., as amended (the "Mediation Rules"). The mediator must be certified or must have experience in the real estate industry. Injunctive relief may be sought without first complying with this Paragraph 16(b). Disputes not settled pursuant to this Paragraph 16 may be resolved by instituting action in the appropriate court having jurisdiction of the matter. This Paragraph 16 shall survive Closing or termination of this Contract.

17. ATTORNEY'S FEES; COSTS: The parties will split equally any mediation fee incurred in any mediation permitted by this Contract, and each party will pay their own costs, expenses and fees, including attorney's fees, incurred in conducting the mediation. In any litigation permitted by this Contract, the prevailing party shall be entitled to recover from the non-prevailing party costs and fees, including reasonable attorney's fees, incurred in conducting the litigation. This Paragraph 17 shall survive Closing or termination of this Contract.

STANDARDS FOR REAL ESTATE TRANSACTIONS ("STANDARDS")

18. STANDARDS:

A. TITLE:

(i) **TITLE EVIDENCE; RESTRICTIONS; EASEMENTS; LIMITATIONS:** Within the time period provided in Paragraph 9(c), the Title Commitment, with legible copies of instruments listed as exceptions attached thereto, shall be issued and delivered to Buyer. The Title Commitment shall set forth those matters to be discharged by Seller at or before Closing and shall provide that, upon recording of the deed to Buyer, an owner's policy of title insurance in the amount of the Purchase Price, shall be issued to Buyer insuring Buyer's marketable title to the Real Property, subject only to the following matters: (a) comprehensive land use plans, zoning, and other land use restrictions, prohibitions and requirements imposed by governmental authority; (b) restrictions and matters appearing on the Plat or otherwise common to the subdivision; (c) outstanding oil, gas and mineral rights of record without right of entry; (d) unplatted public utility easements of record (located contiguous to real property lines and not more than 10 feet in width as to rear or front lines and 7 1/2 feet in width as to side lines); (e) taxes for year of Closing and subsequent years; and (f)

Sample "AS IS" Residential Contract For Sale and Purchase

STANDARDS FOR REAL ESTATE TRANSACTIONS ("STANDARDS") CONTINUED

345 assumed mortgages and purchase money mortgages, if any (if additional items, attach addendum); provided, that, none
346 prevent use of Property for **RESIDENTIAL PURPOSES**. If there exists at Closing any violation of items identified in (b)
347 – (f) above, then the same shall be deemed a title defect. Marketable title shall be determined according to applicable
348 Title Standards adopted by authority of The Florida Bar and in accordance with law.
349 (ii) **TITLE EXAMINATION:** Buyer shall have 5 days after receipt of Title Commitment to examine it and notify Seller in
350 writing specifying defect(s), if any, that render title unmarketable. If Seller provides Title Commitment and it is delivered
351 to Buyer less than 5 days prior to Closing Date, Buyer may extend Closing for up to 5 days after date of receipt to
352 examine same in accordance with this STANDARD A. Seller shall have 30 days ("Cure Period") after receipt of Buyer's
353 notice to take reasonable diligent efforts to remove defects. If Buyer fails to so notify Seller, Buyer shall be deemed to
354 have accepted title as it then is. If Seller cures defects within Cure Period, Seller will deliver written notice to Buyer (with
355 proof of cure acceptable to Buyer and Buyer's attorney) and the parties will close this Contract on Closing Date (or if
356 Closing Date has passed, within 10 days after Buyer's receipt of Seller's notice). If Seller is unable to cure defects
357 within Cure Period, then Buyer may, within 5 days after expiration of Cure Period, deliver written notice to Seller: (a)
358 extending Cure Period for a specified period not to exceed 120 days within which Seller shall continue to use
359 reasonable diligent effort to remove or cure the defects ("Extended Cure Period"); or (b) electing to accept title with
360 existing defects and close this Contract on Closing Date (or if Closing Date has passed, within the earlier of 10 days
361 after end of Extended Cure Period or Buyer's receipt of Seller's notice), or (c) electing to terminate this Contract and
362 receive a refund of the Deposit, thereby releasing Buyer and Seller from all further obligations under this Contract. If
363 after reasonable diligent effort, Seller is unable to timely cure defects, and Buyer does not waive the defects, this
364 Contract shall terminate, and Buyer shall receive a refund of the Deposit, thereby releasing Buyer and Seller from all
365 further obligations under this Contract.
366 **B. SURVEY:** If Survey discloses encroachments on the Real Property or that improvements located thereon encroach
367 on setback lines, easements, or lands of others, or violate any restrictions, covenants, or applicable governmental
368 regulations described in STANDARD A (i)(a), (b) or (d) above, Buyer shall deliver written notice of such matters,
369 together with a copy of Survey, to Seller within 5 days after Buyer's receipt of Survey, but no later than Closing. If Buyer
370 timely delivers such notice and Survey to Seller, such matters identified in the notice and Survey shall constitute a title
371 defect, subject to cure obligations of STANDARD A above. If Seller has delivered a prior survey, Seller shall, at Buyer's
372 request, execute an affidavit of "no change" to the Real Property since the preparation of such prior survey, to the
373 extent the affirmations therein are true and correct.
374 **C. INGRESS AND EGRESS:** Seller represents that there is ingress and egress to the Real Property and title to the
375 Real Property is insurable in accordance with STANDARD A without exception for lack of legal right of access.
376 **D. LEASE INFORMATION:** Seller shall, at least 10 days prior to Closing, furnish to Buyer estoppel letters from
377 tenant(s)/occupant(s) specifying nature and duration of occupancy, rental rates, advanced rent and security deposits
378 paid by tenant(s) or occupant(s)("Estoppel Letter(s)"). If Seller is unable to obtain such Estoppel Letter(s) the same
379 information shall be furnished by Seller to Buyer within that time period in the form of a Seller's affidavit and Buyer may
380 thereafter contact tenant(s) or occupant(s) to confirm such information. If Estoppel Letter(s) or Seller's affidavit, if any,
381 differ materially from Seller's representations and lease(s) provided pursuant to Paragraph 6, or if tenant(s)/occupant(s)
382 fail or refuse to confirm Seller's affidavit, Buyer may deliver written notice to Seller within 5 days after receipt of such
383 information, but no later than 5 days prior to Closing Date, terminating this Contract and receive a refund of the Deposit,
384 thereby releasing Buyer and Seller from all further obligations under this Contract. Seller shall, at Closing, deliver and
385 assign all leases to Buyer who shall assume Seller's obligations thereunder.
386 **E. LIENS:** Seller shall furnish to Buyer at Closing an affidavit attesting (i) to the absence of any financing statement,
387 claims of lien or potential lienors known to Seller and (ii) that there have been no improvements or repairs to the Real
388 Property for 90 days immediately preceding Closing Date. If the Real Property has been improved or repaired within
389 that time, Seller shall deliver releases or waivers of construction liens executed by all general contractors,
390 subcontractors, suppliers and materialmen in addition to Seller's lien affidavit setting forth names of all such general
391 contractors, subcontractors, suppliers and materialmen, further affirming that all charges for improvements or repairs
392 which could serve as a basis for a construction lien or a claim for damages have been paid or will be paid at Closing.
393 **F. TIME:** Calendar days shall be used in computing time periods. **Time is of the essence in this Contract.**
394 Other than time for acceptance and Effective Date as set forth in Paragraph 3, any time periods provided for or dates
395 specified in this Contract, whether preprinted, handwritten, typewritten or inserted herein, which shall end or occur on a
396 Saturday, Sunday, or a national legal holiday (see 5 U.S.C. 6103) shall extend to 5:00 p.m. (where the Property is
397 located) of the next business day.
398 **G. FORCE MAJEURE:** Buyer or Seller shall not be required to perform any obligation under this Contract or be liable
399 to each other for damages so long as performance or non-performance of the obligation is delayed, caused or
400 prevented by Force Majeure. "Force Majeure" means: hurricanes, earthquakes, floods, fire, acts of God, unusual
401 transportation delays, wars, insurrections, acts of terrorism, and any other cause not reasonably within control of Buyer
402 or Seller, and which, by: exercise of reasonable diligent effort, the non-performing party is unable in whole or in part to
403 prevent or overcome. All time periods, including Closing Date, will be extended for the period that the Force Majeure
404 prevents performance under this Contract, provided, however, if such Force Majeure continues to prevent performance

Buyer's Initials _____   Page 7 of 11   Seller's Initials _____
FloridaRealtors/FloridaBar-ASIS-2 Rev.8/13 © 2013 Florida Realtors® and The Florida Bar. All rights reserved.
Serial#: 076445-800140-1810218

Sample "AS IS" Residential Contract For Sale and Purchase

STANDARDS FOR REAL ESTATE TRANSACTIONS ("STANDARDS") CONTINUED

405 under this Contract more than 14 days beyond Closing Date, then either party may terminate this Contract by delivering
406 written notice to the other and the Deposit shall be refunded to Buyer, thereby releasing Buyer and Seller from all
407 further obligations under this Contract.
408 **H. CONVEYANCE:** Seller shall convey marketable title to the Real Property by statutory warranty, trustee's, personal
409 representative's, or guardian's deed, as appropriate to the status of Seller, subject only to matters described in
410 STANDARD A and those accepted by Buyer. Personal Property shall, at request of Buyer, be transferred by absolute
411 bill of sale with warranty of title, subject only to such matters as may be provided for in this Contract.
412 **I. CLOSING LOCATION; DOCUMENTS; AND PROCEDURE:**
413 (i) **LOCATION:** Closing will take place in the county where the Real Property is located at the office of the attorney or
414 other closing agent ("Closing Agent") designated by the party paying for the owner's policy of title insurance, or, if no
415 title insurance, designated by Seller. Closing may be conducted by mail or electronic means.
416 (ii) **CLOSING DOCUMENTS:** Seller shall at or prior to Closing, execute and deliver, as applicable, deed, bill of sale,
417 certificate(s) of title or other documents necessary to transfer title to the Property, construction lien affidavit(s), owner's
418 possession and no lien affidavit(s), and assignment(s) of leases. Seller shall provide Buyer with paid receipts for all
419 work done on the Property pursuant to this Contract. Buyer shall furnish and pay for, as applicable the survey, flood
420 elevation certification, and documents required by Buyer's lender.
421 (iii) **PROCEDURE:** The deed shall be recorded upon **COLLECTION** of all closing funds. If the Title Commitment
422 provides insurance against adverse matters pursuant to Section 627.7841, F.S., as amended, the escrow closing
423 procedure required by STANDARD J shall be waived, and Closing Agent shall, **subject to COLLECTION of all closing**
424 **funds,** disburse at Closing the brokerage fees to Broker and the net sale proceeds to Seller.
425 **J. ESCROW CLOSING PROCEDURE:** If Title Commitment issued pursuant to Paragraph 9(c) does not provide for
426 insurance against adverse matters as permitted under Section 627.7841, F.S., as amended, the following escrow and
427 closing procedures shall apply: (1) all Closing proceeds shall be held in escrow by the Closing Agent for a period of not
428 more than 10 days after Closing; (2) if Seller's title is rendered unmarketable, through no fault of Buyer, Buyer shall,
429 within the 10 day period, notify Seller in writing of the defect and Seller shall have 30 days from date of receipt of such
430 notification to cure the defect; (3) if Seller fails to timely cure the defect, the Deposit and all Closing funds paid by Buyer
431 shall, within 5 days after written demand by Buyer, be refunded to Buyer and, simultaneously with such repayment,
432 Buyer shall return the Personal Property, vacate the Real Property and re-convey the Property to Seller by special
433 warranty deed and bill of sale; and (4) if Buyer fails to make timely demand for refund of the Deposit, Buyer shall take
434 title as is, waiving all rights against Seller as to any intervening defect except as may be available to Buyer by virtue of
435 warranties contained in the deed or bill of sale.
436 **K. PRORATIONS; CREDITS:** The following recurring items will be made current (if applicable) and prorated as of the
437 day prior to Closing Date, or date of occupancy if occupancy occurs before Closing Date: real estate taxes (including
438 special benefit tax assessments imposed by a CDD), interest, bonds, association fees, insurance, rents and other
439 expenses of Property. Buyer shall have option of taking over existing policies of insurance, if assumable, in which event
440 premiums shall be prorated. Cash at Closing shall be increased or decreased as may be required by prorations to be
441 made through day prior to Closing. Advance rent and security deposits, if any, will be credited to Buyer. Escrow
442 deposits held by Seller's mortgage will be paid to Seller. Taxes shall be prorated based on current year's tax with due
443 allowance made for maximum allowable discount, homestead and other exemptions. If Closing occurs on a date when
444 current year's millage is not fixed but current year's assessment is available, taxes will be prorated based upon such
445 assessment and prior year's millage. If current year's assessment is not available, then taxes will be prorated on prior
446 year's tax. If there are completed improvements on the Real Property by January 1st of year of Closing, which
447 improvements were not in existence on January 1st of prior year, then taxes shall be prorated based upon prior year's
448 millage and at an equitable assessment to be agreed upon between the parties, failing which, request shall be made to
449 the County Property Appraiser for an informal assessment taking into account available exemptions. A tax proration
450 based on an estimate shall, at either party's request, be readjusted upon receipt of current year's tax bill. This
451 STANDARD K shall survive Closing.
452 **L. ACCESS TO PROPERTY TO CONDUCT APPRAISALS, INSPECTIONS, AND WALK-THROUGH:** Seller shall,
453 upon reasonable notice, provide utilities service and access to Property for appraisals and inspections, including a walk-
454 through (or follow-up walk-through if necessary) prior to Closing.
455 **M. RISK OF LOSS:** If, after Effective Date, but before Closing, Property is damaged by fire or other casualty
456 ("Casualty Loss") and cost of restoration (which shall include cost of pruning or removing damaged trees) does not
457 exceed 1.5% of Purchase Price, cost of restoration shall be an obligation of Seller and Closing shall proceed pursuant
458 to terms of this Contract. If restoration is not completed as of Closing, a sum equal to 125% of estimated cost to
459 complete restoration (not to exceed 1.5% of Purchase Price), will be escrowed at Closing. If actual cost of restoration
460 exceeds escrowed amount, Seller shall pay such actual costs (but, not in excess of 1.5% of Purchase Price). Any
461 unused portion of escrowed amount shall be returned to Seller. If cost of restoration exceeds 1.5% of Purchase Price,
462 Buyer shall elect to either take Property "as is" together with the 1.5%, or receive a refund of the Deposit, thereby
463 releasing Buyer and Seller from all further obligations under this Contract. Seller's sole obligation with respect to tree
464 damage by casualty or other natural occurrence shall be cost of pruning or removal.

Sample "AS IS" Residential Contract For Sale and Purchase

STANDARDS FOR REAL ESTATE TRANSACTIONS ("STANDARDS") CONTINUED

N. 1031 EXCHANGE: If either Seller or Buyer wish to enter into a like-kind exchange (either simultaneously with Closing or deferred) under Section 1031 of the Internal Revenue Code ("Exchange"), the other party shall cooperate in all reasonable respects to effectuate the Exchange, including execution of documents; provided, however, cooperating party shall incur no liability or expense related to the Exchange, and Closing shall not be contingent upon, nor extended or delayed by, such Exchange.

O. CONTRACT NOT RECORDABLE; PERSONS BOUND; NOTICE; DELIVERY; COPIES; CONTRACT EXECUTION: Neither this Contract nor any notice of it shall be recorded in any public records. This Contract shall be binding on, and inure to the benefit of, the parties and their respective heirs or successors in interest. Whenever the context permits, singular shall include plural and one gender shall include all. Notice and delivery given by or to the attorney or broker (including such broker's real estate licensee) representing any party shall be as effective as if given by or to that party. All notices must be in writing and may be made by mail, personal delivery or electronic (including "pdf") media. A facsimile or electronic (including "pdf") copy of this Contract and any signatures hereon shall be considered for all purposes as an original. This Contract may be executed by use of electronic signatures, as determined by Florida's Electronic Signature Act and other applicable laws.

P. INTEGRATION; MODIFICATION: This Contract contains the full and complete understanding and agreement of Buyer and Seller with respect to the transaction contemplated by this Contract and no prior agreements or representations shall be binding upon Buyer or Seller unless included in this Contract. No modification to or change in this Contract shall be valid or binding upon Buyer or Seller unless in writing and executed by the parties intended to be bound by it.

Q. WAIVER: Failure of Buyer or Seller to insist on compliance with, or strict performance of, any provision of this Contract, or to take advantage of any right under this Contract, shall not constitute a waiver of other provisions or rights.

R. RIDERS; ADDENDA; TYPEWRITTEN OR HANDWRITTEN PROVISIONS: Riders, addenda, and typewritten or handwritten provisions shall control all printed provisions of this Contract in conflict with them.

S. COLLECTION or COLLECTED: "COLLECTION" or "COLLECTED" means any checks tendered or received, including Deposits, have become actually and finally collected and deposited in the account of Escrow Agent or Closing Agent. Closing and disbursement of funds and delivery of closing documents may be delayed by Closing Agent until such amounts have been COLLECTED in Closing Agent's accounts.

T. LOAN COMMITMENT: "Loan Commitment" means a statement by the lender setting forth the terms and conditions upon which the lender is willing to make a particular mortgage loan to a particular borrower. Neither a pre-approval letter nor a prequalification letter shall be deemed a Loan Commitment for purposes of this Contract .

U. APPLICABLE LAW AND VENUE: This Contract shall be construed in accordance with the laws of the State of Florida, and venue for resolution of all disputes, whether by mediation, arbitration or litigation, shall lie in the county where the Real Property is located.

V. FOREIGN INVESTMENT IN REAL PROPERTY TAX ACT ("FIRPTA"): If a seller of U.S. real property is a "foreign person" as defined by FIRPTA, Section 1445 of the Internal Revenue Code requires the buyer of the real property to withhold 10% of the amount realized by the seller on the transfer and remit the withheld amount to the Internal Revenue Service (IRS) unless an exemption to the required withholding applies or the seller has obtained a Withholding Certificate from the IRS authorizing a reduced amount of withholding. Due to the complexity and potential risks of FIRPTA, Buyer and Seller should seek legal and tax advice regarding compliance, particularly if an "exemption" is claimed on the sale of residential property for $300,000 or less.

(i) No withholding is required under Section 1445 if the Seller is not a "foreign person," provided Buyer accepts proof of same from Seller, which may include Buyer's receipt of certification of non-foreign status from Seller, signed under penalties of perjury, stating that Seller is not a foreign person and containing Seller's name, U.S. taxpayer identification number and home address (or office address, in the case of an entity), as provided for in 26 CFR 1.1445-2(b). Otherwise, Buyer shall withhold 10% of the amount realized by Seller on the transfer and timely remit said funds to the IRS.

(ii) If Seller has received a Withholding Certificate from the IRS which provides for reduced or eliminated withholding in this transaction and provides same to Buyer by Closing, then Buyer shall withhold the reduced sum, if any required, and timely remit said funds to the IRS.

(iii) If prior to Closing Seller has submitted a completed application to the IRS for a Withholding Certificate and has provided to Buyer the notice required by 26 CFR 1.1445-1(c) (2)(i)(B) but no Withholding Certificate has been received as of Closing, Buyer shall, at Closing, withhold 10% of the amount realized by Seller on the transfer and, at Buyer's option, either (a) timely remit the withheld funds to the IRS or (b) place the funds in escrow, at Seller's expense, with an escrow agent selected by Buyer and pursuant to terms negotiated by the parties, to be subsequently disbursed in accordance with the Withholding Certificate issued by the IRS or remitted directly to the IRS if the Seller's application is rejected or upon terms set forth in the escrow agreement.

(iv) In the event the net proceeds due Seller are not sufficient to meet the withholding requirement(s) in this transaction, Seller shall deliver to Buyer, at Closing, the additional COLLECTED funds necessary to satisfy the applicable requirement and thereafter Buyer shall timely remit said funds to the IRS or escrow the funds for disbursement in accordance with the final determination of the IRS, as applicable.

Buyer's Initials _____   Page 9 of 11   Seller's Initials _____ _____
FloridaRealtors/FloridaBar-ASIS-2 Rev.8/13 © 2013 Florida Realtors® and The Florida Bar. All rights reserved.
Serial#: 079445-600140-1810218

Sample "AS IS" Residential Contract For Sale and Purchase

STANDARDS FOR REAL ESTATE TRANSACTIONS ("STANDARDS") CONTINUED

525 (v) Upon remitting funds to the IRS pursuant to this STANDARD, Buyer shall provide Seller copies of IRS Forms 8288
526 and 8288-A, as filed.
527 **W. RESERVED**
528 **X. BUYER WAIVER OF CLAIMS:** *To the extent permitted by law, Buyer waives any claims against Seller and*
529 *against any real estate licensee involved in the negotiation of this Contract for any damage or defects*
530 *pertaining to the physical condition of the Property that may exist at Closing of this Contract and be*
531 *subsequently discovered by the Buyer or anyone claiming* by, through, under or against the Buyer. *This*
532 *provision does not relieve Seller's obligation to comply with Paragraph 10(j). This Standard X shall survive*
533 *Closing.*

534 **ADDENDA AND ADDITIONAL TERMS**

535 **19. ADDENDA:** The following additional terms are included in the attached addenda or riders and incorporated into this
536* Contract **(Check if applicable):**

☐ A. Condominium Rider   ☐ M. Defective Drywall   ☐ X. Kick-out Clause
☐ B. Homeowners' Assn.   ☐ N. Coastal Construction Control Line   ☐ Y. Seller's Attorney Approval
☐ C. Seller Financing   ☐ O. Insulation Disclosure   ☐ Z. Buyer's Attorney Approval
☐ D. Mortgage Assumption   ☐ P. Lead Based Paint Disclosure   ☐ AA. Licensee-Personal Interest in
☐ E. FHA/VA Financing   (Pre-1978 Housing)   Property
☐ F. Appraisal Contingency   ☐ Q. Housing for Older Persons   ☐ BB. Binding Arbitration
☐ G. Short Sale   ☐ R. Rezoning   ☐ Other_____
☐ H. Homeowners'/Flood Ins.   ☐ S. Lease Purchase/ Lease Option   _____
☐ I. RESERVED   ☐ T. Pre-Closing Occupancy by Buyer   _____
☐ J. Interest-Bearing Acct.   ☐ U. Post-Closing Occupancy by Seller   _____
☐ K. RESERVED   ☐ V. Sale of Buyer's Property
☐ L. RESERVED   ☐ W. Back-up Contract

537* **20. ADDITIONAL TERMS:** SELLER TO PAY 3% OF BUYERS CLOSING COSTS/PREPAIDS
538 _____
539 _____
540 _____
541 _____
542 _____
543 _____
544 _____
545 _____
546 _____
547 _____
548 _____
549 _____
550 _____
551 _____
552 _____
553 _____

554 **COUNTER-OFFER/REJECTION**

555* ☐ Seller counters Buyer's offer (to accept the counter-offer, Buyer must sign or initial the counter-offered terms and deliver
556 a copy of the acceptance to Seller).
557* ☐ Seller rejects Buyer's offer.

558 **THIS IS INTENDED TO BE A LEGALLY BINDING CONTRACT. IF NOT FULLY UNDERSTOOD, SEEK THE ADVICE OF**
559 **AN ATTORNEY PRIOR TO SIGNING.**

560 **THIS FORM HAS BEEN APPROVED BY THE FLORIDA REALTORS AND THE FLORIDA BAR.**

561 *Approval of this form by the Florida Realtors and The Florida Bar does not constitute an opinion that any of the terms and*
562 *conditions in this Contract should be accepted by the parties in a particular transaction. Terms and conditions should be*
563 *negotiated based upon the respective interests, objectives and bargaining positions of all interested persons.*

Sample "AS IS" Residential Contract For Sale and Purchase

564 AN ASTERISK (*) FOLLOWING A LINE NUMBER IN THE MARGIN INDICATES THE LINE CONTAINS A BLANK TO BE
565 COMPLETED.
566
567
568* Buyer: _____   Date: _____
569
570
571
572
573* Buyer: _____   Date: _____
574
575
576
577
578* Seller: _____   Date: _____
579
580
581
582
583* Seller: _____   Date: _____
584
585 Buyer's address for purposes of notice   Seller's address for purposes of notice
586* _____   _____
587* _____   _____
588* _____   _____
589
590 **BROKER:** Listing and Cooperating Brokers, if any, named below (collectively, "Broker"), are the only Brokers entitled to
591 compensation in connection with this Contract. Instruction to Closing Agent: Seller and Buyer direct Closing Agent to
592 disburse at Closing the full amount of the brokerage fees as specified in separate brokerage agreements with the parties
593 and cooperative agreements between the Brokers, except to the extent Broker has retained such fees from the escrowed
594 funds. This Contract shall not modify any MLS or other offer of compensation made by Seller or Listing Broker to
595 Cooperating Brokers.
596
597* _____   _____
598 **Cooperating Sales Associate, if any**   **Listing Sales Associate**
599
600* _____   _____
601 **Cooperating Broker, if any**   **Listing Broker**

Sample "AS IS" Residential Contract For Sale and Purchase

RECEIPT FOR ESCROW DEPOSIT

Seller:

Buyer:

Property:

Received from: _____ Phone No. _____

Ocala Land Title Insurance Agency, Ltd. has received an escrow deposit for the buyer(s) identified above in the amount of $ ___500 . 00___ for the offer contract dated _____ on the property identified above. All checks received by ____ Land Title Insurance Agency, Inc. will be deposited immediately according to Florida Statutes. Any deposit made by personal check is subject to clearance. Funds will be available for disbursement on _____. Any request for transfer or refund of the escrowed funds must be accompanied by ____ Land Title's Release of Deposit form executed by all parties to the contract.

____ Land Title Insurance Agency, Inc. will [✓]/will not [____] be the closing agent. (check one)

Receipt acknowledged this __6__ day of __May__ , ____

LAND TITLE INSURANCE AGENCY, LTD

By _____

Printed Name: _____

Bank of America 〰〰

Cashier's Check

No.

0109185 00010 0004504510

Remitter(Purchased By):

Pay **FIVE HUNDRED DOLLARS AND 00 CENTS**

To
The
Order
Of: **** **LAND TITLE**

$ **500.00**

Bank of America, N.A.
San Antonio, Texas

VOID AFTER 90 DAYS

Authorized Signature

THE ORIGINAL DOCUMENT HAS REFLECTIVE WATERMARK ON THE BACK   THE ORIGINAL DOCUMENT HAS REFLECTIVE WATERMARK ON THE BACK

Name of the Parties: full legal name is recommended, including the full address

Description of the Land: Somewhere within this section of the form, you must put the book and page number (including the date) that the deed is registered within the county registry. You should also write a couple sentences describing the property, such as "Two-family home on 0.33 acres."

Price (Consideration): The law requires that there must be some form of consideration on this contract. Normally, this money, and the consideration, would then be the value exchanged between two parties.

Deposit: Most P&S agreements will have a deposit paid to the seller's agent as part of the down payment on the property and as a good faith gesture that the buyer is serious about the purchase. Generally, the lower the deposit amount, the less the buyer stands to lose if he or she chooses to default on the purchase. Remember that all deposits *must* be held in an escrow account. It does not have to be an attorney's escrow account. Your broker will have a separate bank account set up to hold all buyer's deposit monies. Also called *earnest money.*

Date: There are two key dates; the date that the P&S is signed by *both* parties and the date of transference/closing. The closing is also called a conveyance, and this is when the property will legally transfer from seller to buyer, by means of a new deed.

Signatures: All parties named on the agreement must sign the agreement. This includes spouses if both husband and wife are current deed holders, for example. Be aware that each page will normally have an area for both seller and buyer to initial. This is important, because without these signatures, one of the parties could say that they did not see one of the numerous pages of the entire contract.

Miscellaneous P&S Agreement concepts and terms

Purchase and Sale Agreement (P&S): This form is used for the sale of real estate.

Bill of Sale: This form is used for the sale of personal property, like a car.

Agreement in Writing: As stated elsewhere, all property transactions must be detailed and agreed to in writing in order to be legally valid. This does not necessarily have to be all on one specific form, but all relevant and detailed correspondence must be in writing between the parties.

Breach of Contract: If either party does not perform all of its requirements under the terms of the contract, there is a breach of contract. Either party may then take court action against the other in typical circumstances, for losses incurred as a result of the breach. In a typical P&S Agreement, if the buyer defaults for any reason, the seller is then allowed to keep the buyer's deposit (earnest money) as a liquidated damage. In many cases, this is the seller's only legal recourse against the buyer. Check with your own state. A breach may occur if one party fails to execute what the agreement specifies as a *specific performance*. Should this occur, it may be the right of a seller to issue a vendor's lien, which attempts to repossess the sold property until the buyer makes all payments for the full purchase price. Any breach of contract may cause the injured party to seek punitive damages, which is typically monetary compensation that exceeds the necessary amount of compensation for losses with the intention of punishing the wrongdoer and acting as a future deterrent.

Assignment: Most contracts are assignable, unless specifically stated otherwise within the document. An assignment of a contract means to transfer the rights of one party to some other third party. In a real estate transaction, this can be tricky, as most mortgage companies do *not* allow the buyer to assign their rights under the P&S to another third-party buyer — unless the mortgage company agrees to that assignment completely. Be wary of a buyer who is trying to assign the contract unless you check with their proposed lender.

Novation: Similar to an assignment, but here an entire new agreement would be formed with a third party to fully replace the existing contract.

Caveat Emptor: This means "buyer beware" or "let the buyer beware" and is often a part of most contracts. However, in real estate, there is increasing pressure toward consumer protection and full property disclosure, which have helped the buyer in many ways.

Deeds

A *deed* is a written instrument that transfers ownership of real property from one party to another. There are many types of deeds that we will describe below.

In general, deeds are recorded in County Land Records or in a Registry of Deeds. They are recorded in large books logged and stored at the Registry, which include a book number, page number, and date. This specific numbered registry info is called the property's *deed reference.* The *grantee* of the deed is typically the buyer; the deed is being written up for their future use and ownership. The *grantor* is the person or entity selling the property.

Every time a property is sold or transferred from one owner to another, a new deed must be created and recorded. Also note that in cases where a property owner refinances their own home, a new deed must be created as well.

Types of deeds

General Warranty Deed (or "Warranty Deed"): This provides the greatest degree of protection for a buyer, compared to other forms of deeds.

Special Warranty Deed: This guarantees the grantee against any defects (or "clouds" on the title as they are called) or claims that arose during the grantor's period of ownership, but not before the period of ownership.

Quitclaim Deed: A quitclaim deed conveys whatever interest the grantor has in the property but makes no warranties or guarantees as to what they include. Due to the prevalence of this type of deed, all lenders require title insurance protection for them, and it is usually a good idea for a buyer to get a "buyer's title insurance policy." These specialized insurance policies protect the new buyer against claims brought against them due to potential title issues (such as multiple ownership).

Other types of deeds: These you may encounter in very specialized situations, and, as such, we will not delve into all definitions in this book. We would recommend you consult your broker or a real estate attorney if you come across any of the following:

- Deed in Trust
- Trustee's Deed
- Bargain and Sale Deed
- Judicial Deed
- Executor's Deed
- Tax Deed
- Sheriff's Deed
- Administration Deed
- Guardian's Deed
- Gift Deed
- Commissioner's Deed
- Referee's Deed in Foreclosure

Sample Special Warranty Deed

SPECIAL WARRANTY DEED

THIS INDENTURE, made the ____ day of _____, 20____, between _____ of the County of _____, State of _____, hereinafter called "Grantor," and _____, whose address is _____, of the County of _____, State of _____, hereinafter called "Grantee" (the terms "Grantor" and "Grantee" are used for the singular and plural, as the context demands).

WITNESSETH that: Grantor, for and in consideration of Ten Dollars ($10.00) and other good and valuable considerations to said Grantor in hand paid by said Grantee, the receipt whereof is hereby acknowledged, has granted, bargained and sold and by these presents does grant, bargain and sell unto the said Grantee, and Grantee's heirs and assigns forever, land situate, lying and being in _____ County, _____ and more particularly described as follows:

(Insert Legal Description)

TO HAVE AND TO HOLD the said tract or parcel of land, with all and singular the rights, members and appurtenances thereof, to the same being, belonging, or in anywise appertaining, to the only proper use, benefit and behalf of the said Grantee forever in FEE SIMPLE.

This conveyance and the warranties contained herein are hereby expressly made subject to those matters set forth on Exhibit "B" attached hereto and made a part hereof.

AND THE SAID Grantor will only warrant and forever defend the right and title to the above described property unto the said Grantee against the claims of those persons claiming by, through or under Grantor, but not otherwise.

IN WITNESS WHEREOF, the Grantor has signed, sealed and delivered this Deed, the day and year above written.

WITNESSES:

_____   _____
                  Seller

_____

STATE OF _____:
                              :
COUNTY OF _____:

THE FOREGOING INSTRUMENT was acknowledged before me this ____ day of _____, 20_(19), by _____.

_____
                  Notary Public

My Commission Expires: _____

Key elements of a deed

1. Grantor (seller)
2. Grantee (buyer)
3. Consideration (usually money; always something of value)
4. Granting Clause (a statement which says that the grantor is conveying all rights to the grantee)
5. Habendum Clause (means "to have and to hold" and re-affirms the granting clause)
6. Limitations/Deed Restrictions
7. Legal Description (this will include a *metes and bounds, lot and block,* and/or a *government survey* method of description; see below)
8. Signature of Grantors
9. Delivery and Acceptance (to buyer/grantee)
10. Acknowledgement (under no duress)
11. Recording (at the County Registry of Deeds; usually requires some minor fee payment made to the Registry)

Metes and Bounds: This form of land description describes land by identifying the perimeter of a lot via length of a side in feet, plus location of the lot line either by compass point (for example, NW 34'8") or by monument (like an iron pipe, nail, oak tree, or stone wall).

Lot and Block: This refers to a map or "plat" that has been placed on file with the county by a developer. The plat identifies each parcel or lot within a block and assigns numbers to them (for instance, lot 12 in Sunnybrook Estates). The individual deed may reference "lot 12, block 21" on that particular plat as a legal description for the property.

Government Survey: This method is used by states and local governments, but not really for private parcels of land. It is a means of determining boundaries of towns, townships, and section of towns.

Other important deed and title terms

Torrens System: A system for recording land titles under which a court may direct the issuance of a certificate of title upon application by the landowner. This system is used in some states, including Massachusetts, for settling land disputes, whereby the issue is taken to a specific Land Court. Please confirm with your broker and state requirements to determine whether you will be required to define and work with the Torrens System.

Title Search/Title Insurance: The mortgage bank will hire an attorney to perform a title search before the loan is administered. The attorney may perform this title search or may subcontract a separate specialist called a title examiner to complete this task. A title search usually involves going to the Registry of Deeds and looking up all deeds recorded for said property for sale. The attorney will prepare a *chain of title* to help determine if there are voids and lapses, which could later result in another party claiming ownership rights of the property. The attorney will then prepare a summary of his findings, or an *abstract of title.*

Due to the fact that these attorney searches are not always foolproof and the fact that many parcels have been transferred upward of 10 to 20 times officially, most banks and many private buyers will elect to purchase a specialized insurance policy called title insurance. As with any insurance policy, the issuer will attach a *certificate of liability insurance*, which summarizes the insured party's insurance policy.

Tax Stamps/Excise Stamps: Many states require fees to be paid to the state when a property is transferred from one owner to another. These stamps indicate that the required excise tax has been paid and can be physically affixed to the deed. They are purchased by the attorney who will affix them to the deed that he records with the registry. This tax is based on a given tax rate and the amount of the purchase price of the property.

Involuntary Alienation: There are several situations in which property transfer without the owner's consent can transpire:

1. **Adverse Possession** (similar to prescription): Ownership or easements can be attained legally after long periods of using and maintaining another's property under some conditions. If a person uses another's land for more than the statues of limitations period prescribed by the state on adverse possession, that person may be able to derive something called an *easement of prescription*. This easement would essentially allow the user to continue ownership rights to the property. Other types of easement include *appurtenant easement*, which affords the right to use adjoining property that transfers with the land, and an *easement in gross*, which attaches a particular right to an individual rather than to the property itself.

2. **Eminent Domain** (also called condemnation): This is the process by which the government (be it local, county, state, or federal) takes ownership of the (private) property for specific use of "the common good." Here, the consent of the property owner is *not* required. However, it is required of the government entity to pay the property owner a fair market value for said property.

3. **Escheat:** As we mentioned earlier, this is when the state can take title of a property where the owner has died and has no will and no heirs.

4. **Foreclosure:** This is when the bank, or other lien holder, forces the sale of a property in order to repay a defaulted and delinquent debt. You would be well advised to become very familiar with the process of buying and selling foreclosed properties, and/ or properties in a state of foreclosure. Speak with your broker, research online, or consult books in print, such as the 2nd edition of "The Complete Guide to Locating, Negotiating, and Buying Real Estate Foreclosures," by Frankie Orlando and Marsha Ford.

5. **Natural Forces:** Nature can often take a property, or at least portions of the property and buildings. This is common in seacoast areas and can also occur through tornados, storm, earthquakes, and the like. Land that is added to land bordering rivers, lakes, and the sea is called *accretion*. When land is gradually lost over time that is called *erosion*. A sudden loss of land via a storm or earthquake is called *avulsion*.

Transfer by Will: When a property is transferred via the wishes of a deceased person (by way of a will), the property is *devised*. The Probate Court is the legal/judicial body that approves and executes the legal title transfer.

Leases and Property Management

Be it residential or commercial, many properties you will work with will not be bought and sold, but will be rented, via a specific lease agreement. In most commercial and larger multifamily residential properties, this can often involve a third-party property management company. We will cover various types of leases and obligations, as well as touch upon some property management basics.

Freehold and non-freehold estates

A freehold estate is an estate that lasts for an indefinite period of time (more than a lifetime). For example, if an owner holds a *fee simple property*, which is property not subject to any limitations or conditions, the owner would have a type of freehold estate. In this section, we will instead be discussing non-freehold estate, which is more customary and also delves into all of the landlord-tenant obligations and two-party lease agreements.

Non-freehold estates are also called "leasehold" estates. Here, the property owner will keep most of his rights to the property but will concede a portion of his rights — via a *Right of Possession* — to the tenant. The right conveyed to the tenant is in return for some payment to the owner — in the form of *rent* — and via the terms of a *lease*. In this case, the property owner is the *lessor* and the tenant (the one paying rent) is called the *lessee*. Leases are drafted for a particular period of time, called the *term*. Note that a lease is personal property, not real property. This comes into play when lease agreements are transferred or assigned.

Types of leasehold estates (or "tenancies")

Estate at sufferance: When a tenant overstays the lease term or has received proper notice to vacate and has not left. It is critical for the landlord to take the proper legal steps as far as eviction and the like during these circumstances.

Estate at will (also known as tenant/tenancy at will): This is when either the lessee or the lessor may end the lease agreement at any time, by giving the other party proper notice as determined within the specific lease agreement. Here, there is no set time or time-limit on the lease.

Estate for years: The most common type of commercial lease agreement, where there is a specific term (in years) and an end date.

Estate from period to period: In this lease there are terms, normally month to month or year to year- but no specified end date. If neither party specifies to the other that they would like to end the lease at the next time the lease runs out, then both parties continue with the lease for another increment of time, at the same lease obligations.

Types of leases

Net Lease/Triple Net Lease (NNN): In a net lease, the tenant is required to pay for some or all applicable expenses, in addition to the base rent. A "triple net lease," or NNN, means that the tenant is paying for all associated property expenses (utilities, insurance, and taxes) in addition to the rental fee.

Gross Lease: This is also called a straight or flat lease. In a gross lease, the landlord/owner pays for all expenses (utilities), and the tenant only pays a flat rental amount.

Percentage Lease: This rent is calculated by a percentage of the gross sales of the tenant. When a tenant's business increases, their rent will increase.

Graduated (or Step-Up) Lease: This is when the rental amount increases over the course of time. It is used in cases where a company needs lower rent and overhead in the beginning of the lease to get established in business.

Ground Lease: This is typically a long-term lease, as lease holders would be unwilling to build costly improvements if the benefit of such improvements could only be realized for a small number of years.

Index Lease: This is a rental agreement that requires changes in rent based on a published record of cost changes.

Sandwich Lease: This is a lease that allows a sub-letting party to sub-let the property.

Sale and Leaseback: This constitutes an arrangement where the seller of an asset leases back the same asset from the purchaser.

Lease Purchase: This is when the two parties will have a lease/rental agreement for a period of time, and then the lessee will purchase the property from the lessor.

Obligations of the lessor and lessee

A lease is a contract whereby both parties are expected to fulfill their portions of the agreement and terms. In addition to what is spelled out specifically within the lease, there are some other "common sense" and legal requirements that both parties must adhere to. Failure to do so results in a breach of the lease and may lead to penalties, fines, and lawsuits.

A tenant who does not fulfill their end of the lease (often associated with failure to pay or late payments) can be *evicted* by the owner. This is a legal process and due diligence must be followed by the owner.

Often, there is a *security deposit* that is associated with a lease. This is earnest money that is given in good faith to the landlord as collateral against tenant-caused damage to the property. When dealing with collateral, a *letter of hypothecation* is devised whereby the debtor pledges collateral to secure a debt or as a condition precedent to the debt, or a third party pledges collateral for the debtor. If there is damage done by the tenant, the landlord has the right to use some or all of these security deposit monies to repair and remedy the physical damage. In this case, the deposit is **not** refunded back to the lessee at the end of the lease term. Often, this deposit is the subject of lawsuits involving leases. On a similar note, the same can be said for deposited or escrowed "last month's rent" payments which are made upfront by the lessee in some lease agreements. This is another measure of protection for the landlord to make sure that as the tenant is ready to leave the property they do not run out on their final month's rental payment.

Lease options

Some leases have included within them an option for the lessee to purchase the property from the lessor at a disclosed time for a disclosed purchase price. As part of the monthly rent, sometimes a portion of this rent will then be deducted from the purchase price or the required deposit at that eventual time of purchase. This "rental partial credit" is not always obligatory.

Similar to a straight option, the lessee may have the "right of first refusal" on said property, whereby the lessee has the first right to purchase the property (and end the lease) if the owner has another (third party) written offer to purchase the property.

Assignment vs. sublease

If a lessee assigns the lease to a third party, then the third party is fully responsible for all terms and obligations within the original signed lease. Be careful to read the lease's fine print, as many leases are *not* assignable by the lessee.

Aside from a true assignment, a lessee may be able to sublease (or "sublet") the property to a third party, while still retaining all the right and responsibilities of the lease with the property owner. This means the lessee is still under all obligations to pay rent and is financially responsible for the condition of the property. However, with a sublease the lessee is essentially contracting out the lease to a third party, and said third party will pay the lessee monthly rent. Subleases can get complicated and are also subjects of numerous lawsuits. Keep in mind that some leases are drafted as to not allow a lessee to sublease the property.

Other lease terms and considerations

Leases within Property Purchases: A new property owner/buyer is obligated under the terms of any existing lease. If the seller of a property is in the middle of a five-year lease agreement with a tenant, the new owner must comply with said lease and allow the tenant to remain under the same rent and conditions. It is wise to include reference to any such leases within a drafted Purchase and Sale Agreement.

99-Year Leases: You may see this term, and it is generally the longest lease term allowed by law without falling into a "permanent" type of agreement, or an estate in fee simple.

State Differences and Consumer Protection Laws: All states will have different regulations and interpretations about what is obligatory to each party in a lease. Much of these differences have to do with the various consumer protection acts and laws, which states write into law. It is best to check with your state and/or your broker. For an overview of land-

lord-tenant laws by state, or landlord legal responsibilities by state, go to: **www.nolo.com/legal-encyclopedia/state-landlord-tenant-laws**.

Property management basics

Depending on the size and niche of the real estate brokerage firm that you go to work for, the company may have its own property management division. Often, real estate sales go hand in hand with property management. An in-house or third party (outside) property management company is essentially responsible for all of the tasks that a typical property owner would have to do, including:

- Evictions
- Account for funds and prepare necessary monthly and year-end reports
- Pay the expenses incurred on the property (especially in "common areas")
- Advertise, screen, interview, and select tenants
- Collect rents
- Maintenance and repairs (sometimes this may include specific tenant customizations or "fit-ups")

Property management firms will provide all of these services and be the main contact person for the tenants, especially in the case of complaints, requests, document preparation, and the like. A property management company also receives an administrative/management fee on top of all actual/direct expenses spent at the property. Often, this fee is a percentage or a flat rate. The fee is normally paid every month by the property owner. A specific and detailed contract between the owner/lessor and the property manager must be signed by both parties.

As a real estate professional, you will probably be asked to recommend a quality property manager. As always, you should feel strongly about any recommendations you give. If a company that you refer performs poorly in a client's eyes, they will remember you for steering them in that direction.

Be careful. If you do not have a good feeling about a company, even if it is a division of your own company, it is best to simply say that you cannot in good faith recommend someone for them. You can also find out what others are saying about property management firms through Zillow's Property Management Finder, available at: **www.zillow.com/agent-finder/property-manager-reviews**. This feature allows you to see ratings and reviews directly from their clients. If you are given the name of a property management firm, you can do some research and provide this feedback to your client.

Real Estate Brokerage

In all cases, as the new real estate sales agent, you will be required to work under the umbrella of a "broker." A broker is a person who, in exchange for some consideration/compensation, sells, buys, exchanges, rents, and negotiates real property. Brokers can specialize in different areas of real estate, including buyer or seller representations, rentals and leasing, residential, commercial, retail, industrial, and so forth. The broker may be more than one person — it could be a partnership, an LLC, or a larger corporation. In this book, it will all be referred to as the "broker."

Broker-related terms and types of agencies

Principal: This is another name for the broker who hires the sales agent.

Fiduciary Relationship: The agent has a fiduciary relationship with the broker, meaning that the agent must always look out for the best interest of the broker in all dealings with the clients (buyer, sellers, tenants) and others.

Buyer Agency: This is becoming more popular, and this is when an agent is representing the buyer, as opposed to the seller. This arrangement can get complicated and misunderstood as to who is paying the commission to the buyer agent/buyer broker. The specific agreement will determine whether the commission is paid by the buyer, the listing agent out of the seller's commission, or by the seller in a separate agreement.

Single Agency: This is the most common agency- whereby the broker represents one party, either the buyer or seller.

Dual Agency: It is possible for one broker to represent both the buyer and the seller in the same property transfer and sale. This can lead to some legal concerns, and specific disclosures must be signed by both the buyer and the seller.

Subagents: This is what happens when a listing broker "co-brokers" with another broker in order to sell the property on behalf of the seller. Most states allow this type of relationship, and often this coincides with use of a Multiple Listing Service (MLS) for a larger marketing reach.

Open Listing: This is not very common, but it is when listing has been given to more than one broker. Any broker can sell the property, and the seller retains the right to sell the property themselves without the use of any broker.

Exclusive Listing: When only one broker is given the opportunity to sell/list the property (this is generally the most common arrangement).

Net Listing: This is when the seller states what he wishes to receive, and then any amount over that base is given to the broker. Net listings can be dangerous and are not legal in some states. This should probably be avoided.

Multiple Listing: A sharing of the listing for practical purposes. Please see the section below.

Commissions: This is how you and the broker will be paid in a transaction. Normally, the full commission in a residential setting is between 4 percent and 7 percent of the sale price, and often, that is broken down between a listing broker and a co-broker. Keep in mind that your portion of the commission will be determined by your agreement with your broker. This is referred to as the broker-agent "split."

Capital Gains: These IRS and accounting-based laws are constantly changing, and it is best to follow up with your broker and/or a Certified Public Accountant (CPA) in your area to determine what capital gain ramifications may be of note to your potential seller clients. In simple terms, if you bought a property three years ago for $200,000, and you sold it today for $300,000, you would have a capital gain (or profit) of $100,000 and would thereby be taxed to some extent on that $100,000. There are many stipulations involved, including short-term and long-term capital gains.

REALTOR®: This copyrighted and registered word is reserved only for those members of the NAR who have agreed to their specific Code of Ethics. This is not a state-specific regulation or entity.

Encumbrances: Anything that lessens the value of a property. This may include liens of any variety, as well as encroachments (whereby a property owner violates his neighbor's rights by building on his or her property) and right of ways.

Escrow Accounts: Agents will often have to make deposits into escrow accounts, which are often held by either their broker or a real estate attorney. An escrow account normally houses a buyer's deposit and may also hold other monies where an independent and safe avenue of holding monies is required. Often times, the release of monies from escrow is in accordance with some type of signed contract.

Termination of Agency: Can be obtained via any of the following:

1. When the property is sold
2. Time limit expiration (most listing agreements are three, six, nine, or twelve months)
3. Mutual consent

4. Revocation of either party (this is unilateral and may
   result in legal action)
5. Death of either party
6. Destruction of property
7. Bankruptcy of either party

Agent's professional responsibilities and strategies

As a real estate sales agent, it is important to remember and focus on the following professional duties.

Reasonable care and diligence: Always represent your broker with a reasonable degree of skill, care, and diligence.

Accountability: An agent must account for all funds given to his control and must not co-mingle any funds (deposits, rents) with their own personal funds or accounts.

Confidentiality: In all matters, the agent must keep items and information confidential to both the client and the broker.

Disclosure (also known as Duty of Notice): The agent must disclose any conflicts of interest to their broker (i.e. agent is related to the property buyer).

Loyalty: The agent must act in the best interest of the broker, even when that may not be in the best interest of the sales agent.

Obedience: The agent must follow all instructions and orders given by the broker, even if said instructions are not in the agent's best interest.

There are four keys to review regarding agency strategy — sometimes called the four Ds:

1. **Document:** Document all relevant transaction and property papers, agreements, disclosures, and the like.

2. **Do:** Do implement all agency obligations that are required by your specific agency contract, state agency law, and fiduciary duties.

3. **Disclose:** Disclose and describe to your client or pending client what all the agency options and relationships are (buyer agency or dual agency, for example).

4. **Decide:** Decide whether you would like to represent the seller, the buyer, or both.

The Multiple Listing Service (MLS)

The MLS is popular and often the key to a wide audience for property marketing and a wide reaching co-broke opportunity. Each state has its own specific MLS, and it is often called something proprietary. Only real estate brokers, agents, and appraisers have full access to the MLS. They pay a fee to a third-party company in order to have access and submit property listings across that state's MLS. *More information on marketing and selling using the MLS will be discussed in a later section of this chapter.*

Marketing strategies and basics

While this book is not designed to be a "marketing-know-how" book, and the license exam does not specifically test on marketing and advertising, it is still important to state a few concepts and ideas. Marketing will be your No. 1 priority as you embark on your real estate career.

As a sales agent, you will be competing with hundreds, and likely thousands, of other agents and brokers in your state and area for business. People will select you to represent them in buying, selling, or leasing a property because of a number of factors, including:

1. Experience level (this will be a hard one to overcome in the first year)
2. Personality (some people will simply like you better than others, and vice-versa)
3. Comfort/how well they know you already
4. Relationships (family and friendly connections)

5. Real estate knowledge base (including how well you know your current local market and its conditions)

6. The broker or company you are working for (some people prefer larger firms with high name recognition, while others prefer a smaller independent outfit)

7. Whether you are working as a full-time or part-time agent

8. What your regular listing commission percentage is

9. What, specifically, the client is getting in marketing and advertising services for said commission percentage

10. Will their listing be on the MLS, and does your office offer co-brokering?

11. How well you promote yourself

12. Your level of real estate sales success (i.e., most homes sold in the county)

13. Your credibility and honesty

14. Your online/website presence and quality

These are a few of the main areas that you will need to focus on as you build your business.

Marketing with the MLS

Most sellers and clients, especially in these days of instant online listings and comparisons, are expecting that their listing will be posted and advertised in the MLS. It ensures that their property listing will quickly and easily reach the largest base of potential buyers and seller brokers, agents, and clients. It is best to work with your broker on how to post your listing on the MLS, how to keep it up to date, and how to work within the system. However, these are the main steps and characteristics:

1. Get a signed listing agreement with the seller (via your broker agency).

2. Fill out the forms (often online) with your state's MLS system (your broker may give you his or her log-in information, or you may have to register in your own name).

3. Add pictures to the online MLS listing server.

4. You will need to state on the system what co-broker percentage you are offering. This should be discussed with your broker and/or the seller. Often, it is simply 50 percent of the total listing commission that was agreed upon with the seller. In some cases, the seller may offer a temporary "co-broke/buyer broker bonus" that may be either a flat fee or an additional 0.5 percent or 1 percent commission. It is important to add this to the MLS, or no other agents will be aware of the incentive.

5. Be sure to update your MLS listing frequently (every day or week) and any time there is a change in the property or sales information (such as a price reduction).

6. Many MLS systems also allow an easy means of gathering marketing data to make comparisons to other properties that are for sale, and to see how often your listing is being viewed and visited by other agents. Often, it will also allow simple comments about your property to be noted by other agents who have been in or to the property.

Land development and building construction

There are many books and sources of information available regarding the intricacies and practicalities of land development as well as homebuilding and other new construction. We will reveal a few items to keep in mind.

You will be working with homebuilders and general contractors. Depending on your area and your broker's niche market, you will likely be representing a builder as the seller of a property that is either being built during your listing agreement or has already been completed in full. If a builder is building a home on a lot but has no end-buyer in mind, it is called a "spec home" or "speculative home." In any event, builders are a unique form of seller, as they are businessmen who are looking at merely the dollars and cents of the deal and have no real emotional attachment to the property.

Do not "dabble" in land development sales and consulting. As a licensed builder myself and someone who has developed land and built upon it, I can say that it is truly its own animal. I will not allow a real estate broker or agent to list my lots or property unless they have some real experience in this type of real estate. It is quite differ-ent, and the terms and details are differ-ent than listing a 50-year-old ranch house or the like.

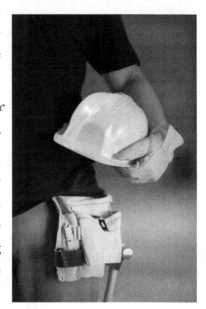

Give yourself, and the builder, plenty of time. I would recommend extending your listing agreement an extra three months, if possible, during any type of new con-struction project. Most construction takes longer than anticipated, and you do not want to be left without a valid listing agreement if the builder takes longer to complete the project than first thought.

Property income analysis

In Chapter 6, we further reveal and show examples of how to analyze some real estate deals from an investment angle. We have also noted some of the important terms of income analysis, including cap rate and Net Operating Income (NOI). As a real estate agent, you will be expected to understand, work with, and extrapolate numbers and income figures when you are try-ing to buy or sell investment property.

Investment property is any property where the owner is expecting monthly cash flow and/or eventual profits as a result of ownership. Often, he will rent out said property and collect rent. Other times, some real estate investors will merely try to quickly buy and sell property quickly, called "flipping."

In most cases, the owner does not live or work in the subject property. Most likely, he will either hire a third party property management company or will have to be available to handle all the circumstances, repairs, and other requirements needed.

CASE STUDY:
BEING LICENSED
IN MULTIPLE STATES

Al P.
Real Estate Investor, 5 years

I have been working as a real estate broker for five years in New Hampshire and four years in Florida. About 50 percent of what I do regularly I learned from the license examination materials. In addition, about 25 percent of my activities I learned from my broker training classes, with the remaining 25 percent being learned via the "school of hard knocks"!

One of the key aspects of real estate is Internet marketing and website development and betterment, which was not discussed much at all during the pre-exam courses or the exam itself. It may be wise for a new agent to get some outside assistance with this important aspect of the industry.

There is always some type of continuing education requirement. In both Florida and New Hampshire, there is a required state-approved test where I needed to achieve either a 70 percent or 75 percent to pass and receive the credits.

It was required that I take a pre-exam course for both states, which I did. I also managed to pass both exams on the first attempt, though I found the sections on real estate legal issues and agency test cases the most difficult.

I studied hard for both New Hampshire and Florida licenses. Florida was the hardest. I took the state test three days after taking the class so that everything was still fresh in my mind. I also replayed audio lessons in my car every day before the state test.

CASE STUDY: TAKING THE EXAM SERIOUSLY

Ron F.
Real Estate Agent, 25 years

After 25 years in the real estate business, I have seen nearly everything. During all this time, I have probably used about 70 to 75 percent of what was learned in the real estate licensing exam. Initially, I felt that much of the material was not useful. Over time I have grown to appreciate the value and depth of what was taught. The course book proved to be a great reference for me to look up items in question — I still use it to this day.

Much of what I do every week correlates directly back to items learned in the pre-exam course and its book. As a student, one should take the study seriously. By doing so and applying oneself, it increases learning for education's sake and not just to pass the exam! This can be difficult, as there are so many terms to memorize.

After taking the state-mandated pre-exam 40-hour course, I was fortunate enough to pass the exam on the first try. The hardest section of my exam was the minutia about the pro-rations that take place on the day of closing. As a REALTOR®, I have never been asked about these numbers by any clients. In New Hampshire, we need to take nine hours of continuing education every two years. Three of those hours need to be "core" courses, with the other six being elective subjects.

Real Estate Law

This chapter presents a general overview of real estate law, along with some key terms and practical working samples. Despite the material offered, it is important to note that what we address is generic in nature, and specific laws in your state may be slightly different. In addition, these regulations can change over time, so it is important to remember the No. 1 rule for a good real estate agent: *Leave the law to an attorney. You are a real estate agent, not a lawyer.*

This kind of thinking will protect you and your broker from potential legal action if you misrepresent a situation or a property deal.

Real Estate Law and Regulations by State

It is important to understand that each state has different intricacies within real estate law, and it is not wise to delve into all of these details. It is important to have working knowledge of all the basic law terms that are used in real estate and to become familiar with the basic forms used in your state or states (if you are planning on getting your sales agent license in more than one state). At a minimum, you should thoroughly review the following real estate contracts and forms for your state:

- Purchase & Sale Agreement (P&S)
- Residential Lease Agreement
- Commercial Lease Agreement
- Listing Agreement(s)
- Property Disclosure Statements and Forms (some states require)
- Offer to Purchase Form (used in some states in conjunction with P&S)
- Agent-Broker Agreement

Sometimes, you will be working with a potential property buyer or seller who is not hiring a professional real estate agent or broker, and they will try to use a generic, national P&S Agreement (or the like) for a transaction. It is strongly recommended that this not be used, as sometimes the basic and national templates do not coincide with all the specific bylaws a state may require for a property transfer. Later, in a court of law, it could be found that it is an invalid contract.

In addition, it is important not to alter clauses and terms within the body of any contract or accepted P&S. For example, the P&S form that your broker allows you to use has been drafted and reviewed (and updated as needed) by various real estate attorneys within your state and has been approved by your local/state Board of REALTORS®. More importantly, it has been authorized for use by the state's Real Estate Commission, which is the governing body of all real estate practice within your state, usually under the jurisdiction of the state's wider Board of Licensure.

Basics of License Law

The State's Board (or Commission) is responsible for overseeing all brokers and agents within the state and to ensure that they are qualified (and licensed). The board is also responsible for certain aspects of consumer protection. The following list describes the typical actions and responsibilities of the board:

- Governor appoints a set number to be on the board (usually five or seven members)
- Board will usually have a chairperson, and all will be citizens of the state as well as experienced and recommended real estate brokers and/or real estate attorneys
- Members of the board will typically serve for three to six-year terms
- Board will meet quarterly to conduct meetings where they will review and vote on necessary business
- Board has the authority to establish new bylaws and rules as they see necessary in regards to real estate
- Board, or its designees (approved third parties) will conduct examinations for licensure of both brokers and sales agents
- Board can conduct hearings and investigations and has authority to enforce all related laws. (Board can require by summons any information or testimony.)
- Board can suspend or terminate any broker or sales agent license if it deems necessary in due course.
- Board can fine a broker or agent in conjunction with its bylaws
- Board decisions will be as a result of a majority vote
- The decision to suspend or terminate any license may be appealed by the affected party (normally to a county court, state court, or superior court)

Licensing requirements

Typically, if a person performs any of the following acts, they must be a licensed agent and working under the supervision of a managing broker:

1. Advertises or represents themselves as a person selling or leasing real estate

2. Sells, exchanges, purchases, rents, leases, negotiates, makes offers, lists real estate to sell, or deals in real estate options

3. Assists or directs in the procuring of prospects for the sale or lease of real estate

4. Assists in the negotiation or completion of any contract or agreement that may or may not result in the sale or lease of real property.

Typical laws and statutes

The following list is *not* exhaustive, but these are the various requirements and prohibitions you will likely find within your state:

*   Agents cannot place "blind ads," meaning you cannot place an ad where you do not disclose the fact that you are (or working for) a licensed broker. You must state the name of the brokerage that you are working for within your advertisement or listing.

*   A sales agent must work for and under the supervision of a broker, and typically an agent can only work for one broker at a time.

*   An agent can be either a true employee of the broker or an independent contractor. (Many brokerages now have their workers as independent contractors instead of true employees. This protects the broker and is also the cheaper option for the broker. Beware of this status as you are comparing different brokerages to work for).

- Commissions are negotiable (in all cases, between any parties).

- An agent must disclose to a buyer, seller, or tenant with whom the agent's allegiances lie (you must declare whom you are working for and representing).

- All offers must be immediately conveyed to the other party in the pending transaction.

- All deposits or other monies paid by a buyer must be immediately given over to the responsible broker (typically the listing broker).

- All brokers must maintain a business address and post their state broker license/certificate in a conspicuous location within the office.

- It is illegal for an agent or broker, while speaking with a client, to recommend not using the services of an attorney.

- There are record-keeping requirements of all brokers to keep proof of all listing advertisements and rental/leasing advertisement for a period of time (normally two to three years). This is to ensure compliance with various provisions of the Fair Housing Act.

- Brokers must maintain records/copies of all checks, money orders, and cash deposits for a period of two to three years (typically earnest deposits)

- Real estate schools must be authorized by the board to certify hours of professional education and credits/hours.

- Board Qualified Instructors (at said schools) have requirements that exceed those of typical real estate brokers.

Contracts and Legal Documents

In dealing with clients, the two most important documents are the P&S Agreement and the Lease Agreement (if applicable). Both are binding contracts and have been discussed in some detail in Chapter 2. In addition, remember that it is not a "contract" unless it is signed, approved, and dated, by *both* parties and both parties are generally aware of the other's acceptance of the terms. Until this is the case, it is merely a document — not a contract or agreement.

Contrary to what may be believed, most states do *not* require buyer and seller signatures on a real estate contract to be *notarized*. Getting a signature notarized is when the person signing a document must sign in front of a state-approved Notary Public, after showing proof of their identification.

As briefly mentioned in the first paragraph of this chapter, it is critical that you, as an agent or broker, do not alter paragraphs, provisions, or wording of these documents. The documents that you see and review have been written by attorneys in your state who are aware of all the bylaws and other legal ramifications of certain wordings and clauses. You, or your client, may believe that certain aspects of the document are unnecessary, but they are written for a specific reason and are a critical aspect of the short and long-term validity of the signed contract. Some other clauses in an agreement may include:

- *Automatic Renewal Clause:* allows for another term after the original agreement reaches its expiration date.

- *Limitation of Liability Clause:* requires both parties to agree on a maximum amount of damages recoverable for a future breach of the agreement.

- *Broker Protection Clause:* entitles the broker to a commission when an entity with whom the broker did not conduct negotiations purchased the property after the expiration of the listing agreement.

The only words or items one should add to a state-specific and authorized real estate form are within those certain areas where there is space to add additional provisions or addenda. An addenda is *multiple* addendums, with an *addendum* meaning "an addition or update for an existing contract between parties. An addendum allows a revision to a contract without creating an entirely new contract. An addendum is only enforceable if both parties agree and sign."

A quick review regarding some (often forgotten) parts of a Real Estate Contract/Legal Document follows. *Note: Most of the following is already incorporated in many state-specific P&S Agreement forms.*

1. **Attorney Review Clause:** Inserting a clause into the real estate contract that allows for a period of attorney review (usually two weeks) provides a key layer of protection for both buyers and sellers.
   Note that in a typical real estate transaction, the attorney that represents the bank or mortgage company is representing the lender and is not truly representing the buyer — although most buyers do not understand this. In addition, said attorney is certainly not representing (to any degree) the seller and their interests.

2. **Timing or Method of Payment:** Simply stating the purchase price is *not* enough. If part of the purchase price is to be paid as earnest money (initial deposits and then installments), that understanding must be stated along with the specific dates on which each such payment is to be made and in what format (i.e., bank/certified check, wire transfer, or cash). Also, there should be a note included as to who is holding said earnest monies.

3. **Mortgage Contingency Clause:** As the majority of property transactions require third party financing, this is essential for

the buyer. Without this clause, a buyer could be liable on a P&S Agreement even if he or she cannot arrange financing (cannot attain a mortgage).

4. **Defeasance Clause:** A mortgage provision indicating that the borrower will be given the title to the property once all mortgage terms are met. If the borrower meets all the mortgage terms, he or she will receive a letter of defeasance.

5. **Inspections Clause:** This allows the buyer to have licensed professionals inspect the property and cancel the contract if those inspections uncover "unsatisfactory" conditions. This limits both the period in which inspections can take place and the nature/ degree (or wording) of defective conditions that can give rise to contract cancellation. These clauses can also protect the seller. *Note that in many cases, the outcome of these property/home inspections (paid by the buyer) can be used by the buyer to gain an advantage in negotiations over the seller. As a sales agent, you should expect this to be the case. Learn how to bring both parties to a reasonable agreement to "save" the deal.*

6. **Pre-Closing Damage/Destruction Clause:** Due to the *doctrine of equitable conversion (see next section)*, depending on the state in which the property resides, and especially in the absence of a well-phrased Damage/Destruction clause, the pending buyer can take the financial responsibility if the property is destroyed (burnt down, etc.) prior to closing.

7. **Prorations:** This is what happens to property taxes and utilities like water, electricity, and heating if the seller moves out and buyer takes possession between the time each of these bills comes due (a very frequent occurrence). Items like these should be prorated at the time of contract formation (the drafting of the

P&S Agreement between both parties) and, if possible, settled at the closing.

Prorations are based on percentages, time, and dollar amounts or value. Examples are shown in the Chapter 6.

8. **Fixtures, Personal Property, and Bill of Sale:** Everyone remembers to put the house down on the contract, but what about all of those "things" inside the house? Which ones are moving out with the seller? Is the buyer aware of this? Which items or fixtures will stay with the house and thus represent a small component of the purchase price? (Terms like "fixtures" were discussed in Chapter 2 in detail.) If such matters are not put in writing, they could become a matter of disagreement later at a much more inconvenient time. A smart real estate agent will help prevent this from happening.

9. **Post-Closing Possession Agreement:** In many cases, the seller will be purchasing a new/separate property and might not be able to move out of the old one by closing day. If this is the case, assuming the buyer agrees to such an extended stay, a final deadline date by which the seller will move out should be included in the real estate contract. A separate agreement outlining such items as the compensation (i.e., rental payment) to be paid by the seller to the buyer for the seller's post-closing period of possession should be attached to the main P&S Agreement — often as an addendum. This is a practical concern that will come up again and again in many property deals.

10. **Condominium/Association Letters and Waivers:** If the property is a condominium, a house belonging to an association, or is tied together in some other type of group living arrangement or co-op, certain additional items need to be clarified/arranged, and these should always be dealt with prior to signing the P&S Agreement. For example, any housing association must be contacted by the buyer (typically, the buyer's attorney) to verify

the amount of assessments levied on the property, to confirm the amount of any current or planned/pending special assessments, and to request a waiver of any *right of first refusal* that may be held by the association.

Destruction of property between P&S Agreement signing and closing

This possible situation can have important consequences for the parties to a real estate contract. For example, what happens if a buyer contracts to purchase seller's house but the house burns down three days later, a full two weeks before the closing? Historically, according to what became known as the *Doctrine of Equitable Conversion*, the answer was that the buyer would be financially liable and responsible. The thinking behind the Doctrine of Equitable Conversion is that although buyer does not obtain *legal* title to the property upon executing the contract, the buyer does obtain *title in equity*. Traditionally in property transactions, the buyer would be liable for any losses resulting from damage to the subject property prior to closing, because the buyer is deemed to be the "true" or *equitable* owner of the property, whereas the seller's interest is limited to a contractual right to the sale proceeds (compensation at closing). Under this generic rule designed to protect the seller's interests, the buyer would still be required to pay the *full* purchase price to the seller, even if the subject property was destroyed (completely or partially) by fire before the buyer received the deed at closing.

In order to mitigate the harsh Doctrine of Equitable Conversion, parties to a real estate contract are always free to add their own rules regarding liability for losses occurring during the pre-closing period. Prior to signing the P&S Agreement, a buyer may insist that a clause be added to the contract making the seller liable for any damage to the property (not caused by the buyer) that occurs prior to the title transfer. In addition, regardless of what rule is in effect regarding pre-closing liability, the buyer, like the seller, typically has an insurable interest in the property after signing the contract and thus can purchase insurance that covers pre-closing damage to the property. This is rarely done in practice, but it is allowable. *Note that your state's P&S Agreement forms may already have a "liability for losses" clause within it.*

Federal Fair Housing Law

The Federal Fair Housing Law, as amended in 1989, was initially formed in 1968 as the Fair Housing Act. For writings within this section, we will refer to the Federal Housing Administration with the acronym FHA (not to be confused with the Federal Housing Authority).

Key provisions of the FHA

* Prohibits housing discrimination against "protected classes" (race, color, religion, national origin, sex, handicapped persons, and families with children). "Handicapped" is defined as any person with physical or mental impairment, which substantially limits one or more significant life activities.

* It is illegal for any lending institution to vary the terms and conditions of a loan because the applicant (borrower) is a member of a protected class. Part of this financing discrimination provision is the ban on "redlining." Redlining is the act of eliminating a portion or section of a town from receiving any loans from the bank — largely due to the makeup of the ethnicity within said area.

* It is illegal to vary terms of, or not offer, brokerage services to members of a protected class. This includes the multiple listing service and any other professional service related to the sale or rental of housing.

* It is illegal for an appraiser to give a specific value or deduction to a property because it is in, or is impacted by, a neighborhood of a strong protected class percentage. For example, the appraiser

cannot calculate a downward adjustment of $12,000 on a property because it is located in a minority neighborhood.

- Specific guidelines (as of 1991 for any newly built property with four or more residential units) mandate that the following design and construction characteristics be handicap-accessible:
  1. Lowered light switches and thermostats
  2. Hallway and doorway designs
  3. Raised electrical outlets
  4. Bathrooms and kitchen design

- Prohibits the following activities:
  - Discrimination against any person in establishing terms or conditions for the sale or rental of housing

  - Refusal to rent, sell, or otherwise deal with any specific person

  - Discrimination in any advertising for the sale or rental of a dwelling

  - Denying that housing is available, when it is available

  - *Blockbusting:* attempting to influence any individual to sell or rent with threats that persons of a particular protected class status are entering the neighborhood

  - *Steering:* showing members of a protected class property in neighborhoods and areas made up mostly of the same minority background while not showing comparable properties in other neighborhoods

Housing not covered by the FHA

- Single-family residences (for sale by a private owner-occupant)

- Rentals of multifamily units that are owner-occupied, as long as it is a two or three family building.

- Religious organizations have a degree of latitude in the (noncommercial) sale or rental of properties they own.

- Private clubs (like the Elk Lodge or Kiwanis Club) may sell or rent their property to members only, as long as it is not for commercial purposes.

Enforcement and fines of the FHA

Violations of the FHA are reported through either the Department of Housing and Urban Development (HUD) or the U.S. District Court.

The court may assess the following fines on the guilty party:

- First offense: $16,000
- Second offense: $42,500 (second offense within five years of first)
- Third offense: $70,000 (third offense within seven years of first)

Truth In Lending Act ("Regulation Z")

Lending money to finance the purchase of property typically involves a financial institution (sometimes called a *warehouse lender*), that lends a line of credit to a borrower in order to initially purchase a property. The Truth in Lending Act (TILA), Title I of the Consumer Credit Protection Act, was established to promote the informed use of consumer credit by requiring disclosures about all relevant terms and costs. This regulation applies to each individual or business that offers or extends credit when the credit is offered or extended to consumers (generally private individuals). The credit is subject to a finance charge (interest payment) or is payable by a written agreement in more than four installments. It is primarily for personal, family, or household purposes, and the loan balance equals or exceeds the new threshold of $50,000 *or* is secured by an interest in real estate.

TILA is intended to easily allow the comparison of the cost of a cash versus credit transaction and the difference in this "cost of credit" among different lenders. The regulation requires a maximum interest rate to be stated in variable rate contracts secured by the borrower's dwelling. It also imposes limitations on home equity plans (Home Equity Lines of Credit: "HELOC" or Home Equity loans) that are subject to the requirements of certain sections of the act and requires a maximum interest that may apply during the term of a mortgage loan. TILA also establishes disclosure standard practices for advertisements that refer to certain credit terms.

In addition to financial disclosure, TILA provides consumers with substantial legal rights in connection with certain types of credit transactions to which it relates. These include a *right of rescission* in certain real estate lending transactions, regulation of certain credit card practices, and a means for fair and timely resolution of credit billing disagreements.

This section will be limited to these aspects of TILA that relate specifically to the mortgage lending process.

Early and final Regulation Z disclosure requirements

TILA requires lenders to make specific disclosures on loans subject to the Real Estate Settlement Procedures Act (RESPA) within three business days after their receipt of a written application. This initial disclosure statement is partially based on the unverified information provided by the consumer. A final (and fully accurate) disclosure statement is provided at the time of loan closing. The disclosure is required to be in a specific format and must include the following information:

1. Name and address of creditor (bank/lending institution)
2. Amount financed
3. Itemization of amount financed [optional, if Good Faith Estimate (GFE) is provided]
4. Finance charge
5. Annual percentage rate, otherwise known as APR (for definition, see Mortgage Terminology in Chapter 4); this is usually a different number than the mortgage or interest rate

6. Variable rate information [for example, Adjustable-Rate Mortgages (ARM)]
7. Payment schedule
8. Total of payments (including all principal plus all interest payments)
9. Demand feature
10. Total sales price
11. Prepayment policy
12. Late payment policy
13. Security interest
14. Insurance requirements
15. Certain security interest charges
16. Contract reference
17. Assumption policy
18. Required deposit information

Disclosure requirements for ARM loans

If the APR on a loan secured by the consumer's principal dwelling may increase after loan commencement and the term of the loan exceeds one year, TILA mandates additional ARM disclosures to be provided, including:

- The booklet titled *Consumer Handbook on Adjustable Rate Mortgages*, published by the Consumer Financial Protection Bureau or a suitable substitute. You can find this book by using their search tool at **www.consumerfinance.gov**.

- A loan program disclosure for each variable-rate program in which the consumer expresses an interest. The loan program disclosure shall contain the necessary information as prescribed by Regulation Z. Note that there are now numerous mortgages available with differing adjustable rate characteristics. One booklet does not cover all available adjustable mortgages.

Right of rescission

In a mortgage transaction involving a consumer's principal dwelling, each consumer whose ownership is or will be subject to the security interest has the right to rescind the transaction. Lenders are required (typically presented at the closing) to deliver two copies of the notice of the right to rescind and one copy of the disclosure statement to each consumer entitled to rescind.

There are specific requirements of how a consumer can legally rescind an applicable credit transaction.

When a consumer rescinds a transaction, the security interest giving rise to the right of rescission becomes void and the consumer will no longer be liable for any amount, including any finance or interest charge. Within 20 calendar days after receipt of a notice of rescission, the lender is required to return any money or property that was given to anyone in connection with the transaction and must take any action necessary to reflect the termination of the security interest.

The consumer may modify or waive the right to rescind under certain specific guidelines.

Advertising disclosure requirements

If a lender advertises directly to a consumer, TILA requires the advertisement to disclose the credit terms and rate in a certain manner. If an advertisement for credit states specific credit terms (rates and payments), it may state only those terms that actually are or will be arranged or offered by the lender. If an advertisement states a rate of finance charge/interest, it may state the rate as an APR. If the APR may be increased after the loan begins (as in many ARMs), the advertisement must state that fact. The advertisement may not state any other rate, except that a simple annual rate or periodic rate that is applied to an unpaid balance may be stated in conjunction with but not more conspicuously than the APR. These mortgage advertising guidelines have been under scrutiny by consumer watchdogs and other politicians since the subprime mortgage crises of 2007.

Property Disclosures and Transferring Ownership

As you can see, there are many regulations of property ownership and ways of transferring the property ownership. Before you take your exam, be sure to review Chapter 2, which includes the following legal terms:

- Deed (all the various varieties)
- Title (all the various varieties)
- Lessee and lessor
- Involuntary transfer
- Lot description
- Registry of deeds
- Tax stamps
- Lease agreement

Regarding property disclosure statements and forms, some states require a seller to fill out and sign a multi-page property condition disclosure statement, while other states have no requirements. All states now recommend such a good-faith document to be transferred from the seller and the seller's agent to the potential buyer.

It is the seller's duty (in specific mandatory states) to complete (in full) the property disclosure form to the "best of their ability." This does not necessarily mean that everything written by the seller on these forms is correct and true, but that the seller believes it to be true. If the seller is legitimately unsure about a property condition, he or she may simply write "unknown" or state "unsure" or "not applicable." A buyer who notices many "unknowns" on a completed seller disclosure form should be sure to do their due diligence on the property, including the use of one or more professional inspectors.

From a legal standpoint, the seller must disclose all known property attributes. Lawsuits and damages have arisen from situations where the old owner (seller) is found later (after the closing) to have purposely lied about or withheld important information on these disclosure forms. As an agent, be sure to tell your seller clients what their duties are under these laws.

CASE STUDY: CONTRACTS & PRACTICING REAL ESTATE LAW NEAR STATE BORDERS

Michael D.
Real Estate Attorney, 31 years

I have been practicing law in both New Hampshire and Massachusetts for 31 years. I have found this dual status key as most of my clients are located along the border in southern New Hampshire. One of the divisions of our law firm focuses on real estate law, where we are typically working on a commercial transaction or zoning and Town Approvals concern.

In New Hampshire, there is a required seller-disclosure form to describe the property details and condition — for residential properties only. This is not required (or expected) for commercial properties.

There have been many times that I have been involved in a case or transaction which resulted from a property buyer or seller using an incorrect P&S Agreement or one that is not the suggested form for the specific state. In generic forms, there can be many deletions, errors, omissions, and language that is incorrect and not the norm for the area. The state of New Hampshire does not mandate any specific P&S Agreement form, but it does suggest that the one endorsed by the state's Board of REALTORS® is used for ease.

In a simple single-family property transfer, our firm is typically hired by the buyer's lender to prepare for and administer the closing. I make sure that the first thing I review with them is the disclosure statement, which tells the buyer and seller that I am only representing the lender and looking after the lender's interests. However, in most cases, the lender's interests will coincide with 90 percent of the buyer's interests.

In commercial or larger transactions, I always recommend that the buyer hire their own private attorney to review documents and to make sure that the buyer's own interests are being protected at the closing.

Real estate agents and brokers could be sued for not explaining the P&S Agreement properly to a buyer, so I think it is important for the real estate professional to be proficient in the clauses and terms that are on their typical P&S form. Note that although they could be sued, that would not be very practical, and I have never seen or heard of it in my professional experience.

Some real estate cases can get very complicated and lengthy. I was involved in a case that took over six years to resolve. It was an urban renewal redevelopment project involving some retail space. The owner/developer was foreclosed upon, and then the bank that held the note went under. There was also a mechanic's lien placed on the property by a subcontractor due to a verbal agreement. The lawsuit involved many parties and was brought on by the eventual title insurance company. The case was finally settled before a retrial, approximately six years after the case was brought to our office.

Real estate lawsuits can also be quite costly. For just a single-family house purchase, I was involved in a $1 million claim involving a buyer who rescinded on a deal because of a blatant misrepresentation of a lot line.

CASE STUDY: ETHICAL STANDARDS

Macie H.
Real Estate Broker, 5 years

I have been practicing real estate in Utah for four and a quarter years and recently got my license in Montana. I received my Associate Broker license in Utah (meaning I am still practicing under another principal broker) last summer, and I have a full Broker's license in Montana. About 95 percent of the exam's materials I have used at some point or another. I have had to refer back to my notes and texts from classes regarding a variety of situations over the years.

Utah does not stress testing on the Real Estate Purchase Contract, which is a state-approved form and the industry standard. There are many agents that still get things wrong or do not understand different supplementary and standard clauses that are in the contract. Also, I think that ethics should be a bigger focus in the agent exam. It is tested in the Broker exam. The reason being, if people are going to make the wrong ethical decisions about their business, they are going to sully the Real Estate Agent and Sales Agent-Broker labels. In addition, I think that it would be great for agents to have to answer practical questions about agency and representation.

The hardest section of the exam involved the types of ownership that exist because there are a variety of deeds that are used to transfer title here. The deeds have specific legal wording that identify what type they are, and if you assume too much in the wording (i.e., do not know and guess) you could really have a mess on your hands.

I did pass the exam on the first try in both states, and I did have help from the required pre-exam courses. It is a 90-hour course in Utah for the Agent license and 120 hours (in addition to the 90 hours) for Broker. Both are state requirements. In addition, for a Broker license, a certain number of sales and/or experience and at least three years in the business is required to apply. I received my Montana license through a reciprocity agreement between Utah and Montana. (Many states have similar reciprocal agreements.)

For continuing education, Utah requires 12 hours every two years, six of which must be core designated and six of which are elective. There is no passive education anymore. Montana requires 12 hours every year.

Chapter 4

Real Estate Finance (Mortgages)

ost real estate purchases involve third party (bank) financing, as most buyers do not have the necessary funds or other liquid assets to pay the entire purchase price. In 2015, the median sales price of a single-family home in the United States, for instance, was approximately $223,500. Average-priced homes in pricier areas, such as San Francisco, New York City, and Boston are much higher. Whatever a buyer does not have in earnest monies will need to be financed. In some cases, there exists "seller financing," where the seller/old owner will essentially act as a bank and hold a mortgage note on the new buyer at terms that both buyer and seller agree upon. Seller financing is relatively rare, so in this chapter the focus will be on traditional (bank-written and held) mortgages.

A mortgage is a specific type of promissory note. A promissory note is any contract in which one party is promising repayment of a debt to another, under some specific terms and length of time. A mortgage is debt that is secured by real property such as a house, a parcel of land, or an apartment building.

Repaying a mortgage will involve paying a certain amount of loan principal and loan interest every month, for a set number of months or years. The total amount paid at the end of the loan will be higher than the simple amount borrowed, especially if it is a long-term mortgage (20 or more years). Most mortgage are written for a 30-year loan term, but over the past few years 40-year mortgages, and even some 50-year mortgages have come to the market.

Although it is not your job to become a mortgage expert, it is important to become well versed in mortgage terminology, the basics of monthly payments, and what potential buyers can truly afford. It is expected with the license exam and in daily work that a sales agent will know how to determine monthly payments and escrows based on the mortgage rate, purchase price, and other factors. One of the easiest ways to handle that task is to purchase and practice on a special real estate/mortgage handheld calculator. *(This may not be allowed in your license exam, so check with your state or broker.)*

Another general comment on the mortgage subject is to work with one or two loan officers that are knowledgeable and that you feel comfortable with. Mortgage brokers (or bank loan officers) are looking to build a professional relationship with you and want to assist in your home and real estate sales, as they could benefit if they were to originate the loan. Most loan officers will be happy to update you on a regular basis on the credit and mortgage market and pass along to you current mortgage rate sheets and any new special loan programs. Often, making a real estate sale is more dependent on finding financing for the buyer than finding a home that the buyer likes.

Mortgage Terminology

1003: Uniform Residential Loan Application (per Fannie Mae).

Acceleration Clause: Allows the lender to speed up the rate at which your loan comes due or even to demand immediate payment of the entire outstanding balance of the loan should you default on your loan.

Adjustment Interval: On an adjustable rate mortgage, the time between changes in the interest rate and/or monthly payment; typically one, three, or five years, depending on the index.

Affidavit: A sworn statement in writing.

Amortized/Amortization: Amortization refers to the principal portion of the loan payment and is the loan payment by equal periodic payments calculated to pay off the debt at the end of a fixed period, including accrued interest on the outstanding balance. A fully amortized loan will be completely paid off at the end of the loan term.

Appraisal: An estimate of the value of real property, made by a qualified professional called an "appraiser." An appraisal will be needed to determine the value of your property.

APR (Annual Percentage Rate): A form of disclosure on the truth and lending form that explains the interest rate after factoring in the cost of obtaining the loan. It is a measure of the cost of credit, expressed as a yearly rate.

ARM (Adjustable Rate Mortgage): A mortgage loan where the interest rate is not fixed for the entire term of the loan but changes during the life of the loan in line with movements in an index rate.

Assumption: The agreement between buyer and seller where the buyer takes over the payments on an existing mortgage from the seller. This must be approved by the lender and be allowed by the note, which was originally signed by the seller.

Balloon: Usually a short-term, fixed-rate loan that involves small payments for a certain period of time and one large payment for the remaining amount of the principal at a time specified in the contract.

Broker: An individual in the business of assisting in arranging funding or negotiating contracts for a client but who does not loan the money himself. Brokers usually charge a fee or receive a commission for their services.

Buy Down: When the lender and/or the homebuilder subsidizes the mortgage by lowering the interest rate during the first few years of the loan. While the payments are initially low, they will increase when the subsidy expires.

Cap: The highest rate that an adjustable rate mortgage may reach. It can be expressed as the actual rate or as the amount of change allowed above the start rate. For example, a 7.99 percent start rate with a 6 percent rate change cap would have a maximum interest rate cap of 13.99 percent.

Clear to Close (CTC): Loan is ready to be closed with no additional conditions.

Closing: The meeting between the buyer, seller, and lender or their agents where the property and funds legally change hands. Also called settlement.

Closing Costs: Usually include an origination fee, discount points, appraisal fee, title search and insurance, survey, taxes, deed recording fee, credit report charge, and other costs assessed at settlement. The costs of closing are usually about three to six percent of the total mortgage amount, or any costs being charged to facilitate granting of the credit request.

Commitment: An agreement, often in writing, between a lender and a borrower to loan money at a future date subject to the completion of paperwork or compliance with stated conditions.

Construction Loan: A short-term interim loan for financing the cost of construction. The lender advances funds to the builder at periodic intervals as the work progresses.

Conventional Loan: A mortgage not insured by FHA or guaranteed by the U.S. Department of Veterans Affairs (VA).

Conversion Clause: A provision in some ARMs that allows you to change the ARM to a fixed-rate loan at some point during the loan term.

Credit Ratio: The ratio, expressed as a percentage, which results when a borrower's monthly payment obligation on long-term debts is divided by his or her net effective income (FHA/VA loans) or gross monthly income (conventional loans).

Credit Report: History of buyer's past credit performance.

Credit Score: The score given to an individual to determine the credit worthiness. These scores come from Equifax, Experian, TransUnion, and other credit reporting agencies.

D.T.I./Debt-to-Income Ratio: The customer's monthly obligations divided by their monthly gross income. Also called back-end ratio.

Deed of Trust: A document that pledges real property to secure a debt. In some cases, a deed of trust can replace a mortgage.

Default: Failure to meet legal obligations in a contract; specifically, failure to make the monthly payments on a mortgage.

Deferred Interest: See **Negative Amortization**.

Delinquency: Failure to make payments on time. This can lead to foreclosure.

Discount Points: Prepaid interest assessed at closing by the lender. Each point is equal to 1 percent of the loan amount (e.g. two points on a $100,000 mortgage would cost $2,000).

Down Payment: Money paid to make up the difference between the purchase price and mortgage amount. Down payments usually are 10 to 20 percent of the sales price on conventional loans and no money down up to five percent on FHA and VA loans.

Due-On-Sale Clause: A provision in a mortgage or deed of trust that allows the lender to demand immediate payment of the balance of the mortgage if the mortgage holder sells the home.

Equity: The difference between the fair market value and current indebtedness. Also referred to as the owner's interest.

Escrow: Refers to a neutral third party who carries out the instructions of both the buyer and seller to handle all the paperwork of settlement or closing. Escrow may also refer to an account held by the lender into which the homebuyer pays money for tax or insurance payments.

Escrow Waiver: The Request for a borrower to pay their own taxes and insurance. Escrow waivers are rarely granted with less than a 25 percent equity position (less than 75 Loan-to-Value Ratio or LTV).

Federal Home Loan Mortgage Corporation (FHLMC): Also known as Freddie Mac. A quasi-governmental agency that purchases conventional mortgages from insured depository institutions and HUD-approved mortgage bankers.

Federal Housing Administration (FHA): A division of the Department of Housing and Urban Development. Its main activity is the insuring of residential mortgage loans made by private lenders. FHA also sets standards for underwriting mortgages.

Federal National Mortgage Association (FNMA): Also known as Fannie Mae. A tax-paying corporation created by Congress that purchases and sells conventional residential mortgages as well as those insured by FHA or are guaranteed by VA. This institution, which provides funds for one in seven mortgages, makes mortgage money more available and more affordable.

Fee Simple: A form of ownership where the owner possesses an absolute title to land, free of any other claim against the title, which one can sell or pass to another through inheritance.

FHA Mortgage Insurance:
Requires an upfront Mortgage
Insurance Premium (MIP) —
about 1.7 percent of the loan
amount. For example, if you use
an FHA-backed mortgage for a
purchase mortgage and your loan
size is $300,000, then your upfront
MIP would be 1.75 percent of
$300,000, or $5,250.

Fixed-Rate Mortgage: A mortgage
on which the interest rate is set for
the term of the loan.

Flood Insurance: A mandatory
insurance for some homeowners
whose property is built in a
designated flood zone.

Foreclosure: A legal procedure
in which property securing debt
is sold by the lender to pay a
defaulting borrower's debt.

Free and Clear: This means the
property is completely paid for and
has no liens attached.

Good Faith Estimate (GFE):
A document that includes the
breakdown of approximate
payments due upon the closing of
a mortgage loan.

Gross Monthly Income: The
total amount the borrower earns
per month, before any expenses
are deducted.

Guarantee: A promise by one
party to pay a debt or perform an
obligation contracted by another
if the original party fails to pay or
perform according to a contract.

Hazard Insurance: A form of
insurance in which the insurance
company protects the insured
from specified losses, such as fire,
windstorm and the like. It would
not cover earthquake, riot, or
flood damage.

**Housing Expenses-to-Income
Ratio:** The ratio, expressed as a
percentage, which results when a
borrower's housing expenses are
divided by his/her net effective
income (FHA/VA loans) or
gross monthly income
(conventional loans).

Impound: The portion of a
borrower's monthly payments held
by the lender or servicer to pay for
taxes, hazard insurance, mortgage
insurance, lease payments, and
other items as they become due.
Also known as reserves.

Index: A published interest rate against which lenders measure the difference between the current interest rate on an adjustable rate mortgage and that earned by other investments. This includes the following: one, three, and five-year U.S. Treasury Security yields, the monthly average interest rate on loans closed by savings and loan institutions, and the monthly average Costs-of-Funds incurred by savings and loans. This is then used to adjust the interest rate on an adjustable mortgage.

Jumbo Loan: A loan that is larger (more than $417,000) than the limits set by the FNMA and the FHLMC. Jumbo loans cannot be funded by these two agencies, so they usually carry a higher interest rate.

LIBOR: London InterBank Offered Rate. LIBOR is the base interest rate paid on deposits between banks in the Eurodollar market.

Loan Committee: A lending or management committee of a bank or other lending institution that analyzes loans for approval or rejection of a loan. Such powers not authorized by the initial loan office and are generally part of the underwriting process.

Loan-To-Value Ratio (LTV): The relationship between the amount of the mortgage loan and the appraised value of the property; expressed as a percentage.

Margin: The number of percentage points the lender adds to the index rate to calculate the ARM interest rate at each adjustment.

Market Value: The highest price that a buyer would pay and the lowest price a seller would accept on a property. Market value may be different from the price a property could actually be sold for at a given time.

Mortgage Insurance: Money paid to insure the mortgage when the down payment is less than 20 percent. See **Private Mortgage Insurance** or **FHA Mortgage Insurance**.

Mortgagee: The lender.

Mortgagor: The borrower or homeowner.

Negative Amortization: Amortization means that monthly payments are large enough to pay the interest and reduce the principal on a mortgage. Negative amortization occurs when the monthly payments do not cover all of the interest cost. The interest cost that is not covered is added to the unpaid principal balance. This means that even after making many payments, a borrower may owe more than was owed at the beginning of the loan.

Origination Fee: The fee charged by a lender to prepare loan documents, make credit checks, inspect, and sometimes appraise a property. Usually computed as a percentage of face value of the loan.

Owner Occupied: Designation given to property used as the owner's residence.

Owners Policy: A policy of the title insurance that protects the buyer against problems with the title.

Piggy Back Loan: Financing obtained, subordinate to the first mortgage, to facilitate closing the first mortgage. Also known as a secondary financing.

Planned Unit Development (PUD): Property owned as a group, where individuals own the specific piece of land and structure they occupy, but also have a divided interest in a common area. A board, often referred to as a Homeowners Association, will govern the development.

Points: A point is equal to one percent of the principal amount of a mortgage. See also **Discount Points**.

Power of Attorney: An authority by which one person enables another to act on his or her behalf. Power of attorney can be limited to specific areas or can be general in some cases.

Preapproval: The buyer has actually begun the application process and an underwriter has approved their income, funds, and credit. Beware of any conditions on the approval.

Prepaid Interest Charge: The portion of interest, collected at loan closing, which covers the time period between funding and the beginning of the first 30-day period covered by the first payment. For example, if the loan closed on 2/15, the first payment due on 4/1 would pay interest from 3/1 to 4/1. The prepaid interest would cover the period from 2/15 to 2/28.

Prepaids: Expenses necessary to create an escrow account or to adjust the seller's existing escrow account. Can include taxes, hazard insurance, private mortgage insurance, and special assessments.

Prepayment: A privilege in a mortgage permitting the borrower to make payments in advance of their due date.

Prepayment Penalty: Money charged for an early repayment of debt. The 2010 Dodd-Frank Act made it so that the new Consumer Financial Protection Bureau rules prohibit prepayment penalties for most residential mortgage loans, except under a few specific circumstances.

Prequalified: The buyer has discussed their financial situation with a loan expert. No attempt has been made to verify the validity of any of the borrower's information. Pre-qualification is only an indication of what the buyer should qualify for.

Principal: The amount of debt, not counting interest, left on a loan.

Principal and Interest (P&I): This refers to the principal and interest portions of the monthly mortgage payment.

Principal, Interest, Taxes, Insurance (PITI): The complete monthly cost associated with financing a property.

Private Mortgage Insurance (PMI): In the event that you do not have a 20 percent down payment, lenders will allow a smaller down payment — as low as five percent in some cases. With the smaller down payment loans, however, borrowers are usually required to carry private mortgage insurance. This requires an initial premium payment of 0.3 percent to 1.5 percent of your mortgage amount per year and may require an additional monthly fee depending on your loan's structure. On a $75,000 house with a 10 percent down payment, this would mean either an initial premium payment of $2,025 to $3,375 or an initial premium of $675 to $1,130 combined with a monthly payment of $25 to $30.

Purchase Agreement: The agreement made between the buyer and seller of a property, containing the purchase price and contingencies of the sale.

Quitclaim: A deed operating as a release. Intended to pass any title, interest, or claim, which the grantor may have in the property, but not containing any warranty of a valid interest or title in the grantor.

Rate Float: Assuming market risk on an interest rate in the hopes that it will go lower prior to closing.

Rate Lock: Choosing to have no change to a rate for a specific length of time.

Ratios: How a buyer's housing expense and debt picture relates to their income.

Real Estate Settlement Procedures Act (RESPA): A federal law enforced by the Consumer Financial Protection Bureau that allows consumers to review information on known or estimated settlement costs once after application and once prior to or at settlement. The law requires lenders to furnish information after application only.

Rescission: The cancellation of a contract. With respect to mortgage refinancing, the law that gives the homeowner three days to cancel a contract in some cases once it is signed if the transaction uses equity in the home as security.

Recording Fees: Money paid to the lender for recording a home sale with the local authorities, thereby making it part of the public records.

Refi: Slang for refinance, which is a new mortgage on a property that does not change ownership.

Servicing: All the steps and operations a lender performs to keep a loan in good standing, such as collection of payments, payment of taxes, insurance, property inspections, and the like.

Settlement Costs:
See **Closing Costs**.

Submission: This refers to a complete loan application package submitted for approval to the underwriting department.

Subordination Agreement: The agreement detailing the contingencies of subordination, filed with the county recorder; if a lien holder agrees to accept a lien position after that of a later recorded lien.

Survey: A measurement of land prepared by a registered land surveyor showing the location of the land with reference to known points, its dimensions, and the location and dimensions of any building.

Suspended: The underwriter cannot yet approve or deny the loan. More information is required.

Title Insurance: The insurance policy insuring the lender and/ or the buyer that the liens are as stated in the title report. Any claim arising from a lien other than that disclosed is payable by the title insurance company.

Title Search: An examination of municipal records to determine the legal ownership of property. Usually performed by a title company.

Title: A document that gives evidence of an individual's ownership of property.

Truth-in-Lending Act (TILA): A federal law requiring disclosure of the APR to homebuyers shortly after they apply for the loan.

Underwriting: Whether or not to make a loan to a potential homebuyer based on credit, employment, assets, and other factors, and the matching of this risk to an appropriate rate and term or loan amount.

VA Mortgage Funding Fee: A premium of up to 2.15 percent (depending on the size of the down payment) paid on a VA-backed loan.

Verification of Deposit (VOD): A document signed by the borrower's financial institution verifying the status and balance of his/her financial accounts.

Verification of Employment (VOE): A document signed by the borrower's employer verifying his/her position and salary.

Wraparound: Results when an existing assumable loan is combined with a new loan, resulting in an interest rate somewhere between the old rate and the current market rate. The payments are made to a second lender or the previous homeowner, who then forwards the payments to the first lender after taking the additional amount off the top.

Taxes

Taxes, including property taxes charged by the town, county, or state, have been detailed elsewhere in this book. All properties (even vacant lots or land) will have assessed on them some amount of tax, even if it is a very small annual amount ($50, for instance). Many banks want to be in charge of paying the property taxes, to ensure that the taxes are paid. In order to do this, the bank will charge extra monies every month to the buyer/borrower, which will then be placed in the bank's escrow account. Then, when those taxes are due to the town/county (quarterly or semi-annually are the most common), the bank or the bank's servicing company will mail the applicable amount to the town/county.

For example: Yearly taxes on a 2,000 square foot colonial-style home are $6,000, due semi-annually. This would equal $3,000 paid twice a year (every region has different due dates and due months — it is wise for the agent to be aware of this in the towns where he or she is working). Most mortgage companies will mandate, or suggest, that the borrower pays an additional $500 every month (along with their basic principal and interest mortgage payment) for property tax use.

The bank prefers to escrow for taxes (and also for homeowner's insurance, which is also a requirement by the lender for the borrower to carry) so that once or twice a year the borrower is not receiving a bill in the mail for $6,000. It is typical that many Americans would have trouble paying this large amount all at once, but it is more manageable when it is spread out over the course of the year.

Real Estate Settlement and Procedures Act (RESPA)

RESPA was enacted in 1974 to provide a uniform method and means of disclosure to consumers regarding fees paid and loan terms for residential real estate. Within this act are also requirements that try to negate un-ethical practices between real estate agents and mortgage/banking officers, such as kickbacks or referral fees.

RESPA is administered by the Consumer Financial Protection Bureau and is part of every loan that is backed by federal agencies, such as VA and FHA. It also is required of any loans sold on the secondary market to the large quasi-governmental agencies: Fannie Mae, Ginnie Mae, and Freddie Mac. In essence, it is the norm in the industry, and your broker will likely have set guidelines in place to make sure that you do not perform your job in a manner against RESPA policy.

One-to-four person family homes (as long as the owner also occupies the building) are covered by RESPA, as well as second mortgages/home equity loans on owner occupied housing. The three key areas as they relate to real estate sales agents are: Controlled Business Arrangements, Computerized Loan Originations, and the HUD-1 Settlement Statement.

Controlled Business Arrangement (CBA)

Especially in today's market where many large conglomerates (like banks) have diversified products and services, this is a key provision of RESPA. Most likely, the agency that you work for will have its own forms that you must require your clients (buyer and sellers) to read and sign. For instance, a real estate brokerage that is working with a client via a listing agreement may also have a division of the main company that is a mortgage broker. It *is* legal for the real estate agent to mention and discuss this separate service and loan offering, but there are forms that are required that are meant to protect the consumer from being "bullied" or "overtly steered" into getting a mortgage through the REALTORS® affiliated lender.

In addition, it is very important that you *not* accept any "referral fees" or anything of value from a mortgage broker/loan officer, even if and when you are leading business to them. If you do receive any form of payment or other compensation, it must be for a tangible service that you have conducted, not merely referring your client to someone. For instance, some real estate agents can also act as a "mortgage/loan originator" in some cases and receive some legitimate payment from a lender. However, it is advised that you discuss this with your broker prior to entering into any such situation.

Computerized Loan Origination (CLO)

In more recent years, consumers have been able to adapt a "one-stop shop" mentality as they venture into the purchase of their new home. Many real estate agents have their own website which may or may not have their own secure online mortgage loan application (often a mini-application). Here the consumer and potential buyer will enter some of their financial information as well as their price range. The real estate agent may then submit this information to an affiliated or chosen lender in order to get a lender's preapproval for the borrower. This is allowable under certain guidelines and restrictions, along with disclosures to the borrower that the real estate agent has these types of business relationships.

CLOs are automated systems for delivering residential mortgage offerings to customers of, or at, a real estate office. On the following pages, you will see an example HUD-1.

HUD-1 — RESPA Uniform Settlement Statement

Sample HUD-1 Settlement Statement

A. Settlement Statement (HUD-1)

OMB Approval No. 2502-0265

B. Type of Loan

1. ☐ FHA 2. ☒ RHS 3. ☐ CONV. UNINS.   6. File Number: 7. Loan Number: 8. Mortgage Insurance Case Number:
4. ☐ VA 5. ☐ CONV. INS.

C. Note: This form is furnished to give you a statement of actual settlement costs. Amounts paid to and by the settlement agent are shown. Items marked "(p.o.c.)" were paid outside the closing; they are shown here for informational purposes and are not included in the totals.

D. Name & Address of Borrower: E. Name & Address of Seller: F. Name & Address of Lender:

G. Property Location: H. Settlement Agent: I. Settlement Date:

Place of Settlement:

J. Summary of Borrower's Transaction		K. Summary of Seller's Transaction	
100. Gross Amount Due From Borrower:		**400. Gross Amount Due To Seller:**	
101. Contract Sales Price	136,435.00	401. Contract Sales Price	136,435.00
102. Personal Property		402. Personal Property	
103. Settlement Charges to Borrower (line 1400)	10,062.85	403.	
104.		404.	
105. Principal Reduction	500.00	405.	
Adjustments for Items Paid by Seller in Advance:		**Adjustments for Items Paid by Seller in Advance:**	
106. City / Town Taxes		406. City / Town Taxes	
107. County / Parish Taxes		407. County / Parish Taxes	
108. Assessments		408. Assessments	
120. Gross Amount Due from Borrower:	146,997.85	420. Gross Amount Due to Seller:	136,435.00
200. Amounts Paid by or in Behalf of Borrower:		**500. Reductions in Amount Due to Seller:**	
201. Deposit or Earnest Money	500.00	501. Excess Deposit (see instructions)	
202. Principal Amount of New Loan	142,857.00	502. Settlement Charges to Seller (Line 1400)	9,857.60
203. Existing Loan(s) taken subject to		503. Existing Loan(s) taken subject to	
204. Daily interest credit		504. Payoff of First Mortgage Loan to Select Portfolio Servicing	111,286.55
205.		505. Payoff of Second Mortgage Loan (Paid by Seller) to Select Portfolio Servicing	7,000.00
206. Good Faith Deposit	350.00	506. Seller Relocation to Juan Jimenez	3,000.00
207. Closing Costs Paid for Buyer by Seller	2,017.02	507. Closing Costs Paid for Buyer by Seller	2,017.02
208. Transfer Tax on Deed POBOB		508. Payoff Mortgage to SunTrust	1,500.00
209. Standard Cost paid by Seller - Owners Title Insurance	757.50	509. Standard Cost paid by Seller - Owners Title Insurance	757.50
Adjustments for Items Unpaid by Seller:		**Adjustments for Items Unpaid by Seller:**	
210. City / Town Taxes		510. City / Town Taxes	
211. County / Parish Taxes	1,016.33	511. County / Parish Taxes	1,016.33
212. Assessments		512. Assessments	
220. Total Paid by / for Borrower:	147,497.85	520. Total Reductions in Amount Due Seller:	136,435.00
300. Cash at Settlement from / to Borrower:		**600. Cash at Settlement to / from Seller:**	
301. Gross Amount due from Borrower (line 120)	146,997.85	601. Gross Amount due to Seller (line 420)	136,435.00
302. Less Amount Paid by/for Borrower (line 220)	147,497.85	602. Less Reductions Amount due Seller (line 520)	136,435.00
303. Cash To Borrower:	**$500.00**	**603. Cash From Seller:**	**$0.00**

The Public Reporting Burden for this collection of information is estimated at 35 minutes per response for collecting, reviewing, and reporting the data. This agency may not collect this information, and you are not required to complete this form, unless it displays a currently valid OMB control number. No confidentiality is assured; this disclosure is mandatory. This is designed to provide the parties to a RESPA covered transaction with information during the settlement process.

Sample HUD-1 Settlement Statement

L. Settlement Charges		Paid from Borrower's Funds at Settlement	Paid from Seller's Funds at Settlement
700. Total Sales / Broker's Commission: $6,186.10			
Division of Commission (line 700) as follows			
701. 4,093.05 to			
702. 4,093.05 to			
703. Commission Paid at Settlement			6,186.10
704. Warehousing Fee			
800. Items Payable in Connection with Loan:			
801. Our origination charge	(from GFE #1) $1,675.00		
802. Your credit or charge (points) for the specific interest rate chosen	(from GFE #2) $-200.00		
803. Your adjusted origination charges	(from GFE #A)	1,475.00	
804. Appraisal Fee	(from GFE #3)		
to Executive Appraisal Solutions, Inc.		390.00	
805. Credit Report	(from GFE #3)		
to Kroll Factual Data		15.93	
806. Tax Service			
807. Flood Certification	(from GFE #3)		
to First American Flood		13.00	
808. Guarantee Fee	(from GFE #3)		
to USDA		2,857.14	
900. Items Required by Lender to be Paid in Advance:			
901. Daily interest charge from	(from GFE #10)	34.24	
days			
902. Guarantee Fee	(from GFE #3)		
903. Homeowner's Insurance for 1.00 years	(from GFE #11)		
to AIIC		915.00	
1000. Reserves Deposited with Lender:			
1001. Initial deposit for your escrow account	(from GFE #9)		
to Inlanta Mortgage, Inc.		1,563.23	
1002. Homeowner's Insurance 3 months @ $76.25 per month			
to Inlanta Mortgage, Inc.	$228.75		
1003. Mortgage Insurance			
1004. Property Taxes 11 months @ $153.34 per month			
to Inlanta Mortgage, Inc.	$1,686.74		
1005. USDA Annual Fee 2 months @ $47.26 per month	$94.52		
1099. Aggregate Adjustment	$-446.78		
1100. Title Charges:			
1101. Title services and lender's title insurance	(from GFE #4)	800.95	
1102. Settlement or Closing Fee			
to	$475.00		697.50
1103. Owner's Title Insurance	(from GFE #5)		
to		757.50	
1104. Lender's Title Insurance			
to			
- Lender's Premium (Risk Rate Premium: $57.00)	$182.00		
- Endorsement 8.1	$50.00		
- Endorsement FL Form 9	$93.95		
1105. Lender's Title Policy Limit $142,857.00			
1106. Owner's Title Policy Limit $136,435.00			
1107. Agent's Portion of the Total Title Insurance Premium	$758.41		
1108. Underwriter's Portion of the Total Title Insurance Premium	$325.04		
1109. Title Search $85 Paid Outside of Closing FATIC by OLTIA			
1200. Government Recording and Transfer Charges:			
1201. Government Recording Charges	(from GFE #7)	105.00	
1202. Deed $10.00 Mortgage $95.00 Releases $0.00			
1203. Transfer Taxes	(from GFE #8)	785.86	
1204. City/County tax/stamps Deed $0.00 Mortgage $0.00			
1205. State tax/stamps Deed $955.50 Mortgage $500.15			955.50
1206. Intangible Tax			
to Clerk of the Circuit Court	$285.71		
1207. Other Tax 2			
1208. Title Clearing Affidavit (3 Liens)	(from GFE #7)		
to Clerk of the Circuit Court			18.50
1300. Additional Settlement Charges:			
1301. Required services that you can shop for	(from GFE #6)	350.00	
1302. Survey Inspection			
to	$350.00		
1303. Pest Inspection			
1304. 2013 RE Taxes PA# 35996-018-00 Paid Outside of Closing by Seller $1,784.87			
1305.			
1306.			
1400. Total Settlement Charges (Enter on line 103, Section J and line 502, Section K)		$10,062.85	$9,857.60

Sample HUD-1 Settlement Statement

Comparison of Good Faith Estimate (GFE) and HUD Charges

Charges That Cannot Increase	HUD Line No.	Good Faith Estimate	HUD
Our origination charge	# 801	1,675.00	1,675.00
Your credit or charge (points) for the specific interest rate chosen	# 802	-200.00	-200.00
Your adjusted origination charges	# 803	1,475.00	1,475.00
Transfer taxes	#1203	2,241.36	765.86

Charges That in Total Cannot Increase More Than 10%	HUD Line No.	Good Faith Estimate	HUD
Government Recording Charges	#1201	105.50	105.00
Appraisal Fee	# 804	390.00	390.00
Credit Report	# 805	30.00	15.93
Flood Certification	# 807	13.00	13.00
Guarantee Fee	# 808	2,857.14	2,857.14
Total		3,395.64	3,381.07
Increase between GFE and HUD Charges		-14.57	-0.43%

Charges That Can Change	HUD Line No.	Good Faith Estimate	HUD
Initial deposit for your escrow account	#1001	1,084.58	1,563.23
Daily interest charge from Jul 30, 2014 to Aug 1, 2014 @ 17.1200 / day for 2 days	# 901	462.24	34.24
Homeowner's Insurance	# 903	920.00	915.00
Title services and lender's title insurance	#1101	975.00	800.95
Owner's Title Insurance	#1103	790.00	757.50
Survey Inspection	#1302	350.00	350.00

Loan Terms

Your initial loan amount is	$142,857.00
Your loan term is	30 years
Your initial interest rate is	4.375 %
Your initial monthly amount owed for principal, interest, and any mortgage insurance is	$713.28 includes [X] Principal [X] Interest [ ] Mortgage Insurance
Can your interest rate rise?	[X] No. [ ] Yes, it can rise to a maximum of ____%. The first change will be on _____ and can change again every _____ after _____. Every change date, your interest rate can increase or decrease by ____%. Over the life of the loan, your interest rate is guaranteed to never be LOWER than ____% or HIGHER than ____%.
Even if you make payments on time, can your loan balance rise?	[X] No. [ ] Yes, it can rise to a maximum of $_____.
Even if you make payments on time, can your monthly amount owed for principal, interest, and mortgage insurance rise?	[X] No. [ ] Yes, the first increase can be on _____ and the monthly amount owed can rise to $_____. The maximum it can ever rise to is $_____.
Does your loan have a prepayment penalty?	[X] No. [ ] Yes, your maximum prepayment penalty is $_____.
Does your loan have a balloon payment?	[X] No. [ ] Yes, you have a balloon payment of $_____ due in _____ years on _____.
Total monthly amount owed including escrow account payments	[ ] You do not have a monthly escrow payment for items, such as property taxes and homeowner's insurance. You must pay these items directly yourself. [X] You have an additional monthly escrow payment of $276.85 that results in a total initial monthly amount owed of $990.11. This includes principal, interest, any mortgage insurance and any items checked below: [X] Property taxes [X] USDA Annual Fee [ ] Flood insurance [ ] [X] Homeowner's insurance [ ]

Note: If you have any questions about the Settlement Charges and Loan Terms listed on this form, please contact your lender.

Sample HUD-1 Settlement Statement

Buyers

Sellers

Property Addresses

I have carefully reviewed the HUD-1 Settlement Statement, and to the best of my knowledge and belief, it is a true and accurate statement of all receipts and disbursements made on my account or by me in this transaction. I further certify that I have received a copy of HUD-1 Settlement Statement.

Borrower: _____ Seller: _____

The HUD-1 Settlement Statement which I have prepared is a true and accurate account of this transaction. I have caused or will cause the funds to be disbursed in accordance with this statement.

Settlement Agent: _____ Date:

WARNING: It is a crime to knowingly make false statements to the United States on this or any other similar form. Penalties upon conviction can include a fine and imprisonment. For details see Title 18 U.S. Code Section 1001 and Section 1010.

As shown in this example HUD-1, you should be very familiar with this form, the terminology, and payouts. You should be able to explain this form in full to your client, be it the buyer or seller.

The HUD-1 settlement statement is a standardized form at closing that lists all financial information affecting both buyers and sellers. This must include all charges and fees, and all prorations.

The Loan Process

Getting a loan can be confusing. We have tried to simplify the loan process by outlining the steps involved. The language is geared primarily toward consumers/borrowers, but all of the information is relevant for a real estate agent as well.

Step one: find out how much you can borrow

The first step in obtaining a loan is to determine how much money you can borrow. In the case of buying a home, you should determine how much home you can afford before you begin looking. By answering a few simple questions, we will calculate your buying power based on standard lender guidelines.

You may also elect to get pre-approved for a loan, which requires verification of your income, credit, assets, and liabilities. It is recommended that you get pre-approved before you start looking for your new house. This will help you to do the following:

1. Look for properties within your range.

2. Be in a better position when negotiating with the seller (seller knows your loan is already approved).

3. Close your loan quicker.

More on Pre-qualification

LTV and Debt-to-Income Ratios: LTV, or Loan-to-Value ratio, is the maximum amount of exposure that a lender is willing to accept in financing your purchase. Lenders are usually prepared to lend a higher percentage of the value, even up to 100 percent, to creditworthy borrowers. Another consideration in approving the maximum amount of loan for a particular borrower is the ratio of monthly debt payments (such as auto and personal loans) to income. Rule of thumb states that your monthly mortgage payments should not exceed 1/3 of your gross monthly income. Therefore, borrowers with high debt-to-income ratio need to pay a higher down payment in order to qualify for a lower LTV ratio.

FICO Credit Score: FICO Credit Scores are widely used by almost all types of lenders in their credit decision. It is a quantified measure of creditworthiness of an individual, which is derived from mathematical models developed by Fair Isaac and Company in San Rafael, California. FICO scores reflect credit risk of the individual in comparison with that of the general population. It is based on a number of factors including past payment history, total amount of borrowing, length of credit history, search for new credit, and type of credit established. When you begin shopping around for a new credit card or a loan, every time a lender runs your credit report, it adversely affects your credit score. It is, therefore, advisable that you authorize the lender/broker to run your credit report only after you have chosen to apply for a loan through them.

Self-Employed Borrowers: Self-employed individuals often find that there are greater hurdles to borrowing for them over an employed person. For many conventional lenders, the problem with lending to the self-employed is documenting an applicant's income. Applicants with jobs can provide lenders with pay stubs, and lenders can verify the information through their employer. In the absence of such verifiable employment records, lenders rely on income tax returns, which they typically require for two years.

Source of Down Payment: Lenders expect borrowers to come up with sufficient cash for the down payment and other fees payable by the borrower at the time of funding the loan. It is generally expected that these funds be the borrower's own saving, although a borrower may receive non-returnable gifts toward down payment and other loan fees.

Step two: select the right loan program

Home loans come in many shapes and sizes. Deciding which loan makes the most sense for your financial situation and goals means understanding the benefits of each. Whether you are buying a home or refinancing, there are three basic types of home loans. Each have different advantages.

Fixed Rate Mortgage

Fixed rate mortgages usually have terms lasting 15 or 30 years. Throughout those years, the interest rate and monthly payments remain the same. You would select this type of loan when you:

- Plan to live in home more than seven years
- Like the stability of a fixed principal/interest payment
- Do not want to run the risk of future monthly payment increases
- Think your income and spending will stay the same

Adjustable Rate Mortgage

Adjustable Rate Mortgages (often called ARMs) typically last for 15 or 30 years, just like fixed rate mortgages. But during those years, the interest rate on the loan may go up or down. Monthly payments increase or decrease. You would select this type of loan when you:

- Plan to stay in your home less than five years

- Do not mind having your monthly payment periodically change (up or down)
- Are comfortable with the risk of possible payment increases in the future
- Think your income will probably increase in the future

Combination Rate (often called "Hybrid ARM") Mortgage

Combination rate mortgages combine fixed interest rates and adjustable interest rates. Lenders often refer to these loans as hybrid loans. For the first few years (three to seven), the interest rate is fixed. It remains the same and so does your monthly payment. During the remaining years of the loan, your interest rate becomes adjustable and can vary. You would select this type of loan when you:

- Want the stability of a fixed principal/interest payment in the short term
- Want to repair your credit by demonstrating your ability to make regular payments, then refinance for a lower interest rate
- Have a lot of consumer debt (these loans typically allow more)
- Want to borrow more and get a lower monthly payment than a standard fixed rate loan

By carefully considering the above factors and seeking professional advice, you should be able to select the loan that matches your present condition as well as your future financial goals.

Step three: apply for a loan

Most loan applications take only ten minutes to complete, with mini/preliminary applications. This information can then be given to the lender or mortgage broker in order to pre-qualify the borrower for a maximum loan amount. The real estate agent then uses this loan amount to determine what price range the potential house should be in.

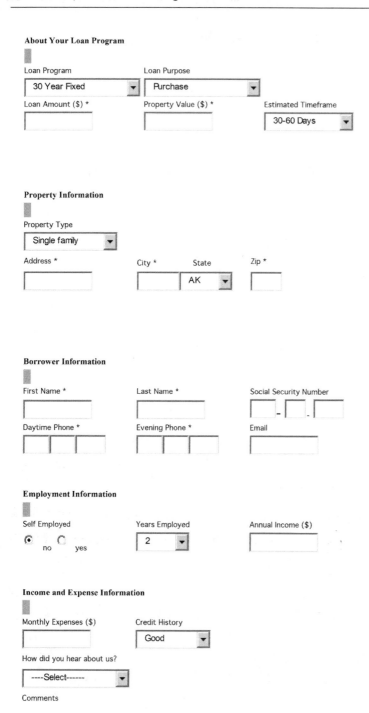

About Your Loan Program

Loan Program
| 30 Year Fixed ▼ |

Loan Purpose
| Purchase ▼ |

Loan Amount ($) *
| |

Property Value ($) *
| |

Estimated Timeframe
| 30-60 Days ▼ |

Property Information

Property Type
| Single family ▼ |

Address *
| |

City *
| |

State
| AK ▼ |

Zip *
| |

Borrower Information

First Name *
| |

Last Name *
| |

Social Security Number
| | - | | - | |

Daytime Phone *
| | | | | |

Evening Phone *
| | | | | |

Email
| |

Employment Information

Self Employed
⊙ no ○ yes

Years Employed
| 2 ▼ |

Annual Income ($)
| |

Income and Expense Information

Monthly Expenses ($)
| |

Credit History
| Good ▼ |

How did you hear about us?
| ----Select----- ▼ |

Comments

Step four: begin loan processing

Loan processing is the act of reviewing all of the required documents (W2s, bank statements, P&S Agreements, and tax returns) to ensure that all paperwork is present to be submitted to the underwriter. The Lender's Administrative Assistants and their underwriting department conduct loan processing. At the beginning of the loan processing, the appraisal of the property is also ordered. Overall, processing can take anywhere from two to four days, and underwriting could take up to seven to ten days from there.

Underwriting is the bank's risk management and policy department, and it is their ultimate decision on whether the bank will give the borrower the stated loan, on terms previously discussed. Once all conditions of the borrower are met, the underwriter will state that the loan is clear to close.

Step five: close your loan

The borrower will then be contacted by the bank's closing attorney and will set a closing time, day, and location over the following two to three days. The attorney's office will also give you the exact check amounts for any checks that the buyer (or seller) will need to bring to the closing. Note that most checks required of you at closing will need to be certified bank checks (personal checks are typically not accepted). The most important check that the buyer usually is responsible for is the balance of the down payment on the property, and this will definitely need to be a certified check.

At the closing, the new deed will be drafted and recorded by the bank's attorney. The borrower will receive keys to the house and any other peripherals.

Mortgage application checklist

Below is a list of documents that are required when you apply for a mortgage. However, every situation is unique, and you may be required to provide additional documentation. So, if you are asked for more information, be cooperative and provide the information requested as soon as possible. It will help speed up the application process.

Your property:

- Copy of signed sales contract including all riders (or addendums)
- Verification of the deposit you placed on the home
- Names, addresses, and telephone numbers of all REALTORS®, builders, insurance agents, and attorneys involved
- Copy of listing sheet and legal description, if available (if the property is a condominium, provide condominium declaration, bylaws and most recent budget)

Your income:

- Copies of your pay stubs for the most recent 30-day period and the year-to-date income
- Copies of your W-2 forms for the past two years
- Names and addresses of all employers for the last two years
- Letter explaining any gaps in employment in the past two years
- Work visa or green card (copy front and back)

Self-employed; receive commissions or bonuses, interest/dividends, or rental income:

- Provide full tax returns for the last two years **plus** year-to-date Profit & Loss Statement. (Provide complete tax return including attached schedules and statements. If you have filed an extension, please supply a copy of the extension.)

- A Schedule K-1 for all partnerships and S-Corporations for the last two years. (Double-check your return. Most K-1s are not attached to the 1040.)

- Completed and signed Federal Partnership (1065) and/ or Corporate Income Tax Returns (Form 1120) including all schedules, statements and addenda for the last two years. (Required only if your ownership position is 25 percent or greater.)

Alimony or child support used to qualify:

- Provide divorce decree/court order stating amount as well as proof of receipt of funds for the last year.

Social Security income, disability, or VA benefits:

- Provide award letter from agency or organization.

Source of funds and down payment:

- *Sale of your existing home:* Provide a copy of the signed sales contract on your current residence and statement or listing agreement if unsold (at closing, you must also provide a settlement/closing statement).

- *Savings, checking, or money market funds:* Provide copies of bank statements for the last three months.

- *Stocks and bonds:* Provide copies of your statement or certificates from your broker.

- *Gifts:* Provide Gift Affidavit and proof of receipt of funds.

- Based on information appearing on your application and/or your credit report, you may be required to submit additional documentation.

Debt or obligations:

- Prepare a list of all names, addresses, account numbers, balances, and monthly payments for all current debts with copies of the last three monthly statements.

- Include all names, addresses, account numbers, balances, and monthly payments for mortgage holders and/or landlords for the last two years.

- If you are paying alimony or child support, include marital settlement/court order stating the terms of the obligation.

- Check to cover Application Fee(s).

Conventional mortgage information & techniques

Conventional is also called "conforming" or "A-paper," and it relates to the largest pool of borrowers in the residential market. It is sometimes called "prime." There are also subprime or nonprime mortgages and borrowers.

Prime

Prime mortgages are loans that meet the standards set forth by Fannie Mae and Freddie Mac. Those who qualify for prime mortgages are required to have a good credit history with no records of late payments against their credit. Income is also factored into whether or not a person meets the standards for a prime mortgage. Usually, monthly income levels must be three to four times greater than the monthly mortgage payments. Money lenders will offer prime mortgages to their best customers, and these loans are coveted, because they are offered with interest rates as low as the current prime rate offered by the Federal Reserve (or lower in some cases). They require a down payment of roughly 10-20 percent on the home sale price. The most common type of prime mortgage is a fixed rate prime mortgage because it's interest rate remains stable over the life of the loan.

Subprime

Subprime would be considered those credit-challenged and minimum or zero-down payment borrowers who in most years past could not attain a mortgage. In 2008, there were once again a few options, if any, for many subprime borrowers, due to widespread defaults and problems with many of the subprime mortgages on the secondary market.

However, the Wall Street Journal reported that in 2015, loans to consumers with low credit scores had reached their highest level since the start of the financial crisis in 2008, driven by a new crop of companies extending credit. Almost four out of every 10 loans went to subprime customers during the first 11 months of 2014, according to Equifax. The secondary market is typically influenced by Wall Street or Fannie Mae (or one of the other large, government-backed agencies). Another type of mortgage that involves buyers who do not qualify for mortgages through traditional lending practices is called a purchase-money mortgage. This type of mortgage is called seller financing because the financing is provided by the seller of the property.

Nonprime

A nonprime mortgage is somewhere between a prime mortgage and a subprime mortgage. It is not a prime loan because these buyers do not qualify for them, but they are not subprime because they adhere to stricter requirements than subprime, yet still allow those who don't qualify for prime loans to obtain financing. Given the damaged reputation of the subprime market following the real estate collapse of 2008, lenders are now calling subprime mortgages "nonprime," but with different requirements.

Nonprime mortgages require 30 percent down to safeguard their investment. According to chief executive officer of Skyline Financial Corp, "You're going to have to make all types of loans, ones that conform to all the new standards and ones that don't, to keep powering the housing recovery. There needs to be a solution for people who don't fit in the box, and rebuilding nonprime lending is it." Today's lenders are looking for creative ways to offer financing without taking too much risk. For example, *wraparound loans* act as a form of secondary financing where the seller lends the buyer the difference between the existing loan and the purchase price.

The secondary market

The secondary mortgage market has become increasingly critical over the past two decades. During this time, banks have realized that it is usually more profitable for them to sell their mortgages (notes) to another entity. This selling of all rights and future profits and interest fees is called the secondary market. The buyers of these notes are more often than not Freddie Mac and Fannie Mae, quasi-governmental agencies. In this manner, the federal government does have some influence on the mortgage and housing market. Also, there are numerous privately-held financial and investment companies (many on Wall Street in New York) that will buy mortgage notes from banks. The bottom line is that the bank that owns your loan at the closing will typically not be the note-holder in two or three months' time.

When Fannie Mae announces new guidelines or restrictions, it has a dramatic effect on mortgage accessibility, which will affect your buyer and seller clients. This is why it is important to stay knowledgeable about key financing news. The loan officers that you will come to know will be a valuable asset in this manner.

Special Financing Agreements

As an agent, you will find out that the sale of property is not limited to homes. Due to the changing nature of residency, different types of real estate sales have given rise. As a real estate agent, you may end up brokering deals that involve nontraditional types of property and non-traditional types of loans. The following section provides a brief overview.

Condominiums

Condos are usually more difficult to finance, as the bank will have more guidelines than for a

typical, single-family house. Sometimes, a newer condo development will need to be submitted to be placed on that lender's approved condo list. This can take time, and there are no guarantees of approval. Most banks require that a new condo development be at least 50 percent sold out before they will offer a mortgage to a buyer. In addition, there are many other stipulations.

Condotels

A relatively new arrangement, this is a combination of a condo and hotel room. There are very few lenders who will offer a mortgage to a buyer on this type of new development scheme. It is difficult to secure financing for condotels, because they cannot be financed by Freddie Mac or Fannie Mae. However, some banks offer rates, but these typically run a half-percent higher than for a comparable conventional mortgage, and minimum down payments start at 20 percent.

Half-share and quarter-share mortgage

This is another new loan program, which allows for two to four different property owners to each have their own partial share and loan of one residential property. Often used as a competitor of timeshare operations and in vacation areas. Not all banks will accept this kind of ownership. However, if you are interested in securing a mortgage for a half-share or quarter-share, check **www.sharetobuy.com** for more information.

Real Estate Investment Trusts (REITs)

This is more of a shared investment tool involving the purchase of one or more properties, and they are not owner-occupied. Most real estate agents do not work much with REITs.

Credit Unions

Members of a credit union (a nonprofit lending institution, as opposed to a for-profit bank) can often times receive better mortgage rates and deals from their credit union than out in the regular mortgage marketplace. Always ask your buyer clients if they are members of a credit union. If so, they may want to apply for a loan there.

State-specific housing authorities and home financing authorities: Most states have specific state-subsidized agencies that will help low-to-moderate income buyers qualify for a mortgage. It is best to seek out specific details with help from your broker.

USDA Rural Housing Service

The federal government has a subsidized loan program that is meant to help rural America with home purchasing. There are income and town population requirements, among other important loan characteristics.

Committed to the future of rural communities.

Mobile homes/ manufactured homes

Single and double-wide mobile homes (built in full at a factory and placed either on blocks or permanently attached to a concrete foundation) can be difficult to finance conventionally. If a housing unit has a HUD number or stamp on it or on its deed, it is considered "manufactured," and most lenders will not accept this as collateral on a mortgage loan. However, there are loan options. Most are for a maximum of 20 years, and their interest rates are higher than regular conventional mortgage rates.

Private lending ("hard money")

In addition to banks and credit unions, there are also private individuals, or small groups of private individuals, who will lend out money in a mortgage facility. Private money is used when the buyer or the property will not fit into typical lender guidelines. Many real estate investors use private money. Rates and points (lender fees) are much higher than in conventional bank financing.

Bridge (or blanket) loan

In a situation where a buyer must purchase a home but their former home is *not* sold yet, the buyer will often need to take out a bridge loan. This bridge loan is usually three to six months in length and will provide the client with the means of affording both (new and former) house mortgage payments. Buyers try to avoid bridge loans, as they are typically costly. This is why it is a better idea to first have the former house under a sales agreement before the client puts in an offer to purchase their next home.

Land contracts

An agreement for sale of property in which the buyer takes possession while making payments, but the seller holds title until full payment is made.

CASE STUDY:
DEALING WITH
REFERRAL PARTNERS

David K.
Mortgage Broker, 5 years

I have been in the mortgage industry for more than five years, and I work for a mortgage broker as a branch manager.

As a mortgage professional, I need to know certain aspects of RESPA to do my job properly. The part of RESPA that I work with on a daily basis is proper disclosures and making sure the information on the disclosures is accurate. We must make sure that we are disclosing to the borrower all the required information per RESPA in a timely manner.

My number one goal with referral partners, including real estate agents, is to treat their customers the same way I would want them to treat mine. They can be assured that I will be upfront with the client and provide them with excellent customer service.

The reason REALTORS® recommend their buyers to me is because they have the confidence and understanding that their client will be taken care of. They know that if I provide them with a preapproval, the loan will close. REALTORS® also like the fact that I am on top of my loans and that I communicate with all parties involved on a regular basis.

I do not work with just any REALTOR®. My goal is to surround myself with REALTORS® that have a focus on a certain market. When I refer a client to a REALTOR®, I look to match the market they are looking at and also if they would fit on a personality level.

In today's market, the most difficult part of the job is to keep up with the market and changing guidelines. I have to read and understand the guidelines and make sure that you find out as much information as possible on your borrower.

My advice to new REALTORS® is:

1. Educate yourself on financing: I see so many REALTORS® that waste their time on clients that will never get financing.

2. Partner with a mortgage lender: Establish at least three relationships with mortgage lenders. Use them all as a resource and when you can, refer your client to all three.

3. Focus: Pick a market that you want to sell into, and develop a sales strategy as well as goals on how you will sell into this market. Become the "Real Estate Resource" for your market.

4. Network: The successful REALTORS® that are selling homes are the ones that are networked well in their market. Referrals are a great way to do business.

CASE STUDY:
REAL ESTATE &
AFFORDABLE HOUSING LAW

Jessica B.
Financial Writer, 5 years

Statistics say that nearly eight million Americans occupy neighborhoods of poverty where at least 40 percent of the residents are below the poverty line. In order to bring these families above the poverty line, the government provides different kinds of financial aid — rental, housing, and healthcare assistance.

Creating affordable housing opportunities is a key element of any socially responsible housing policy. The government-backed loans provide housing assistance to low income and poor credit borrowers who otherwise do not meet the criteria for traditional lending options offered through private lenders, banks, and mortgage companies. Such loans are available even with low down payments and closing costs that are at comparatively lower interest rates. When the government backs a loan for an otherwise unqualified borrower, lenders are more interested to offer the loan, because even if the borrower defaults, the lender will be paid by the government.

Government-backed mortgages such as the FHA loans help buyers qualify with as low as three percent down payment and poor credit score (around 580). (Please note that the FHA does not provide loans but insures them.) More than simply checking a buyer's score, the FHA-approved lenders care about whether buyers have been paying all their bills on time for at least the past two years. Moreover, the underwriting standards are easier, and there are housing counselors to assist a buyer when it comes to choosing the right loan option. Government-backed mortgages are best suited for first-time buyers with low-to-moderate income, not-so-good credit, and who are capable of making payments at comparatively lower rates of interest. One may even get a comparatively bigger loan. Apart from the FHA and VA, the Rural Housing Service and state and local governments also encourage buyers to go for government-backed loans.

REALTORS® should become knowledgeable about FHA/HUD loans. FHA loans have flexible qualifying criteria (low income or poor credit). As such, buyers can easily qualify if they fulfill the basic requirements. Any buyer can easily get prequalified for an FHA loan and then look out for suitable homes. Thus, REALTORS® come to know whether they have a customer who's ready to buy before they show any homes. It gets easier for the REALTOR® to find a suitable home for the buyer because the latter is prequalified and likely to get a mortgage in order to finance the purchase.

There is more paperwork involved in government-backed loans. Usually government-backed loans, such as the FHA insured mortgage, take around 45 to 60 days to close. The underwriting and closing time depend more upon the lender, irrespective of whether it is a government-backed loan or any conventional mortgage.

The FHA has been through significant changes in terms of coming up with new products, reformed guidelines, closing cost, and appraisal requirements etc. A new, streamlined 203k program has been in place with less documentation being required. In addition, home inspection for repair costs under $15,000 has been eliminated.

The FHA Modernization Act has been in effect since 2008. Use of risk-based upfront mortgage insurance premiums and enhancement of reverse mortgage products for seniors are some of the components of this act. The primary purpose is to expand the reach of FHA loans to a wider section of borrowers.

Besides this, there is a change in the FHA loan limit, especially in high-cost areas, and reforms have helped the FHA in raising loan limits for high-cost areas, thereby insuring larger mortgages at an affordable price. As such, the highest loan limit is currently $625,000 and is thereby designed to ensure economic stability to communities.

FHA-insured loans are the most popular government-backed loans having the following features:

1. Helps in financing 97 percent of the purchase with the remaining 3 percent being the down payment.

2. One can have low credit (580 FICO score) and high debt-to-income ratio (31/43) to qualify for FHA loan.

3. Allows for down payment in the form of assistance programs and gifts.

4. The borrower pays 3.5 percent of the loan amount as upfront mortgage insurance premium at closing. Often the premiums are included into the loan amount. New borrowers with a FICO score of less than 580 are required to put down at least ten percent.

5. FHA 203k loans can help you finance both the purchase and repair work needed for the home.

CASE STUDY: REAL ESTATE & HOME FINANCING

Dan H.
Senior Mortgage Planner, 10+ years

The FHA is a critical part of home financing. Historically, the FHA steps in where private, market-driven lenders have feared to tread. FHA does it without penalizing homebuyers with higher rates, variable rates, or prepayment penalties. Originally, FHA was the government's answer to private lenders' reluctance to finance prospective homebuyers who had less-than-perfect credit. Since its start in 1934, FHA has helped Americans purchase more than 34 million homes — Americans who might have otherwise been stopped from owning a home.

The key benefit is that homebuyers with less-than-perfect credit can qualify for an affordable fixed-rate mortgage. Also, the down payment hurdle to home ownership is lower with FHA. The program requires a 3 percent down payment, and all of it can be in the form of a gift from family, a grant from a community or state agency, or borrowed funds [like a loan from your 401(k) and, in some cases, even an unsecured personal loan]. Essentially, FHA has lowered or removed two of the big barriers to home ownership: credit and down payment savings. And with the recent collapse of so-called sub-prime lending and the retreat of private lenders, especially in serving less-than-prime homebuyers, FHA has helped the real estate industry weather a "perfect storm" of challenges.

A REALTOR® who is savvy about FHA loans can spot problem properties or situations that would keep their clients from closing. FHA does have minimum property standards, designed to protect homebuyers. Knowing what type of repairs FHA appraisal standards will flag can give you a jump start on raising the issue with the seller's agent and laying the groundwork for quick negotiations to resolve the property issue. For condominiums, there is a database of FHA-approved projects that can streamline the financing. Getting so-called spot approval for a condominium that is not in the database is more difficult and time-consuming. Before listing a condominium property, check the FHA website to see if the property is already approved. The database is not a guarantee of FHA approval but can attract a wider range of buyers and signal that financing will be easier to secure.

For the homebuyer, the FHA application does contain a little more paperwork. In many parts of the country, a pest inspection is required, but that can often be done at the same time as the customary home inspection.

In 2008, FHA business was booming because many other lending options retreated or disappeared altogether. This boom overwhelmed some lenders, making it important for mortgage loan officers to place loans carefully, especially when the buyer needs a quick closing. At the same time, the boom in FHA business has spurred a number of lenders to beef up their FHA underwriting staff to more quickly handle the volume. In this area of the country, there are half a dozen lenders that can turn around an FHA mortgage commitment in less than a week. Working with a loan officer who can craft a complete loan file from the start can also save lots of time in underwriting.

Today, the FHA is still popular with mortgage borrowers, as it has raised its loan limits and reduced insurance premiums in many parts of the country to help finance a wider group of homebuyers and home owners looking to refinance riskier home loans. FHA has also temporarily loosened its rules against financing the purchase of foreclosure properties and began tying the price of its mortgage insurance to homebuyer's credit and down payment.

Chapter 5

Real Estate Appraisal

An appraisal is merely "an estimate of market value." This appraisal does not set the value or price of a property. It simply estimates what the value might be under normal circumstances. In the real estate world, it is important to distinguish exactly what an appraisal is and who can perform it. These terms are important for a variety of reasons, including legal, regulatory, and false advertising concerns.

An appraisal is often deemed a "certified appraisal." For the sake of this chapter, the two words will be interchangeable. Only a licensed appraiser can perform an appraisal. The appraiser is licensed through their state of work, after many hours of training under the tutelage of another licensed appraiser. A licensed appraiser must show sufficient knowledge of the local real estate market and generally be good with numbers and statistical analysis. They also must have a strong and practical knowledge of housing and building styles and terms. An appraiser is not a "home inspector," and the appraisal report should not be relied on by the buyer, seller, or REALTOR®

as to the quality and habitability of the house or building in question. *For an example of a uniform appraisal report, see Appendix D.*

Most appraisers focus on the residential real estate market, while others become further qualified and appraise commercial, industrial, and other types of properties.

There are different types of appraisal forms used, most of which are accepted by every bank and mortgage company. The different form numbers are set by Fannie Mae and HUD/FHA based on loan program parameters and underwriting guidelines.

Before dissecting how an appraiser arrives at a market value, it is important to review what a certified appraisal is and what it is not, and how these terms vary and why:

Appraisal: A multi-page report of estimated market value from one of the acceptable appraisal methods, conducted by a state-licensed real estate appraiser.

Comparative Market Analysis (CMA): A comparison of the prices of recently sold homes similar to a listing seller's home in terms of location, style, and amenities. Also known as a competitive market analysis. CMA's are allowed to be performed by any real estate agent or broker and are normally offered to a pending seller client for *free* and typically are not as accurate as a certified appraisal.

Broker Price Opinion (BPO): The estimated value of a property as determined by a real estate broker. A broker price opinion is based on the characteristics of the property being considered. Some of the factors that a broker will consider when pricing a property include the value of similar surrounding properties, sales trends in the neighborhood, an estimate of any of the costs associated with getting the property ready for sale, and/ or the cost of any needed repairs. Sometimes when a full appraisal is not required, a lender or an investor will ask for a BPO, as its cost is normally between $100 and $125 to complete.

Automated Valuation Model (AVM): AVM reports rely on available data from sales reports, tax records, and loan information, and are compiled without human interaction. These reports are not intended to be used as a replacement for an actual appraisal. There is no property inspection of any kind, and data used to compile an estimated market value may be inaccurate or outdated. AVM's can be ordered quickly and easily online, arriving at an "instant" property value. AVM's are cheap, costing between $15 and $35 in most cases.

Assessment: The value placed on a home, determined by a (town/county) tax assessor to calculate a tax base. Assessments are often confused by sellers as an appraisal or a market value. Some towns will have very accurate tax assessments, while others will be more broad-based and potentially outdated. Generally, town assessment values run a little lower than a true market value, but not always.

All of this information points to one key outcome: *market value*. This is the highest price a buyer is willing to pay and the lowest price a seller is willing to accept. The market value assumes:

- Both buyer and seller are knowledgeable of the property and area market
- The property is on the market a reasonable amount of time
- Neither party is acting under duress

The *value* of the property is what it is worth and not necessarily the agreed on purchase price.

For instance, the value of a property may be $300,000, but in a case where the seller is desperate and must sell quickly, he may accept an offer at $285,000.

The *cost* of a property typically has little or nothing to do with the value of a property. This fact becomes evident in both new construction as well as existing/older homes.

When an Appraisal is Needed

Loans/mortgages

Lending institutions will require an appraisal to insure that their position is secured adequately via the value of the property. Most banks will lend up to 90 percent of the appraised value of a property, and some will lend up to 95 or even 97 percent.

Real estate taxes

In some cases, a town may require an appraisal to be conducted to assist them in arriving at an assessed value. However, in most cases, a town assessor (often a town employee) will conduct the property valuation on their own without the use of a certified appraiser.

Insurance

Insurance companies will need to arrive at an estimated market value to make sure that they are insuring the property for an adequate total sum, in case of total loss.

Estate settlement

The heirs of an estate may want to get an impartial estimate of property value to assist them in their decisions of inheritance or tax planning.

Condemnation

This is the term for how the government takes ownership of a property via eminent domain. The government must pay a fair market value for the property in transfer.

Business acquisition

This would be the case in a commercial real estate transaction, as in a restaurant where the owner of a business is selling the business *plus* the property.

Exchanges

This has become increasingly popular, via the IRS code 1031. One owner, or investment group, will essentially trade a property for another property. Here, it is necessary to arrive at a fair market value for both (or all) properties involved.

Value Elements

The following criteria are what create value in a property:

Transferability: The owner should be able to pass along full ownership rights to another without any severe restrictions.

Demand: The need or desire of a potential buyer to own a piece of property.

Utility: The property must be able to be used for the sought-after purpose (i.e.. a lot that cannot be built upon due to environmental hazards has no value as a potential residential building lot).

Scarcity: An effect of supply and demand; how much of like-properties are available at any particular time in a particular area/region.

Influences and Variables to Value

Social Forces: Social trends can affect neighborhoods as well as entire regions. This can include changes in population growth, age groups, and size of the family unit among other factors.

Economic Forces: Overall economic trends may include job opportunities, industrial growth rates, financing availability, cost of living, real estate taxes, and selling prices of other homes.

Physical Forces: Typically, people have little control over physical characteristics, such as the lay of the land, water table, and inability to access town utilities or drill for a water well.

Governmental Forces: These include all the master planning, zoning ordinances, and other local bylaws that are often political in nature. Building code moratoriums on new permits would also fall into this category.

Highest and Best Use: Real estate is constantly changing, often due to different zoning districts. A parcel may have a value of $200,000 as a single-family residential lot, but if that neighborhood suddenly becomes zoned commercial, that same (unchanged) property may have a market value of $325,000. Property values are always concerned with whether or not the property is being used to its highest value and use.

Contribution: Home and property owners will often make alterations, additions, and other improvements to the property that had a cost associated with them. These contributions do *not* always result in an increased market value of the property, and if the value is increased it is almost always *less* than the cost associated with performing said alteration. Magazines like Remodeling (**www.remodeling.hw.net**) perform annual reports on which residential improvements have the highest rate of return at the eventual house sale. Most home improvements increase the value of the home between 50 and 80 percent of the actual cost.

Supply and Demand: Just like the latest Christmas toy craze, if there is not enough of a certain desirable property, its value at that time will increase.

Conformity: Properties that have similar properties in their immediate vicinity often hold their values better than an oddity (such as a three-family house in the middle of a section of town that only has single-family homes). In this case, the three-family home is suffering from *regression*. On the contrary, a 1,200 square-foot home located on a street with all 2,500 square foot homes would benefit from *progression*. The smaller home would be worth slightly more than it would normally be due to the immediate neighborhood (and neighborhood value) it is located in.

Plottage (or Assemblage): Increasing the value of two or more contiguous lots by combining them into a larger lot that would then have more use and worth. This often comes into play due to various zoning ordinances that have been developed. For instance, if two adjacent lots separately do not have the necessary street frontage to allow for the building of a house, there is a motivation for the owners of the lots to somehow legally join the lots together to form one new lot, which then could be sold as a "buildable" lot in a conforming sense.

Substitution: This theory relates to the fact that a potential buyer will substitute the second or third house they see for the first one they saw if it has all the same perceived benefits but costs less. Essentially, the buyer substitutes one home with a better value for another. This can only be done if property benefits and features are relatively similar to each other.

Anticipation: Often, buyers will value a property based on *anticipated* pleasure or profit due to said property in the future. For instance, a buyer may anticipate that they will install an in-ground pool in the back yard of a property with a nice and large/level backyard. Psychologically, that buyer may put an additional value on that *future* benefit.

Change: It is important to try to foresee an appropriate use of a parcel of land. Real estate is always in a state of flux and change, due to physical or economic variables.

The Appraisal Process

When a buyer or seller works with an agent on the sale of property, the mortgage lender will require an estimated value of the property called an appraisal. The sale of a property requires an appraisal because the underlying asset serves as collateral for the loan. In other words, the value of the property is pledged as security for repayment of the loan in case the purchaser of the property winds up defaulting on the loan. If the mortgages lender winds up seizing the property, the appraisal gives them an idea of its value, and they can then attempt to liquidate to recoup the loan. As an agent, you must know the following steps in the appraisal process.

1. Identify the property by street address *and* by legal description (book and page number).

2. What is the purpose of the appraisal? Who is the client? Is this for a purchase? For a cash-out refinance?

3. What type of property is it? This will help determine what method of cost valuation will be used: *comparison, income,* or *cost* approaches.

4. Evaluate the neighborhood to see if there are any key zoning changes.

5. Data selection, collection, and analysis: this includes all data needed per the method of value listed above. Data needed may require construction cost estimates, income statements, and assumptions for income-producing property.

6. Land value estimate: most appraisal forms require a separate value of the land, separate from the building or improvements on it. Is this parcel being used to its best and highest use?

7. Apply the three value approaches: it is always best for the appraiser to attempt to use two or three methods of value analysis, not just one. In most residential (single family) appraisals, the comparison method is the most important.

8. Reconciliation of value estimates: here is where the appraiser's experience and knowledge will show. No two properties are *exactly* the same, so there must be additions and subtractions calculated to arrive at a fair market value for the subject property. For instance, one comparable home may have an additional half-bathroom that the subject property does not have. Here the appraiser would need to make a deduction to arrive at a fair estimated value for the subject property.

9. Final report of value estimate: this is a conclusion/summary in a report that states the appraiser's final estimated market value of the subject property.

See Appendix D for a blank sample Uniform Residential Appraisal Report.

Market approach

The market approach, sometimes called the sales comparison approach, is most often used in residential real estate, and it involves comparing the subject property (its attributes and detractions) to other local, similar properties. An example of such can be found in the above sample appraisal. In the first column, there is the subject property (here a single family home), and then there are typically three comparable sale properties.

As the key features of all properties are listed, there is a dollar adjustment (or partial reconciliation) right next to it. At the bottom of the three comparable columns there is an "adjusted sale price," which is a fair market value after the various reconciliations.

Income approach

In our example shown above, there is no income approach conducted because in a single-family home (owner-occupied), there is no income being produced. Therefore, we will detail the main steps below.

There are three keys in assessing a market value for an income-producing property. They are: *market value, net income,* and *capitalization rate.* The basic formula is:

Value = Net Income / Capitalization Rate

Example: A five-family house generates income of $700 per apartment per month. The expenses per year are:

Real estate taxes	$3,000
Insurance	$1,500
Utilities	$1,000
Maintenance/Repairs	$1,200
Misc.	$400

The appraiser has reviewed similar area investment properties and found that the appropriate cap rate is 12 percent. What should the value of this property be?

Gross (Total) Income = $700 per Unit × 5 units × 12 months = $42,000
Total Expenses = $7,100
Net Income = $42,000 - $7,100 = $34,900

Using the given cap rate of 12 percent, Value = $34,900 / .12 = $290,833

Appraisers also use something called a Gross Rent Multiplier (GRM) to arrive at a quick ballpark value approximation. This is the relationship between a monthly gross rent and the property's value. Often times, an area's

GRM could be between 80 and 90. For example, a multi-family property sold for $275,000, with a gross (not "net") monthly income of $3,200. The GRM would be 85.9.

$$\$275,000 \: / \: \$3,200 = 85.9 \: (GRM)$$

An appraiser might pool this sale with two other multi-family sales in the town to arrive at an average GRM for the area. The appraiser would then use the average GRM to arrive at a quick estimate of value for a subject's multi-family property.

Cost approach

As evidenced in the sample appraisal above, the appraisal will often include the cost approach as at least a secondary means (and proof) of a market value. In our sample, it is shown that the value based on the cost approach would be $399,985. This is much higher than the summary value of $342,000, which was based on the comparable sales approach. To a buyer of a property, it may not matter how much it would *cost* to build the property/building from scratch if they can purchase a similar property for significantly less money.

Cost approach is based on first setting a value on the land itself and then building the structures and features in a systematic way using accepted construction costs. Usually, these construction costs are based on the square-foot approach. Square foot costs are a basic means of arriving at an approximate cost of an item or building based solely on its size.

CASE STUDY: BEING CAUTIOUS ABOUT HOME VALUATIONS

Michael L.
Real Estate Appraiser, 6+ years

I have been working as a real estate appraiser for six years. (More recently, I have also been working as a licensed real estate agent, as well.) In the past year, the main changes in my business have been a decrease in volume and tightening of lender guidelines.

Many real estate agents (and buyers and sellers) see various home "prices" and "values" in print and online. None of these are certified appraisals. For instance, assessed values can never keep pace with a fluid, changing market. Assessed values are based on historic, not current, market data. Over the past four to five years, instant home valuations are also available on the Internet, but they are not very accurate. They have gotten better as technology advances and accurate market data becomes more readily available. In general, I would say "fair market value" changes every six months. "Volatile markets" change plus or minus 10 percent in a 12-month period.

Similar in many ways to real estate agent continuing requirements, in Massachusetts, we need 45 hours during each 3-year licensing cycle including USPAP updates.

Here's my list of do's and don'ts for listing agents to make friendly with the appraiser during the inspection:

Do arrive on time for the appointment. If the appraiser is having a bad day and has to wait an extra 15 to 20 minutes for you, usually in the rain, it just starts the whole thing off on the wrong foot.

Do bring a copy of the P&S Agreement. A house is only worth what an educated buyer in the market is willing to pay for it, and a signed purchase and sale agreement is the strongest piece of evidence you have to support your case.

If it is not fully executed yet, give them an unsigned or partial copy and tell them you'll fax/e-mail it over as soon as a fully signed one is available. They will need the information contained in the P&S for their appraisal report.

Do include a copy of the field card and the deed. You *did* pull both of these documents when you listed the home, right? The appraiser will most likely have these documents already, but if not, you may have saved them a trip. Plus, it shows a level of professionalism on your part.

Feel free to include relevant comps. With "relevant" being the key word. It is an appraiser's job to research the comps, but if your house is a particularly tricky or unique one, it does not hurt to make some suggestions. If the comps are less than three months old (yes, these days three months is the preferred time frame!), less than a mile away, and within a 25 percent range (smaller or larger) than your house, throw them in the folder.

Appraisers (and the lenders they work for) like to look at sold comps. Do not tell the appraiser about all the great active listings in the neighborhood that support the purchase price. Active sales do not set the market; closed sales do.

CASE STUDY: LEARNING BEYOND THE EXAM

Barbara G.
Real Estate Broker, 5+ years

I have been working as a real estate agent for Coldwell Banker Residential Brokerage for about five years. There has been much that I have had to learn after the license exam in order to be successful. I would say I only use about 50 percent of what I learned from the preparation and completion of the exam.

I wish that the exam would focus more on how to write up good written offers. What should be included or excluded? In my opinion, the hardest part of the exam itself was not knowing exactly what section or subject to focus on in my studying. I remember I studied long and hard on one or two subject headings that were rarely touched on in the Massachusetts state exam.

There was no required pre-exam course needed, and as such I did not take any prep course. However, I did pass the exam on my first attempt. In my state, we need 12 hours of continuing education credits every two years, which is not that much compared to some other states.

Chapter 6

Math Review for the
Real Estate Professional

A s noted earlier, basic math skills are necessary in order to excel on the real estate exam. Do not assume that you remember what a "denominator" and all the other middle school math rules from yesteryear are. Because of that, a brief tutorial on the necessary math skills are shown and detailed below, including some examples and problems. There is an answer key to these problems at the end of this chapter. (It is recommended that you use a scrap piece of paper to do these practice problems, and you should do the same for your actual real estate exam.)

Decimals

A decimal is an expression that divides a whole number into subdivisions of ten.

$$1/5 = .20$$

$$1/5 \text{ of } 1/5 \text{ [or } 1/25] = .04$$

Addition of decimals

Line up the decimal points, and then add the numbers as you would any other numbers, making sure to also include the decimal point at the bottom in the answer/sum value.

Remember that the number .2 can also be written as 0.2 or .20

Example: 1.12 + .4 + 6.3 =   1.12

$$
\begin{array}{r}
1.12 \\
.40 \\
+ \quad 6.30 \\
\hline
\mathbf{7.82}
\end{array}
$$

Subtraction of decimals

Similar to addition above, make sure you line up the decimal points in the numbers being subtracted, and then subtract as you would normally.

Example: 2.34 – 1.03 =   2.34

$$
\begin{array}{r}
2.34 \\
- \ 1.03 \\
\hline
\mathbf{1.31}
\end{array}
$$

Complete the following decimal problems:

1) 16.24 – 4.07 =   2) 14.30 + .78 =   3) 2.2 + 1.45 =
4) 3.29 – 1.20 =   5) 5.67 – 4.07 =   6) 0.02 + 0.102 =

Multiplication of decimals

Here we do *not* line up the decimal points. Instead, we simply multiply the numbers as normal, and then we add the quantity of decimal points in each number to arrive at the number of digits to the right of the decimal point in the answer.

Example: .35 × .03 = .0105 (or 0.0105)

Complete the following decimal problems:

7) 1.0 × 5.67 =   8) 0.1 × 56.70 =   9) 212.08 × 2.5 =

10) 0.02 × 100.09 =   11) 1.6 × 6.1 =   12) 4 × .25 =

Division of decimals

The value on the left is called the "divisor" and the value on the right is called the "dividend." For example:

$$4 \longrightarrow \text{quotient}$$
$$\text{divisor} \longleftarrow 2 \overline{)8} \longrightarrow \text{dividend}$$

However, the opposite is true in the easier manner of expressing division herein:

$$8 / 2$$

(Here "8" is the dividend and "2" is the divisor; "2" is going into "8." The answer here is 4)

When dividing decimal numbers, the decimal has to be "removed" from the divisor, by moving to the right within the number until the decimal point is immediately after the last (nonzero) number. However, to calculate the math correctly, one must do the same — move the decimal point to the right, to the other number (the dividend) — by the same amount.

$$4.5 / .20 = 22.5 \text{ (or 22.50)}$$

Complete the following decimal problems:

13) 10.4 / 3.25   14) 56 / 0.3   15) 3.34 / 0.12

16) .8 / 4.2   17) .15 / 0.5   18) 35.4 / 1.6

Fractions

Any number that is not a whole number must be expressed as a fraction. When we say "one half" of something, it is written as 1/2.

Here are some common fraction terms:

Numerator: the number "1" in the fraction "1/2"; the top number of a fraction.
Denominator: the number "2" in the fraction "1/2"; the bottom number of a fraction.
Proper Fraction: a value that is less than 1; for example, 1/4 or one quarter is less than "1"
Improper Fraction: a value that is more than 1; for example, 3/2 is more than "1")
Mixed number: a whole number plus a fraction; for example, 3 1/2

Addition of fractions

1. To be added, fractions must have the same denominator.
2. If needed, fractions should be converted into their lowest common denominator (LCD).
3. Numerators are then added, while the denominator should be the same as the LCD.
4. Mixed numbers need to be converted to improper fractions before adding.
5. Answers are then converted back to mixed numbers (from improper fractions).
6. Reduce, if needed.

Example

Problem: 2/3 + 1/6
The LCD is 6.

Therefore, change the fraction "2/3" to "4/6"

Now, add. 4/6 + 1/6 = 5/6

Complete the following fraction problems:

19) 3/4 + 1/2 =   20) 4/7 + 10/14 =   21) 1 1/3 + 5/6 =

22) 8/2 +2/3 =   23) 2 1/6 + 3/4 =

Subtraction of fractions

In subtraction, the basic rules of fraction addition are maintained.

1. To be subtracted, fractions must have the same denominator.
2. If needed, fractions should be converted to their LCD.
3. Numerators are then subtracted, while the denominator should be the same as the LCD.
4. Mixed numbers need to be converted to improper fractions before subtracting.
5. Answers are then converted back to mixed numbers (from improper fractions).
6. Reduce, if needed.

Example

Problem: 1 3/4– 5/6

Change "1 3/4" to a single fraction: "7/4"

The problem now looks like this: 7/4 – 5/6

The LCD is 12.

Therefore, change the initial problem to the following: 21/12 – 10/12

Now, subtract. 21/12 – 10/12 = 11/12

Complete the following fraction problems:

24) 3/4 – 1/2 =   25) 1 1/2 – 5/6 =   26) 2 2/5 – 4/10 =

27) 6/4 – 3/8 =   28) 3/4 – 1/12 =

Multiplication of fractions

Multiplication of fractions can be expressed or written in three ways:

1. $1/3 \times 1/2 =$
2. $1/3 * 1/2 =$
3. $1/3 \ (1/2) =$

Here are the basic rules of multiplying fractions.

1. Change mixed numbers to improper fraction (i.e., 3 1/2 change to 7/2)
2. In multiplication, you do not need to convert to the lowest common denominator.
3. Multiply the numerators together.
4. Multiply the denominators together.
5. Reduce, if needed.
6. Convert answer from an improper fraction to a mixed number, if applicable.

Example

Problem: $2 \ 1/3 \times 2/7$

Change "2 1/3" to a single fraction: "7/3"

The problem now looks like this: $7/3 \times 2/7$

$7/3 \times 2/7 = (7 \times 2) \ / \ (3 \times 7) = 21/14$

Reduce 21/14 to 3/2

The answer is: 1 1/2

Complete the following fraction problems:

29) $2/3 \times 4 \ 1/4 =$ 30) $1/2 \times 6 \ 1/6 =$ 31) $1/2 \times 1/4 =$

32) $10 \ 4/6 \times 6/4 =$ 33) $2 \ 2/7 \times 1/10 =$

Division of fractions

The language associated with division is demonstrated in the following sentence: the divisor into the dividend equals the quotient (the quotient is the answer). In an equation, this will appear as follows: Dividend/Divisor = Quotient.

Here are the basic rules of dividing fractions.

1. Change mixed numbers to improper fractions.
2. In division, there is no need to convert to the LCD.
3. Invert (flip) the numerator and denominator of the second number in problem.
4. Proceed as in multiplication (see steps above).

Example

Problem: [4/7] / [2/3]
Flip the numerator and denominator of the second number: "2/3" to "3/2"
Now, multiply. 4/7 × 3/2= 12/14
Reduce. The answer is: 6/7

Complete the following fraction problems:

34) [2/3] / [1/2] =   35) [2 1/3] / [3/4] =   36) [1 8/7] / [2/6] =

Percentages

Percentage is a means of expressing a part of a whole, where the whole is taken to be "100." If we considered a dozen eggs as the whole, or 100 percent, and 3 of the dozen were broken from the store, we would say that 3/12 were broken, or 25 percent. For the purposes of this book, the term "percent" will be used as the indicator for the term "percent," not the symbol.

When working with percentages in real estate calculations, you have to be able to convert the percentage to either a fraction *or* a decimal to then proceed with the calculation.

This first intro is a series of steps on those conversions — and back again.

Percent to decimal

To convert a percent to a decimal, simply drop the percent sign and move the decimal point *two* places to the *left*.

Example

Problem: 35 percent
Drop the percent sign: 35 percent = 35
Move the decimal two places to the left: **.35** (or **0.35**)

Complete the following percentage problems:

37) 50 percent =   38) 110 percent =   39) 6 percent =
40) 25.4 percent =

Decimal to percent

To convert a decimal to a percent, move the decimal point *two* places to the *right*, and add the percent sign.

Example

Problem: .15
Move the decimal two places to the right: .15 = 15
Add the percent sign: **15 percent**

Complete the following decimal problems:

41) 2 =   42) 76 =   43) .04 =   44) 13.23 =

Percent to fraction

In order to convert a percent to a fraction, put the number over 100, drop the percent sign, and then reduce the fraction (to the greatest common divisor if applicable).

Example

Problem: 12 percent

Put the number over 100: 12/100

Reduce the fraction: 3/25

Complete the following percentage problems:

45) 8 percent =   46) 34 1/2 percent =   47) 45 percent =
48) 123 percent =

Fraction to percent

To convert a fraction to a percent, multiply the number by 100 and add the percent sign. If the fraction is a mixed number, first convert it to an improper fraction.

Example

Problem: 3/12

Multiply by 100: 3/12 × 100/1 = 300/12

Reduce and add the percent sign: 25 percent

Complete the following fraction problems:

49) 7/8 =   50) 1/4 =   51) 2 3/4=   52) 5/4 =

Decimal to fraction

To convert a decimal to a fraction, first remove the decimal point and put the number over *1 multiplied by as many zeros* as there are decimal places. Reduce the answer if needed.

Example

Problem: .20

Remove decimal point: 20

Put the number over 1 multiplied by as many zeroes as there are decimal places: 20/100

Reduce. The answer is: 1/3

Complete the following decimal problems:

53) .32 =   54) .120 =   55) .8 =   56) 18.5 =

Fraction to decimal

In order to convert a fraction to a decimal, divide the denominator into the numerator. If the number is a mixed number, you must first convert it to an improper fraction.

Example

Problem: 2 2/3

Convert to an improper fraction: 8/3

Divide the denominator into the numerator. The answer is: 2.67

Complete the following fraction problems:

57) 1/3 =   58) 4 1/4 =   59) 2 1/5 =   60) 3/10 =

Measurement of Distance, Area, and Volume

It is part of a real estate professional's regular work to deal with a variety of issues involving measurements. Basic questions could be as follows:

- How many acres of land are part of this development? (Note: 1 acre = 43,560 square feet; this is very close to the size/area of a football field.)
- Are you listing any 1,500 square-feet, cape-style homes?

- How many miles away is the closest fire station?

We will first review the following key points: area, volume, acreage, and perimeter.

Area

Area is always expressed using the term "square." For example, we refer to area by using the phrases "square feet" or "square miles." Whenever you multiply area or volume, you must only multiply "like" units of measure. In other words, you cannot multiply 5 feet by 20 centimeters.

Another way of signifying "squared" is to simply multiply said number by the same number. For example, "4 squared" = 4 × 4. The answer would be 16.

Rectangle

A rectangle is a four-sided shape where all angles/corners are right angles (90 degrees).

The basic equation for a rectangle is Area = Length × Width.

width   Area = $l \bullet w$

length

Example

Problem: How many square feet are in a rectangular lot that is 125 feet long × 200 feet wide?
Answer: 125 feet × 200 feet = **25,000 square feet**

Triangle

A triangle is any three-sided figure. A "right triangle" is a triangle that has one angle that is a right angle (90 degrees).

The basic equation for any triangle is Area = ½ (Base × Height)

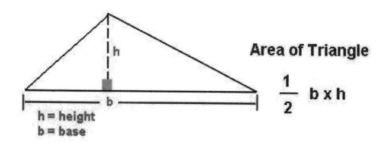

h = height
b = base

Area of Triangle

$$\frac{1}{2} \; b \times h$$

Trapezoid

A trapezoid is a four-sided shape where only two sides are parallel. The other two (opposite) sides are not parallel to each other. It is a "squashed" rectangle or square.

The basic equation for a trapezoid is Area = 1/2 (B1 + B2)(H), where B1 and B2 are the lengths of the two sides which ARE parallel to each other, and H is the height or the distance that B1 and B2 are apart.

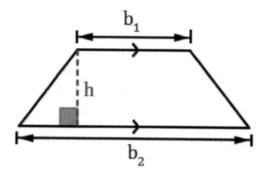

Circle

The area of a circle equals pi (π) or π times the radius squared. π = approximately 3.14 or 31/7.

The radius of a circle is half of the diameter; the diameter is the longest straight line drawn from one side of the circumference to the opposite side of the circle.

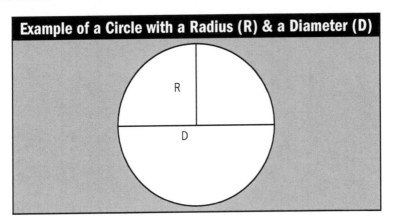

Example of a Circle with a Radius (R) & a Diameter (D)

Example

Problem: What is the area of a circular lot whose radius is 200 feet?
The equation would be π × 200 squared.
Area = 3.14 × (200)(200)
Answer: 3.14 × 40,000 = **125,600 square feet**

Complete the following problems:

1. What is the area of a square lot with street frontage of 225 feet?

2. What is the area of a rectangular lot that is 150 feet wide be 300 feet deep?

3. What is the area of a triangular lot where two sides are 100 feet and 125 feet, if the angle between the 2 sides is 90 degrees?

4. What is the area of a triangular lot with a base of 300 feet and a height/altitude of 150 feet?

5. What is the area of a trapezoidal-shaped lot with the following sides: 75 feet, 45 feet, 125 feet, and 45 feet, plus a height of 40 feet (see below)?

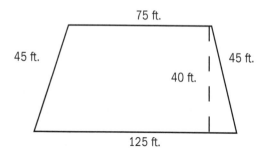

1. What is the area of a circular lot with a diameter of 300 feet?
2. What is the area of a man-made circular pond with a radius of 80 feet?

Acreage

An acre is an area of land equal to 43,560 square feet. To easily grasp the size, keep in mind that an acre is more or less the size of a full football/ soccer field.

Today, many conversion sites exits online to calculate any measurement for easy use, but if you do it manually, the formula for converting square feet to acres is [acres = ft2 ÷ 43,560]. Conversely, the formula for converting acres into square feet is [ft2 = acres × 43,560].

Volume

In everyday real estate tasks, "area" is used more frequently than "volume," but there will be times when a volume calculation is needed. Volume is three-dimensional, whereas area is two-dimensional.

Remember that Area = Length × Width (two measurements being calculated together), whereas **Volume = Length × Width × Height** (three measurements being calculated together).

Rectangular volume

The volume of a rectangular figure (which would include a square shape) is length × width × height (or depth).

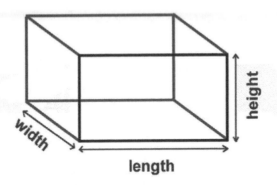

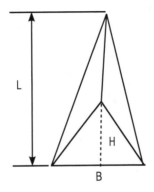

Example

Problem: What is the volume of a room that is 12 feet wide × 18 feet long × 8 feet high?

Use the equation V = L × W × H.

Answer: 12' × 18' × 8' = **1,728 cubic feet (or c.f.)**

Triangular volume

The volume of triangular shape is ½ the base times the height times the length.

Example

Problem: What is the volume of a camping tent that has a base width of 7 feet, a height of 6 feet, and a length of 10 feet?

Use the equation V = ½ base × height × length.

Answer: ½ (7' × 6') × 10' = **210 cubic feet**

Cylinder (circular volume)

The volume of a cylinder is the area of the circular base (3.14 × radius squared) times the height.

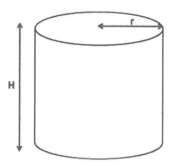

Example

Problem: What is the volume of a cylinder 4 feet high with a base whose diameter is 6 feet?

First, convert the diameter measurement to a radius measurement. R equals ½ the diameter.

R = ½ (6) = 3

Now, use the equation V = (3.14 × radius squared) × height

Answer: 3.14 (3')(3') × 4' = **113.04 cubic feet**

Complete the following problems:

1. An A-Frame type ski chalet has a triangular shape to it. To determine the size of an air-conditioning unit, the cubic footage

of space inside needs to be determined. The roof height is 24 feet, the base width is 24 feet and the base length is 28 feet. What is the volume of this chalet?

2. A cylindrical barrel has a base radius of 1.5 feet and a height of 3.5 feet. What is its volume?

3. What is the volume of a basement whose dimensions are 34 feet long, 24 feet wide and 7.5 feet high?

Perimeter

Perimeter is the distance around the exterior of a figure or shape. For non-circles, the perimeter is found by adding all the lineal dimensions of all the sides. For circles, the perimeter is called a circumference. The calculation involves π; Perimeter = $(\pi)(D)$, where D equals the diameter.

Examples

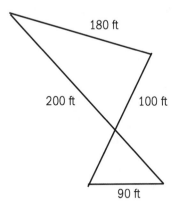

180 ft

200 ft   100 ft

90 ft

Answer: 100' + 90' + 200' + 180' = **570 feet (or lineal feet)**

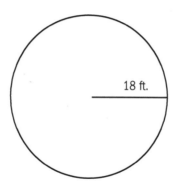

Answer: $(3.14)(36') =$ **113.04 feet**

Complete the following problems:

1. What is the perimeter of a pentagon-shaped lot with dimensional sides of 225 feet, 130 feet, 87 feet, 200 feet, and 32 feet?

2. What is the perimeter of a triangle with a base of 8 feet and both sides measuring 6 feet?

3. What is the perimeter of a circular pool with a diameter of 16 feet?

Formulas and Formula Aids

Much of the real estate exam will involve definitions, but many problems will also require you to be able to use a formula to determine the correct answer. Most formulas that you will use are simple multiplication and division problems, often in the form of a fraction.

The following Table of Formula Aids will assist you in correctly answering the exam's math problems. Feel free to use this guide as you are attempting your practice exams at the end of this book. In addition, you may want to ask your state's testing facilitator if you can bring such a general formula guide into your examination. If you are someone who prefers using an app, iTunes offers a free one called "Real Estate Licensing Exam Prep" that offers flash cards and study guides.

Table of Formula Aids

Formula	Aid
Length x Width = Area $\qquad$ L x W = A	$\dfrac{A}{L \times W}$
Principal x Rate x Time = Interest $\qquad$ P x R x T = I	$\dfrac{I}{P \times R \times T}$
Base x Rate = Percentage $\qquad$ B x R = P	$\dfrac{P}{B \times R}$
*Sell Price x Rate = Commission $\qquad$ SP x R = C	$\dfrac{C}{SP \times R}$
*Amount x Rate = Interest $\qquad$ A x R = I	$\dfrac{I}{A \times R}$
*Appraised Value x Assessment Rate $\qquad$ AppV x AssR = AssV = Assessed Value	$\dfrac{AssV}{AppV \times AssR}$
*Assessed Value x Tax Rate = $\qquad$ AssV x TR = Tax Annual Tax	$\dfrac{Tax}{AssV \times TR}$
*Cost x Depreciation Rate = Depreciation $\quad$ C x R = D	$\dfrac{D}{C \times R}$
*Investment x Rate of Profit = Profit $\qquad$ I x R = P	$\dfrac{P}{I \times R}$
* Investment x Rate of Loss = Loss $\qquad$ I x R = L	$\dfrac{L}{I \times R}$
*Investment x Rate of Return = Net Income $\quad$ I x R = NI	$\dfrac{NI}{I \times R}$
*Value x Capitalization Rate = Net Income $\quad$ V x CR = NI	$\dfrac{NI}{V \times CR}$

Other Math Notes and Useful Terms

In real estate work, the agent will be required to have a thorough and working understanding of numerous math-related terms and functions, and we will highlight many of those herein. Please refer to the Table of Formulas above, which will correspond to the terms described.

Interest

Interest is the charge or fee for the use of the principal on a loan or mortgage.

Interest equals $P \times R \times T$.

P = Principal (the amount borrowed)
R = Rate (the percent — usually an annual percent — charged for use of the money)
T = Time (the duration/length, in years, of the loan/mortgage)

If the terms of a loan are portions of years (for example, two years and three months), that would need to be converted to years via a fraction or a decimal in order to enter it into a formula to arrive at a needed rate, principal, or interest value: two years and three months = 2.25 years.

Note that for banking purposes, it is usually figured that there are 30 days in every month, although many months do not have exactly 30 days in them. This helps to keep the math and escrows simple.

Amortization

Amortization is the systematic reduction and liquidation of debt. It is often referred to in regard to mortgages. A 30-year mortgage amortizes (is fully paid off including all principal and interest payments) in exactly 30 years. There are many tables, charts, calculators, and online tools that can be used to determine the exact values at different times during a loan term. A real estate agent does not need to be an expert in these formulas but should know how to find the correct answers from online tools, handheld real estate calculators or their various lender and mortgage partners.

In typical mortgages, each month the borrower is making a principal payment as well as an interest payment. Using the example above, after 30 years, the loan's principal amount and all of the required interest payments will be completely paid in 30 years. Please note that there are "interest-only" mortgages that are now available which do *not* pay down any loan principal for a specific period of time. These types of mortgages can be dangerous for some borrowers, as they are not building much, if any, equity in their homes.

Profit & Loss

In business, real estate investments and rental properties, ongoing and annual accounting will determine the Profit & Loss Statement of the business venture. Investors, REALTORS®, and bankers are often interested in the return on investment (ROI). For example, if a man invests $8,000 and one year later his investment has grown to $10,000, he has a 25 percent profit, not 20 percent. We must compare the $2,000 profit to the original $8,000 amount.

Investment

Normally, this is equal to the purchase price. This is the amount of money the buyer puts into a business/investment transaction. With some investments, a cost basis can be adjusted for financial and corporate developments.

Rate of Return

This is expressed as a percentage. It is a comparison of the net income to the investment itself.

Net Income

This is expressed annually. Net income is the income less all expenses.

For example, an apartment house that sells for $200,000 with an annual return on investment of 10 percent has an annual net income of $20,000.

Taxation

Taxation comes for many different jurisdictional levels, including federal, state, county and town. Real estate agents are primarily concerned with property taxes, which are normally assessed by either the town or the county where the property is located.

In general, the Assessed Value × Tax Rate = Annual Tax.

The annual tax needs to be paid by the property owner. Normally, the town expects payment either twice or four times per year. When there is a mortgage involved, most lenders have an option (and actually prefer) to escrow for the property taxes each and every month. In this way, the borrower is paying a smaller portion every month that is set aside in the lender's escrow account or third party provider. Then, the town is paid the applicable property taxes via this escrow account.

It is important to understand that an appraisal is *not* the same as an assessment. The entire point of an assessment, and assessed value, is solely to determine the tax due to be paid. It may or may not have anything to do with the market value of the property. On the other hand, an appraisal is a statistical analysis and opinion of what the property will sell for in the current market.

Tax rates can be expressed in a variety of ways, and different towns or counties may calculate it differently, so it is important for the real estate agent not to assume. Tax rates may be listed as so much money per $1,000, per $100, per $10 of assessed value and so forth. Some towns use a "mill rate." A mill rate of 52 = $52/$1,000 of assessment.

Proration & Settlement

At the closing, or transference, of real property, there are always charges that need to be figured and credited to and from the buyer and seller. In most cases, the mortgage lender (if there is one) and the real estate attorney involved will take the lead role in determining the exact dollar figures that each party is responsible for based on the specific day of the month the closing takes place.

However, it is important for any real estate agent or broker to be very comfortable in ascertaining these values or at least being able to double-check these numbers for the benefit of their client, be it buyer or seller.

A debit is money that must come *from* a party. A credit is money that will go *to* a party.

Some examples of items that must be prorated and settled at the closing are:

1. Property taxes

2. Interest charge on the new and former mortgage loan

3. Utility bills or unused fuel remaining at the home (as in propane and oil tanks for home heating)

4. State or county property *transfer* taxes (if applicable in your area)

5. "Stamps" as they are often called — referring to the county registry that stamps the new deed created

As shown below, the physical settlement form is called an HUD-1 Settlement Statement. This is the generic sheet that is approved by the federal Housing and Urban Development department. On this sheet, there are all the critical figures that a buyer, seller, and a real estate agent should be reviewing before and during the property closing. See the example on the following pages:

Sample HUD-1 Settlement Statement

A. Settlement Statement (HUD-1)

OMB Approval No. 2502-0265

B. Type of Loan

1. ☐ FHA 2. ☒ RHS 3. ☐ CONV. UNINS.   6. File Number: 7. Loan Number: 8. Mortgage Insurance Case Number:
4. ☐ VA 5. ☐ CONV. INS.

C. Note: This form is furnished to give you a statement of actual settlement costs. Amounts paid to and by the settlement agent are shown. Items marked "(p.o.c.)" were paid outside the closing; they are shown here for informational purposes and are not included in the totals.

D. Name & Address of Borrower:

E. Name & Address of Seller:

F. Name & Address of Lender:

G. Property Location:

H. Settlement Agent:

I. Settlement Date:

Place of Settlement:

J.	Summary of Borrower's Transaction		K.	Summary of Seller's Transaction	
100. Gross Amount Due From Borrower:			**400. Gross Amount Due To Seller:**		
101.	Contract Sales Price	136,435.00	401.	Contract Sales Price	136,435.00
102.	Personal Property		402.	Personal Property	
103.	Settlement Charges to Borrower (line 1400)	10,062.85	403.		
104.			404.		
105.	Principal Reduction	500.00	405.		
Adjustments for Items Paid by Seller in Advance:			**Adjustments for Items Paid by Seller in Advance:**		
106.	City / Town Taxes		406.	City / Town Taxes	
107.	County / Parish Taxes		407.	County / Parish Taxes	
108.	Assessments		408.	Assessments	
120.	Gross Amount Due from Borrower:	146,997.85	420.	Gross Amount Due to Seller:	136,435.00
200. Amounts Paid by or in Behalf of Borrower:			**500. Reductions in Amount Due to Seller:**		
201.	Deposit or Earnest Money	500.00	501.	Excess Deposit (see instructions)	
202.	Principal Amount of New Loan	142,857.00	502.	Settlement Charges to Seller (Line 1400)	9,857.60
203.	Existing Loan(s) taken subject to		503.	Existing Loan(s) taken subject to	
204.	Daily interest credit		504.	Payoff of First Mortgage Loan to Select Portfolio Servicing	111,286.55
205.			505.	Payoff of Second Mortgage Loan (Paid by Seller) to Select Portfolio Servicing	7,000.00
206.	Good Faith Deposit	350.00	506.	Seller Relocation to Juan Jimenez	3,000.00
207.	Closing Costs Paid for Buyer by Seller	2,017.02	507.	Closing Costs Paid for Buyer by Seller	2,017.02
208.	Transfer Tax on Deed POBOB		508.	Payoff Mortgage to SunTrust	1,500.00
209.	Standard Cost paid by Seller - Owners Title Insurance	757.50	509.	Standard Cost paid by Seller - Owners Title Insurance	757.50
Adjustments for Items Unpaid by Seller:			**Adjustments for Items Unpaid by Seller:**		
210.	City / Town Taxes		510.	City / Town Taxes	
211.	County / Parish Taxes	1,016.33	511.	County / Parish Taxes	1,016.33
212.	Assessments		512.	Assessments	
220.	Total Paid by / for Borrower:	147,497.85	520.	Total Reductions in Amount Due Seller:	136,435.00
300. Cash at Settlement from / to Borrower:			**600. Cash at Settlement to / from Seller:**		
301.	Gross Amount due from Borrower (line 120)	146,997.85	601.	Gross Amount due to Seller (line 420)	136,435.00
302.	Less Amount Paid by/for Borrower (line 220)	147,497.85	602.	Less Reductions Amount due Seller (line 520)	136,435.00
303.	**Cash To Borrower:**	**$500.00**	**603.**	**Cash From Seller:**	**$0.00**

The Public Reporting Burden for this collection of information is estimated at 35 minutes per response for collecting, reviewing, and reporting the data. This agency may not collect this information, and you are not required to complete this form, unless it displays a currently valid OMB control number. No confidentiality is assured; this disclosure is mandatory. This is designed to provide the parties to a RESPA covered transaction with information during the settlement process.

Previous editions are obsolete   Page 1 of 4   HUD-1

Sample HUD-1 Settlement Statement

L. Settlement Charges		Paid from Borrower's Funds at Settlement	Paid from Seller's Funds at Settlement
700. Total Sales / Broker's Commission: $8,186.10			
Division of Commission (line 700) as follows			
701. 4,093.05 to			
702. 4,093.05 to			
703. Commission Paid at Settlement			8,186.10
704. Warehousing Fee			
800. Items Payable in Connection with Loan:			
801. Our origination charge	(from GFE #1) $1,675.00		
802. Your credit or charge (points) for the specific interest rate chosen	(from GFE #2) $-200.00		
803. Your adjusted origination charges	(from GFE #A)	1,475.00	
804. Appraisal Fee	(from GFE #3)		
to Executive Appraisal Solutions, Inc.		390.00	
805. Credit Report	(from GFE #3)		
to Kroll Factual Data		15.93	
806. Tax Service			
807. Flood Certification	(from GFE #3)		
to First American Flood		13.00	
808. Guarantee Fee	(from GFE #3)		
to USDA		2,857.14	
900. Items Required by Lender to be Paid in Advance:			
901. Daily interest charge from	(from GFE #10)	34.24	
days			
902. Guarantee Fee	(from GFE #3)		
903. Homeowner's Insurance for 1.00 years	(from GFE #11)		
to AIIC		915.00	
1000. Reserves Deposited with Lender:			
1001. Initial deposit for your escrow account	(from GFE #9)		
to Inlanta Mortgage, Inc.		1,563.23	
1002. Homeowner's Insurance 3 months @ $76.25 per month			
to Inlanta Mortgage, Inc.	$228.75		
1003. Mortgage Insurance			
1004. Property Taxes 11 months @ $153.34 per month			
to Inlanta Mortgage, Inc.	$1,686.74		
1005. USDA Annual Fee 2 months @ $47.26 per month	$94.52		
1099. Aggregate Adjustment	$-446.78		
1100. Title Charges:			
1101. Title services and lender's title insurance	(from GFE #4)	800.95	
1102. Settlement or Closing Fee			
to	$475.00		697.50
1103. Owner's Title Insurance	(from GFE #5)		
to		757.50	
1104. Lender's Title Insurance			
to			
- Lender's Premium (Risk Rate Premium: $57.00)	$182.00		
- Endorsement 8.1	$50.00		
- Endorsement FL Form 9	$93.95		
1105. Lender's Title Policy Limit $142,857.00			
1106. Owner's Title Policy Limit $136,435.00			
1107. Agent's Portion of the Total Title Insurance Premium	$758.41		
1108. Underwriter's Portion of the Total Title Insurance Premium	$325.04		
1109. Title Search $85 Paid Outside of Closing FATIC by OLTIA			
1200. Government Recording and Transfer Charges:			
1201. Government Recording Charges	(from GFE #7)	105.00	
1202. Deed $10.00 Mortgage $95.00 Releases $0.00			
1203. Transfer Taxes	(from GFE #8)	785.86	
1204. City/County tax/stamps Deed $0.00 Mortgage $0.00			
1205. State tax/stamps Deed $955.50 Mortgage $500.15			955.50
1206. Intangible Tax			
to Clerk of the Circuit Court	$285.71		
1207. Other Tax 2			
1208. Title Clearing Affidavit (3 Liens)	(from GFE #7)		
to Clerk of the Circuit Court			18.50
1300. Additional Settlement Charges:			
1301. Required services that you can shop for	(from GFE #6)	350.00	
1302. Survey Inspection			
to	$350.00		
1303. Pest Inspection			
1304. 2013 RE Taxes PA# 35996-018-00 Paid Outside of Closing by Seller $1,784.87			
1305.			
1306.			
1400. Total Settlement Charges (Enter on line 103, Section J and line 502, Section K)		$10,062.85	$9,857.60

Sample HUD-1 Settlement Statement

Comparison of Good Faith Estimate (GFE) and HUD Charges

Charges That Cannot Increase	HUD Line No.	Good Faith Estimate	HUD
Our origination charge	# 801	1,675.00	1,675.00
Your credit or charge (points) for the specific interest rate chosen	# 802	-200.00	-200.00
Your adjusted origination charges	# 803	1,475.00	1,475.00
Transfer taxes	#1203	2,241.36	785.86

Charges That in Total Cannot Increase More Than 10%	HUD Line No.	Good Faith Estimate	HUD
Government Recording Charges	#1201	105.50	105.00
Appraisal Fee	# 804	390.00	390.00
Credit Report	# 805	30.00	15.93
Flood Certification	# 807	13.00	13.00
Guarantee Fee	# 808	2,857.14	2,857.14
Total		3,395.64	3,381.07
Increase between GFE and HUD Charges		-14.57	-0.43%

Charges That Can Change	HUD Line No.	Good Faith Estimate	HUD
Initial deposit for your escrow account	#1001	1,084.58	1,563.23
Daily interest charge from Jul 30, 2014 to Aug 1, 2014 @ 17.1200 / day for 2 days	# 901	462.24	34.24
Homeowner's Insurance	# 903	920.00	915.00
Title services and lender's title insurance	#1101	975.00	800.95
Owner's Title Insurance	#1103	790.00	757.50
Survey Inspection	#1302	350.00	350.00

Loan Terms

Your initial loan amount is	$142,857.00
Your loan term is	30 years
Your initial interest rate is	4.375 %
Your initial monthly amount owed for principal, interest, and any mortgage insurance is	$713.26 includes [X] Principal [X] Interest [ ] Mortgage Insurance
Can your interest rate rise?	[X] No. [ ] Yes, it can rise to a maximum of ____%. The first change will be on ____ and can change again every ____ after ____. Every change date, your interest rate can increase or decrease by ____%. Over the life of the loan, your interest rate is guaranteed to never be LOWER than ____% or HIGHER than ____%.
Even if you make payments on time, can your loan balance rise?	[X] No. [ ] Yes, it can rise to a maximum of $_____
Even if you make payments on time, can your monthly amount owed for principal, interest, and mortgage insurance rise?	[X] No. [ ] Yes, the first increase can be on _____ and the monthly amount owed can rise to $_____. The maximum it can ever rise to is $_____.
Does your loan have a prepayment penalty?	[X] No. [ ] Yes, your maximum prepayment penalty is $_____.
Does your loan have a balloon payment?	[X] No. [ ] Yes, you have a balloon payment of $_____ due in ____ years on _____.
Total monthly amount owed including escrow account payments	[ ] You do not have a monthly escrow payment for items, such as property taxes and homeowner's insurance. You must pay these items directly yourself. [X] You have an additional monthly escrow payment of $276.85 that results in a total initial monthly amount owed of $990.11. This includes principal, interest, any mortgage insurance and any items checked below: [X] Property taxes [X] USDA Annual Fee [ ] Flood insurance [ ] [X] Homeowner's insurance [ ]

Note: If you have any questions about the Settlement Charges and Loan Terms listed on this form, please contact your lender.

Sample HUD-1 Settlement Statement

Buyers

Sellers

Property Addresses

I have carefully reviewed the HUD-1 Settlement Statement, and to the best of my knowledge and belief, it is a true and accurate statement of all receipts and disbursements made on my account or by me in this transaction. I further certify that I have received a copy of HUD-1 Settlement Statement.

Borrower: _____   Seller: _____

The HUD-1 Settlement Statement which I have prepared is a true and accurate account of this transaction. I have caused or will cause the funds to be disbursed in accordance with this statement.

Date:

Settlement Agent:

WARNING: It is a crime to knowingly make false statements to the United States on this or any other similar form. Penalties upon conviction can include a fine and imprisonment. For details see Title 18 U.S. Code Section 1001 and Section 1010.

Commissions

This is a key aspect of being a real estate agent or broker, as this is primarily the only means you will have of being paid. Sales agents will receive a portion of the commission from a property sale. The agent will share this commission payment with the broker that he or she works under. Said broker will often share the total commission with a co-broker (depending on circumstances).

In a typical scenario, a seller will sign an agreement with a real estate broker for the broker to list, market, and sell the property for a set percent of the purchase price. Normally this "full-service" commission is between 4 percent and 6 percent. A typical example for a sales agent is as follows (your exact payment and details will likely vary):

- Property sales price (not the *listing price*) = $300,000
- Seller's agreement with listing broker = 5.0 percent = $15,000 total commission
- Listing broker splits commission with buyer's broker = $7,500 seller's commission
- Sales agent has negotiated a 60 percent / 40 percent split with his broker.
- 60 percent of $7,500 = **$4,500**

From the final amount, in most cases, the agent will be taxed; most sales agents are "independent contractors" of brokers and/or their companies and are not truly "employees."

Note that **S**ell **P**rice × **C**ommission **R**ate = **C**ommission (SP × CR = C)

Depreciation

Depreciation is a reduction in the value of a property. That depreciation could be for a variety of reasons, but, in general, it is an accepted accounting practice by the IRS and all investors, property managers and owners. Per the IRS, only the buildings can depreciate. The land itself cannot lose value.

Some key terms to review are:

Depreciation: a reduction in value
Appreciation: an increase in value
Useful life: the number of years an asset will last before needing replacement
Book value: value remaining after depreciation (equals the original cost minus accrued depreciation)
Accrued depreciation: total depreciation to date (yearly depreciation times number of years)
Depreciation Rate: the yearly rate times the number of years

Example

A building costs $240,000 and has a useful life of 20 years.
Original Cost = $240,000; Useful Life = 20 years; Depreciation = $12,000/year ($240,000 divided by 20 years)
After two years, what is the accrued depreciation and book value?
Answer: Original Cost ($240,000) – Depreciation ($24,000) = Book Value ($216,000)

Answer Key:

1. 12.17	2. 15.08	3. 3.65
4. 2.09	5. 1.60	6. 0.122
7. 5.67	8. 5.67	9. 530.20
10. 2.0018	11. 9.76	12. 1.0
13. 3.20	14. 186.67	15. 27.83
16. 0.19	17. 0.30	18. 22.13
19. 1 1/4	20. 12/7	21. 2 1/6
22. 4 2/3	23. 2 11/12	24. 1/4

25. 2/3	26. 2	27. 1 1/8
28. 2/3	29. 2 5/6	30. 3 1/12
31. 1/8	32. 16	33. 8/35
34. 1 1/3	35. 3 1/9	36. 6 3/7
37. 0.50	38. 1.10	39. .06
40. .254	41. 200 percent	42. 7600 percent
43. 4 percent	44. 1323 percent	45. 2/25
46. 69/200	47. 9/20	48.123/100
49. 87.5 percent	50. 25 percent	51. 275 percent
52. 125 percent	53. 8/25	54. 3/25
55. 4/5	56. 37/2	57. .333
58. 4.25	59. 2.20	60. 0.30
61. 50,625 SF	62. 45,000 SF	63. 6,250 SF
64. 22,500 SF	65. 4,000 SF	66. 70,650 SF
67. 20,096 SF	68. 8,064 CF	69. 24.73 CF
70. 6,120 CF	71. 674 ft.	72. 20 ft.
73. 50.24 ft.		

Chapter 7

Practice Tests
and Answer Keys

*T*he following sample tests are based on the national criteria and real estate regulations. The reader will need to seek out state-specific regulations and laws.

National Practice Exam #1

1. A homeowner has a balance of $149,570.75 remaining on the mortgage. The interest rate is 7.5 percent and the monthly payment is $1150.00. After the next two payments, the balance will be:

    A. $149,451.30
    B. $149,355.57
    C. $149,139.04
    D. $149,570.05

2. The lender's right to call in the loan in case of default and put the secured property up for sale is based on the mortgage document's

   A. fine print
   B. equity of redemption
   C. defeasance clause
   D. acceleration clause

3. Commercial banks would rather make short-term loans like construction loans and 90-day business loans. The reason for their preference is that:

   A. The source of their lending funds is primarily from CDs.
   B. The source of their lending funds is primarily from checking accounts.
   C. The source of their lending funds is primarily from savings accounts.
   D. The source of their lending funds is primarily from issuing bonds.

4. After the sale of the collateral property, it is determined that the net proceeds did not clear the debt. In this situation, the borrower is likely to receive a

   A. letter of defeasance
   B. notice of a deficiency judgment
   C. certificate of liability
   D. notice of foreclosure

5. FHA mortgage insurance premium is calculated at a rate of ½ percent annually. How much is the premium for the month in which the remaining principal owed is $184,694?

   A. $0.05
   B. $24.00
   C. $76.96
   D. $92.34

6. The Corcorans have a gross income of $60,000. The lender wants them to spend no more than 33 percent of their income on their housing expense. A house they can buy for $240,000 has $2,400 in annual property taxes. Homeowners insurance would cost about $400 per year. At today's interest rates, monthly payments would be $6.65 per $1,000 borrowed on a 30-year mortgage. What is the smallest amount they can expect to spend for a cash down payment?

   A. $20,000
   B. $48,000
   C. $53,940
   D. $26,970

7. What is the difference between MIP and PMI?

   A. MIP is required only on VA mortgages
   B. PMI is the older form of mortgage insurance
   C. PMI insures conventional mortgages, and MIP insures FHA loans
   D. There is no difference; the two terms mean the same thing

8. The Meningers needed two different loans to buy their first home. The loan that will have first claim on the value of the house in case of foreclosure is the one that was first

   A. recorded
   B. signed
   C. applied for
   D. satisfied

9. In a loan closing, proper signatures on the promissory note create

   A. recordation of the lien on the land records
   B. the lien on the property
   C. a nonbinding fiscal contract
   D. the indebtedness of the borrower

10. Which clause, if included in a mortgage, permits a lien recorded subsequent in time to have a superior position to the mortgage that was recorded prior in time?

    A. Subordination clause
    B. Release clause
    C. Subjective clause
    D. Superior clause

11. Express covenants that protect the grantee are found in a

    A. quitclaim deed
    B. deed of trust
    C. general warranty deed
    D. sheriff's deed

12. How may FHA insured and VA guaranteed loans be assumed?

    A. On payment of an assumption fee to the seller
    B. Either freely or on qualification of the buyer, depending on the date of the loan
    C. Only if the new buyer is a veteran
    D. With guaranteed agreement of the selling broker

13. Can a ranch contain a basement?

    A. Yes, many ranches have a downstairs level.
    B. No, ranches are built on a cement slab and do not have a true basement.
    C. Yes, one of the habitable areas is located somewhat underground.
    D. No, ranches have cellars.

14. Which of the following statements is/are true regarding the FHA (Federal Housing Authority)?

    I. FHA loans are funded by conventional lenders.

II. FHA has a program 203b that is for one-to-four family dwellings.

III. FHA insures loans but does not guarantee them.

    A. I only.

    B. 1, II, and III.

    C. II and III only.

    D. No statement is true.

15. Land consisting of a quarter section (160 acres) is sold for $1805 per acre. The total sale price is

    A. $288,800

    B. $72,200

    C. $396,000

    D. $45,125

16. A purchaser contracts for a new home for $250,000 and, after making a 10 percent down payment, applies for a fixed rate loan at the rate of 7.5 percent. At the settlement on April 10, the lender collects interest up to May 1. What is the interest charge to the buyer shown on the settlement statement?

    A. $1250.00

    B. $492.19

    C. $984.38

    D. $833.33

17. The entity that relinquishes ownership through a deed of trust mortgage foreclosure is the

    A. lender

    B. beneficiary

    C. mortgagor

    D. mortgagee

18. The purchase contract is the most important document in the sales process because

    A. it provides the road map for the closing
    B. the agent is not guaranteed payment without it
    C. preparing sales agreements is good for the legal business
    D. verbal real estate contracts can only be recorded in select counties

19. Which of the following phrases is *not* discriminatory in an advertisement to lease a nonexempt 50-unit apartment complex under the current Federal Fair Housing Act?

    A. no handicapped alteration will be made
    B. adults only; no children
    C. no propane or charcoal grills on premises
    D. females only

20. The purpose of RESPA is to

    A. help a buyer know how much money is required
    B. make sure that buyers do not borrow more than they can afford
    C. allow the REALTOR® to accept kickbacks from the buyer's lender
    D. see that a buyer and seller know all settlement costs

21. Important provisions of RESPA include all of the following except

    A. the settlement location must be at an attorney or bank office
    B. a uniform settlement statement
    C. the lender's estimate of settlement costs
    D. the disclosure of controlled business

22. Which method of foreclosure is used in a deed of trust mortgage lien?

   A. Deed in lieu of accepted by lender
   B. Probate court ordered sale
   C. Sheriff's sale at the courthouse
   D. Non-judicial power of sale

23. Mark Stuart, a widower, died without leaving a will or other instruction. His surviving children received ownership of his real estate holdings by

   A. adverse possession
   B. law of intestate succession
   C. beneficiary's writ
   D. eminent domain

24. An abstract of title contains

   A. the summary of a title search
   B. an attorney's opinion of title
   C. a registrar's certificate of title
   D. written opinion of title from the County Registrar's Clerk

25. A bookstore in the North Mall pays a base rent each month plus additional rent based on the amount of business it does. It is operating under a

   A. ground lease
   B. holdover lease
   C. net lease
   D. percentage lease

26. Tammi Coady lives in one side of a duplex house. She wants to advertise the other side as non-smoking. Can she legally do so?

   A. Yes, because she occupies part of the house herself.

B. Yes, because the right to smoke is not protected by law.

C. No, because a property owner cannot advertise discriminatory practices.

D. No, because each housing unit is its own Book and Page number.

27. The term "walk-through" refers to

A. the buyer's final inspection of the property to check its condition

B. an FHA-approved termite inspection

C. a seller's check of the premises before an open house is held

D. an appraiser's inspection of the interior of the subject property

28. An owner who transfers real property through a will is known as

A. devisee

B. legatee

C. testator

D. beneficiary

29. Kelly has a three-year lease on her apartment. At the end of the three years

A. the landlord must notify her if he wants her to vacate

B. she must give the landlord one month's notice of termination or departure

C. the landlord must give her an Option to extend at the current rent amount plus are market escalation

D. neither party need give the other any notice of termination

30. Property managers often make management decisions about tenant selection and budgets for their clients. In these relationships, the property manager is acting as a(n)

    A. subagent

    B. power of attorney

    C. general agent

    D. independent contractor

31. Net operating income (NOI) is found by

    A. subtracting yearly operating expenses from effective gross income

    B. dividing effective gross income by the cap rate

    C. subtracting yearly operating expenses from the appraiser's estimate of potential gross income

    D. multiplying effective gross income by the cap rate

32. An oral agreement between a lessor and lessee is legally

    A. a valid tenancy for one year

    B. unenforceable due to the statute of frauds

    C. unenforceable due to the statute of limitations

    D. a valid tenancy at will

33. A prospect for the lease of a commercial property feels the need for adversarial representation and hires a broker to negotiate the lease on his behalf. The contract entered into between the prospect and the broker is called

    A. an authorization to negotiate with limited Power of Attorney

    B. a cooperative brokerage agreement

    C. a property management agreement

    D. a buyer broker agreement

34. The seller of a house built before 1978 is required by law to furnish the buyer with a

    A. Good Faith Estimate (GFE) of settlement costs

B. lead paint information booklet

C. seller's property information disclosure

D. proof of flood insurance

35. Rufus Chaffee hires Chris Brown, a property manager, to lease a house that he owns. Rufus is Chris's

   A. client

   B. customer

   C. fiduciary

   D. subagent

36. The responsibilities of the property manager include all of the following except

   A. maintaining the property while preserving finances

   B. marketing for a constant tenant base

   C. preparing and submitting budgets

   D. seeking interested buyers

37. The landlord has the right to access the premises

   A. in case of emergency

   B. for the purposes of making unannounced "spot" checks

   C. when the tenant is away for an extended time

   D. none of the above

38. What would you pay for a building producing $20,000 net income annually and showing a minimum rate of 8 percent?

   A. $50,000

   B. $250,000

   C. $160,000

   D. $200,000

39. The correct formula for estimating value using the cost approach is

    A. cost to reproduce + value of land = value
    B. depreciation + value of land – cost to reproduce = value
    C. value of land + cost to reproduce _ depreciation = value
    D. cost to reproduce – depreciation + value of land = value

40. The right to occupy a property without interference for a specified period of time is known as a

    A. leasehold
    B. prescriptive easement
    C. trespass
    D. eminent domain

41. The Civil Rights Act of 1866 prohibits discrimination in real estate based on

    A. race
    B. race and gender
    C. handicap and country of origin
    D. whether buyer is from one of the former Confederate states

42. Market data approach appraising may require adjustments of sold comparables by an appraiser for all of the following except

    A. sale date of comparable
    B. financing made available by seller
    C. replacement cost of existing homeowner's recent improvements
    D. lot size and location

43. When an appraiser deducts depreciation using the reproduction cost of a building, the depreciation represents

    A. loss of value due to any cause

B. costs to modernize property

C. lack of site improvements

D. loss of value due only to age of improvements

44. A residential property was built 105 years ago. Three of the five bedrooms have no closets, the basement floor is heavily cracked, and the original wood shake roof needs repairs. To the appraiser, the most important consideration is

   A. how the bedrooms could be reconfigured to provide some storage

   B. how much it would cost to finish the basement floor

   C. the sale price of a nearby similar property

   D. the life expectancy of the roof

45. Assuming the NOI remains constant, what will happen to the present value of the property if the cap rate increases? The present value will

   A. increase

   B. decrease

   C. stay the same

   D. increase at first and then decrease

46. The closed sale price of an income property divided by its gross monthly rent equals the

   A. unit density ratio

   B. gross rent multiplier

   C. gross income multiplier

   D. capitalization rate

47. For appraising a 15-year-old single family house, the best data is the

   A. probable rent figure

B. replacement cost

C. recent sale prices of nearby houses

D. owner's original cost plus money spent on improvements + market appreciation

48. Prices are likely to rise when there is a

    A. seller's market

    B. buyer's market

    C. thin market

    D. local employer introducing a new product line

49. What will the amount of taxes payable be if the property's assessed value is $170,000 and the tax rate is 50 mills in a community where the equalization factor is 120 percent?

    A. $12,000

    B. $10,200

    C. $3,460

    D. $8,500

50. The most profitable way in which a particular property can be utilized is known as its

    A. highest and best use

    B. plottage value

    C. condoization

    D. principle of progression

51. In the market or sales data approach of appraisal, the sales prices of similar, recently sold properties are

    A. adjusted

    B. analyzed

    C. assessed

    D. only used if the sales have occurred within the past six months

52. A single family property located in an industrial area has a minimum value because of the principle of

    A. conformity
    B. contribution
    C. noise and air pollution
    D. diminishing returns

53. The most accurate way to uniquely locate and bound a parcel of real property is to use

    A. points that are shown on the lender's plot map
    B. a metes and bounds survey
    C. the assessor parcel number
    D. latitude and longitude bearings

54. The purchaser of a cooperative apartment receives shares in the cooperative and a

    A. bargain and sale deed
    B. proprietary lease
    C. joint tenancy
    D. limited partnership

55. A small ranch is being established on a newly acquired 25-acre parcel of land. The new owner plans to enclose the property with a chain link fence. The rectangular lot has 1,089 feet of frontage on the state road. How many feet of fencing will be needed?

    A. 2,090 feet
    B. 4,595 feet
    C. 4,270 feet
    D. 4,178 feet

56. The type of ownership that would give an investor the greatest flexibility when selling his or her interest would be

    A. a general partnership

    B. joint tenancy

    C. ownership in severalty

    D. a limited partnership

57. Of the following, which lien has the lowest property?

    A. unsecured judgment

    B. a mortgage or trust deed

    C. property taxes

    D. mechanic's lien

58. Rob has the right to cross Scott's property to get to his property. What is the right called?

    A. a right of way

    B. an easement by prescription

    C. an easement in gross

    D. an appurtenant easement

59. Mike owned fee simple title to a lot next door to a zoo. He gave the lot to the zoo as a gift. However, he wanted to make sure it would always be used for zoo purposes. His attorney prepared his deed to convey ownership of the lot to the zoo "so long as it is used for zoo purposes." The zoo owns a

    A. fee simple estate

    B. fee simple absolute

    C. fee simple determinable

    D. subordinate estate

60. An acre contains approximately

    A. 5270 square yards

    B. 45,000 square yards

    C. one quarter square mile

    D. 43,560 square feet

61. A zoning commission may grant a variance to property use when which of the following exists?

    A. limitation of feasible building sites due to land contours
    B. property improvement will be beneficial for neighborhood
    C. alternative building site that increase owner's costs
    D. over-budget development costs to a subdivider

62. Tenancy by the entirety is a special form of ownership available only to

    A. sole owners
    B. limited liability corporations
    C. married couples
    D. civil unions

63. Which of the following is not a physical characteristic of land?
    A. wetland concentration
    B. indestructibility
    C. non-homogeneity
    D. situs

64. A purchase in which the seller holds title until a specified number of payments have been made is known as a

    A. future delivery purchase
    B. deferred transfer mortgage
    C. contract for deed
    D. collateral mortgage

65. Which of the following actions is legally permitted?

    A. advertising property for sale only to a special ethnic group
    B. refusing to make a mortgage loan to a minority individual because of a poor credit history

C. altering the terms of a loan for a member of a minority group

D. telling a minority individual that an apartment has been rented when in fact it has not been rented

66. A deed restriction is also known as a land use covenant. Which of the following is an example of a land use covenant?

A. minimum square footage of homes within a subdivision

B. type of fencing constructed by owner

C. Energy-Star fixtures within a structure

D. Both A and B

67. A valid deed must contain

A. a legal description

B. a survey of the property

C. date stamp from the County Registrar

D. the signature of the grantee

68. An appraiser may take this factor into consideration when appraising a property

A. familial status

B. age of property

C. religions of area churches

D. race of neighborhood

69. Which is not an exemption to the Federal Housing Act?

A. An owner who occupies a one-to-four family dwelling may limit the rental of rooms or units.

B. Housing may be limited for use by senior citizens if occupied by one person at least 55 years of age or older.

C. A man with two children

D. Religious organizations may limit the occupancy of real estate that it owns to its members if the units are not owned for business purposes

70. Which of the following statements best describes a real estate agent's liabilities concerning environmental hazards?

   A. Residential real estate agents do not need to know about environmental conditions.
   B. Unless the buyer notices something, the real estate agent does not have to worry about it.
   C. Disclosure of environmental hazards is the responsibility of the seller.
   D. A real estate agent licensee could be liable if he or she should have known about a condition, even if the seller neglected to disclose it.

71. Which of the following would not be allowed under the Federal Housing Act?

   A. The owner of a nine-unit apartment building renting to men only
   B. A landlord refuses to rent his double home in which he lives to a woman with two children and two cats.
   C. An Elks Lodge will rent rooms only to members who belong to the Elks Lodge
   D. Housing limited to persons age 62 or older

72. When describing the particulars about a property, the agent does not disclose that a capital improvement project has been approved that will result in a special assessment to the owner in the near future. The broker has

   A. acted in accordance with the duties of a fiduciary
   B. committed a fraud

    C. refrained from disclosing anything that would weaken the principal's bargaining position

    D. acted in an unethical manner, but not fraudulently

73. A broker would not be violating a law for making the statement, "This is the most beautiful harbor view in the state," because it is considered harmless

    A. puffing

    B. showmanship

    C. advertising

    D. misrepresentation

74. Agent Harris has just returned from a closing for a property that sold for $125,000. The property was listed by ABC Realty. Harris received 2 percent of the sale price total commission for the transaction from the closing agent. Harris is on a 55/45 split with his company. How much commission will Harris receive?

    A. $5,000

    B. $3,750

    C. $1,375.20

    D. $1,320.20

75. All are protected classes except

    A. a 34-year-old man

    B. national origin

    C. race

    D. handicap

76. When may a broker functioning as an intermediary appoint one licensee to communicate with the seller and another licensee to communicate with the buyer?

    A. when in the judgment of the broker it is best to make such appointments

    B. when written permission to do so has been obtained from the parties

    C. when the parties have given verbal approvals to make such appointments, after shaking hands in agreement

    D. when the seller has given written consent for the broker to do so

77. When a buyer makes an offer and a seller changes a few of the terms before he signs and returns it, that is a

    A. rejection

    B. seller concession

    C. counteroffer

    D. conditional rejection

78. Which of the following listings is risky and open to fraudulent dealings?

    A. listing your brother's home, under applicable guidelines

    B. a net listing

    C. an exclusive agency

    D. an exclusive right to sell

79. In a real estate transaction, a broker does not affirmatively represent either the buyer or the seller as agent. He is acting as

    A. a non-representing dual agent

    B. an undisclosed dual agent

    C. a transaction broker

    D. an illegal real estate subagent

80. Which of the following would not be permitted under the Federal Fair Housing Act?

A. The owner of a 30-unit residential apartment building renting only to black men

B. An Arabian owner refusing to rent his home to an Israeli

C. The USO in NY renting rooms only to service personnel

D. An owner who lives on one side of a duplex refusing to rent to a family with 5 children on the other side of the duplex

81. A broker takes a sales agreement to his seller for full price. The seller states he will not accept this agreement because the buyers are Mexican. The broker should do which of the following?

A. Abide by the principle directions and return the offer to the selling broker

B. Explain to the owner that his refusal to sign because of the buyer's race violates federal laws

C. Bring sales agreements to the seller from non-Mexican buyers only

D. Tell the buyers that they'll need to find another property

82. After a purchase contract is accepted, the parties may later make additional agreements without changing the original document by use of

A. a time extension

B. a revision

C. an addendum

D. a contingency

83. The buyer has been held to be in default on a contract of sale. If buyer and seller had not agreed on liquidated damages, the seller could do which of the following?

A. Sue the buyer for compensatory damages

B. Obtain a court order preventing the buyer from purchasing another property

C. Have the buyer incarcerated

D. Only keep the buyer's earnest deposit

84. The statute of frauds requires that

A. certain contracts, including those of real estate, must be in writing to be enforceable

B. the seller of real estate provide a written disclosure about the condition of the property

C. real estate brokers answer buyers' and sellers' questions honestly

D. property deeds must be recorded in the appropriate County Registry

85. The buyer makes an offer to purchase a property and specifies that the owner accept or reject the offer within 48 hours. Before hearing back from the owner, the buyer locates a more attractive property and withdraws the offer. Is the buyer legally permitted to withdraw his offer?

A. Yes; an offer with a condition to respond in 48 hours is not valid

B. No; the offer is binding until the 48-hour time period expires

C. Yes; either party may withdraw an offer or counteroffer at any time prior to its acceptance

D. Yes; until the seller physically signs an acceptance, it is not a valid contract

86. The broker's only responsibility at the conveyance is to

A. verify and receive the brokerage fee/commission

B. explain the clauses found in the deed

C. review the title report for clouds or other problems

D. interpret the terms and conditions contained in the loan documents

87. One effect of a clause in a sales agreement that states that "time is of the essence" might be that

   A. the seller can take care of matters at their convenience

   B. the buyer must deal with the details of the contract as they occur

   C. all parties, exclusive of the agent, must attend to details quickly

   D. all parties must attend to those details called for in the agreement in a timely manner

88. At a general meeting of a brokers' trade association, several members begin talking about fees and business practices. This sort of activity could be considered

   A. a good way for brokers to learn about the different practices regionally

   B. activity endorsed by the Chamber of Commerce

   C. an appropriate activity within the association

   D. a violation of the Sherman Anti-Trust Act

89. An appraiser estimates annual rental collections on an investment property of $99,000. The vacancy factor is 5 percent and operating expenses run 25 percent of gross income. A similar investment should generate a ROI of 15 percent. Using the income approach to value, what is the market value of this property?

   A. $462,000

   B. $627,000

   C. $396,000

   D. $660,000

90. The Beans put their house on the market, the Browns made a written purchase offer, and the Beans accepted the offer in writing. When is the contract valid?

    A. Immediately
    B. As soon as the signatures are notarized
    C. When it is placed in the public records
    D. When the Browns are notified of the acceptance, verbally or in writing

91. The investor criterion for a home mortgage is an uninsured LTV ratio of 90 percent of the appraisal. The sales agreement and appraisal is in the amount of $180,000. Following underwriting guidelines, the buyer qualifies for a loan of $155,000. How much of the purchase will be financed by this investor?

    A. $162,000
    B. $135,000
    C. $108,750
    D. $155,000

92. The seller offers to pay 3 points on the buyer's 80 percent loan. If the house sells for $350,000, what is the expense to the seller?

    A. $10,500
    B. $2,400
    C. $3,000
    D. $8,400

93. David and Sandra Schneider have paid a total of $10,500 in mortgage interest and $1,500 in property taxes in this tax year. If they are in the 30 percent tax bracket, their tax savings is

    A. $3,600
    B. $1,000
    C. $8,400
    D. $12,000

94. The area of a lot that measures 425 feet × 425 feet is how many square yards?

    A. 26,759
    B. 120,416
    C. 40,139
    D. 361,251

95. Closing occurs on October 10. Annual property taxes of $9,000 are paid at the end of the year. What is the correct entry for the closing statement for the proration of taxes?

    A. $750
    B. $700
    C. $7,500
    D. $7,000

96. The Sherman Anti-Trust Act prohibits real estate brokers from

    A. selling each other's listings
    B. discriminating on the basis of religion or ethnicity
    C. advertising the amount of down payment needed on a property
    D. agreeing to set standard co-broker commission rates

97. House A sold for $132,000. It had three bedrooms, two bathrooms, and a two-car garage. In the same neighborhood one month later, house B sold for $142,000. It had a three-car garage, but otherwise was similar to House A. House C (subject property) has a two-car garage. What would the appraiser adjust for the extra garage space on House B?

    A. $10,000 deduction from the value of House B
    B. $8,000 deduction from the value of House A
    C. $10,000 addition to the value of House B
    D. $8,000 addition to the value of House A

98. If a lender agrees to make a loan based on a 95 percent LTV, what is the amount of a loan for a property appraised for $135,000 and a sale price of $137,800?

    A. $130,910

    B. $105,920

    C. $128,110

    D. $128,250

99. Tom Corcoran, a property owner, just received a bill from her local taxing authority in the amount of $3,060. Property taxes in this town are based on 80 percent of an assessed value, and the rate is $1.50 per hundred. What value has the assessor placed on Tom's property?

    A. $204,000

    B. $163,200

    C. $255,000

    D. $285,000

100. What is the square footage of a living room measuring 32 feet by 23 feet?

    A. 637

    B. 906

    C. 550

    D. 736

National Practice Exam #2

1. Jeff Kosarka has $86,576 left on his 8.5 percent mortgage. His monthly payment is set at $852.56 for principal and interest (he pays his own taxes and insurance). How much of his next payment will go toward the loan interest?

    A. $116.76

    B. $239.31

    C. $735.80

    D. $613.25

2. Theresa Henchey is buying a new home for $200,000. She makes a $47,000 down payment and finances the balance with a 7.5 percent 30-year conventional loan. The factor for repayment is $7.00 per thousand. After making the first payment, what is the remaining balance on Theresa's loan?

    A. $152,885.25

    B. $152,808.75

    C. $152,635.25

    D. $153,135.25

3. Which of the following instruments would contain the loan amount, term of the loan, interest rate, and monthly payments?

    A. lease

    B. mortgage

    C. deed

    D. none of the above

4. A developer received a loan that covers numerous parcels of real estate and provides for the release of the mortgage lien on each parcel as it is sold and an agreed-upon amount of the original loan is paid. This type of loan is called a

    A. package loan

    B. wraparound loan

    C. purchase-money loan

    D. blanket loan

5. In a loan execution, proper signatures on the promissory note create

    A. the lien on the property

    B. the indebtedness of the borrower

    C. the transfer of ownership to a trustee

    D. recording of the lien on the land records

6. When negative amortization occurs, the

    A. loan balance increases

    B. term of the loan increases

    C. monthly payment increases

    D. term of the loan decreases

7. The borrower conveys legal title to the property to a disinterested third party for safekeeping in order to obtain a loan. In this situation, the document required is a

    A. general warranty deed

    B. involuntary conveyance

    C. trust deed

    D. mortgage

8. A borrower obtains a $100,000 mortgage at 7.5 percent. If the monthly payment of $902.77 is credited first to interest and then to the principal, what will the balance of the principal be after the borrower makes their first payment?

    A. $99,772

    B. $99,375

    C. $99,097

    D. $99,722

9. A collateral property is sold. It is then determined that the net proceeds did not clear the debt. In this situation, the borrower will likely receive a

    A. notice of foreclosure

    B. letter of defeasance

C. certificate of liability

D. notice of deficiency judgment

10. One of the newer developments in mortgage lending is the use of

    A. fixed-rate 30 year mortgages

    B. adjustable rate mortgages

    C. wraparound mortgages

    D. computerized loan origination

11. How may FHA insured and VA guaranteed loans be assumed?

    A. on payment of an assumption fee to the seller

    B. only if the second borrower is related to the original borrower

    C. either freely or on creditworthiness of the buyer, depending on the date of the loan

    D. under no circumstances

12. A tenant paid rent of $500 due the first of September and a $500 security deposit. The property then sold on September 15. How much money will the sellers owe the buyer at closing?

    A. $500

    B. $750

    C. $1,000

    D. $1,500

13. A borrower notices that he is paying an MIP on his HUD Settlement Statement. What kind of loan does he have?

    A. 80 percent LTV conventional loan

    B. VA loan

    C. FHA 203b loan

    D. Graduated payment loan

14. Using real property, while retaining the property itself, as collateral to secure a loan is called

    A. hypothecation
    B. encumbrance
    C. mortgage
    D. promissory intent

15. An accrued charge on a settlement statement is paid

    A. in advance
    B. always by the seller
    C. always by the buyer
    D. in arrears

16. Any federally backed loan may require the borrower to carry special insurance if the property is located in

    A. an earthquake area
    B. a desert
    C. an ocean hazard district
    D. a flood zone

17. Which method of foreclosure is used in a deed of trust mortgage lien?

    A. Sheriff's sale at the courthouse
    B. Judicial court-ordered sale
    C. Non-judicial power of sale
    D. Deed in lieu of accepted by the lender

18. If real estate property taxes are paid in arrears, what would the seller be debited on a September 14 closing with annual taxes of $5,400? (Use the statutory method whereby taxes accrue from January 1 through closing date, and the seller is responsible for day of closing.)

A. $3,800

B. $3,814

C. $3,810

D. $2,700

19. Which of the following phrases is allowable in an advertisement to lease a non-exempt 80-unit apartment complex under the current Federal Fair Housing Act?

    A. No handicapped alterations will be made

    B. Adults only; no children

    C. Females only

    D. No smoking on premises

20. The provisions of RESPA apply to

    A. all residential mortgage loans

    B. one-to-four family residential mortgage loans

    C. all mortgages except home equity loans

    D. commercial mortgages up to $2,000,000

21. When representing a buyer in a real estate transaction, the agent must disclose to the seller all of the following except

    A. any potential for the agent to benefit from referring the parties to a subsidiary of the agent's firm for transaction-related services

    B. the agent's relationship with the buyer

    C. any agreement to compensate the agent out of the listing broker's commission

    D. the buyer's financial situation

22. The term "walk-through" refers to

    A. the buyer's final inspection of the property before closing to check its condition

    B. empty office buildings where the vacancy rate in the community is high

    C. a seller's check of the premises before an open house is held

    D. an appraiser's inspection of the interior of the subject property

23. The seller delivers the deed and the buyer pays the purchase price in the step referred to as

    A. commitment

    B. underwriting

    C. closing

    D. warehouse lending

24. The entity that loses ownership through a deed of trust foreclosure is the

    A. lender

    B. mortgagor

    C. mortgagee

    D. beneficiary

25. Steve Lee owns an apartment building that was constructed in 1965. According to federal law, which of the following must be attached to the leases Steve prepares for prospective tenants?

    A. a lead-based paint disclosure statement

    B. a report of the building's radon level

    C. a diagram of all underground storage tanks (USTs)

    D. any known instances of groundwater contamination in the building's water supply

26. While Dana Mawn spends six months in Europe, he continues to pay rent to his landlord, but actually collects rent from his

friend Brian, who is living there while he is gone. The situation is knows as

    A. an assignment

    B. a temporal rental

    C. a lease option

    D. a sublet

27. One advantage of condominium ownership over cooperative ownership is that

    A. condominium owners can mortgage their units individually

    B. condominium owners pay no maintenance fees

    C. a cooperative owner must put down at least 20 percent down payment

    D. there is basically no difference in the two forms of ownership

28. All are examples of involuntary transfer of title except

    A. adverse possession

    B. condemnation through eminent domain

    C. dedication

    D. tax sale

29. Key provisions of RESPA include all of the following except

    A. the lender's estimate of settlement costs

    B. a settlement location

    C. a uniform settlement statement

    D. the disclosure of controlled business

30. Scott Roberto's tenants all had a few months remaining on their leases when he entered into a contract to sell his six-unit apartment building to Mike Ciak. Tenants in this situation normally

    A. need to do nothing and may remain until the end of their leases

    B. can be required to leave with 60 day's notice

    C. lose their leases unless they pay a 10 percent resale fee

    D. must renegotiate their leases with the new property owner

31. Which of the following would be classified as "limited" common elements in a condominium development?

    A. elevators

    B. hallways

    C. unassigned parking spaces

    D. assigned parking spaces

32. The federal ban on housing discrimination based on familial status is aimed at providing equal access to rentals for

    A. unmarried couples

    B. retired individuals with or without pets

    C. single tenants

    D. people with children

33. A tenant in an office park pays a monthly rent that includes all property maintenance charges, cleaning services, and utilities. This is a

    A. tenant-at-will

    B. triple net lease

    C. net lease

    D. gross lease

34. The management agreement does all of the following except

    A. identify the parties

    B. state the owner's overall goals for the property

    C. describe the manager's responsibilities and authorities

D. authorize the manager to make personal deals resulting in outside compensation by suppliers

35. The penalty for a first violation of federal fair housing laws can be as much as

    A. $1,000
    B. $5,000
    C. $100,000
    D. $10,000

36. A type of lease that is common in retail properties requires the tenant to pay a portion of gross sales to the landlord. This is often referred to as a

    A. net lease
    B. sales lease
    C. gross lease
    D. percentage lease

37. Candy Coady lives in one side of a three-family house. She wants to advertise the other side as non-smoking. Can she legally do so?

    A. No, because a property owner cannot advertise discriminatory practices.
    B. Yes, because she occupies part of the house herself.
    C. Yes, because the right to smoke is not protected by law.
    D. Yes, because it is an owner-occupied property.

38. An appraiser is appraising a house that had an estimated economic life of 30 years when the property was purchased 20 years ago. If the appraiser currently estimates that the house is one-third depreciated, what is the remaining economic life?

    A. 10 years
    B. 15 years

C. 20 years

D. None of the above

39. A house was built 75 years ago. Two of the five bedrooms have no closets, the basement floor is gravel and dirt, and the original slate roof needs repairs. To the appraiser, the most important consideration is

A. how the bedrooms could be reconfigured to provide some storage

B. are there lead paint hazards onsite?

C. the sale price of a nearby similar property

D. the life expectancy of the roof

40. Which of the following would most likely be considered incurable depreciation?

A. improvements beyond those of other homes in the area

B. a roof with curled and cracked shingles

C. a broken window

D. septic system has failed

41. When an appraiser deducts depreciation using the reproduction cost of a building, the depreciation represents

A. loss of value due to any cause

B. costs to modernize property

C. lack of site improvements

D. current cost to construct a similar building

42. What will the amount of taxes payable be if the property's assessed value is $85,000 and the tax rate is 50 mills in a town where the equalization factor is 110 percent?

A. $9,350

B. $4,250

C. $3,460

D. $4,675

43. Randy Cross hires Jeff Railsback, a property manager, to lease a house that he owns. Randy is Jeff's

A. customer

B. fiduciary

C. client

D. lessor

44. A tenant is delinquent on his lease payments. The owner can

A. disconnect natural gas service to the tenant's unit

B. bring court action

C. personally evict the tenant after giving 24-hour constructive notice

D. turn off the electricity and water

45. A property is valued at $850,000 by an appraiser and generates an annual net income of $152,000. What capitalization rate percentage did the appraiser use in determining value?

A. 11.5

B. 18

C. 14.45

D. 13

46. Which of the following is not necessary in order for a property to have value?

A. The owner of the property is unknown.

B. There is minimal supply in the regional market.

C. The property is unique.

D. The property has a useful purpose.

47. While the objective in the cost approach generally is to estimate the value of both land and improvements, the land typically is appraised using the

    A. HUD taxation maps and charts
    B. market data approach
    C. gross rent multiplier approach
    D. option approach

48. The correct formula for estimating value using the cost approach is

    A. cost to reproduce + depreciation – financing cost = value
    B. depreciation + value of land – cost to reproduce = value
    C. value of land + cost to reproduce + depreciation = value
    D. cost to reproduce – depreciation + value of land = value

49. The most profitable way in which a particular property can be utilized is known as its

    A. highest and best use
    B. plottage value
    C. zoning conformance
    D. principle of progression

50. An income approach appraisal would include which of the following information?

    A. Building value based on cost per square foot
    B. Gross operating income over the past three years
    C. Replacement cost of structure and site improvements
    D. Annual NOI generated

51. In comparing a competitive market analysis to a comparative market analysis, what is the differing factor?

    A. Properties currently for sale in the same market area
    B. Amenity differences between the comparables

    C. Adjustments for time of sale, such as location and property condition

    D. Comparative market analysis must be completed be a certified appraiser

52. Mark Sogofsky refuses to sell his farm to the state, which needs it to complete the route for a new highway. The state may go to court and ask that his farm be condemned, allowing the state to purchase the land using its right of

    A. eminent domain

    B. adverse possession

    C. easement by necessity

    D. best and proper use

53. Which of the following effects, if any, does zoning have on property values?

    A. Value is enhanced because of the principle of conformity.

    B. Values are unchanged because owners have the freedom to develop land as they wish.

    C. Value is diminished because of the lack of creative use of land.

    D. Value is not related to zoning; an owner can always seek a variance.

54. Which of the following statements is true of joint tenancy?

    A. When one of the tenants dies, his interest is spread among the survivors.

    B. Destruction of the property terminates the co-ownership.

    C. One of the tenants can assign their rights of the deed to a third party.

    D. Unless another form of ownership is described in the deed, co-owners who are not spouses of each other are presumed to be tenants in common.

55. A planned unit development consists of

    A. subdivisions designed by a board-certified Master Planner

    B. parcels owned separately and areas owned in common for use by parcel owners

    C. high-rise building that includes apartments as well as commercial units, such as stores and Laundromats.

    D. residential apartment building units that share common elements, such as hallways and recreational areas within a larger building

56. A subdivider must place in the public records a map of the property known as a

    A. plat

    B. before and after schematic

    C. plot

    D. plan

57. Danielle owned fee simple title to a lot next door to the church. She gave the lot to the church as a gift. However, she wanted to make sure the lot would always be used for related purposes. Her attorney prepared her deed to convey ownership of the lot to the church "so long as it is used for church purposes." The church owns a

    A. fee dimple determinable

    B. fee simple estate

    C. fee simple absolute

    D. taxable business property

58. Which approach to value is best when appraising a seven-unit apartment building?

    A. market rent escalation or depreciation
    B. replacement cost
    C. the income approach to value
    D. reproduction cost

59. To determine an encroachment, the purchaser should obtain

    A. a survey
    B. title insurance
    C. a title search
    D. a current opinion from the town assessor

60. An owner is planning to build on a newly purchased lot. Zoning laws state that no improvement may exceed 50 feet in height, architectural guidelines limit improvements to 45 feet in height, and the deed restriction states that the maximum height is 35 feet. What is the tallest building the owner can legally construct?

    A. 50 feet
    B. 45 feet
    C. The new building can be any size that complies with the State Building Code
    D. 35 feet

61. The right that a power company acquires in order to lay a service line across a customer's property is called

    A. a variation
    B. a license
    C. an easement in gross
    D. a restrictive covenant

62. An odorless substance created by decaying radioactive materials in the soil is known as

    A. radon gas
    B. urea formaldehyde
    C. carbon monoxide
    D. ultraviolet degradation

63. Soil that builds up gradually along a river bank is called

    A. alluvion
    B. avulsion
    C. peat
    D. silt

64. A seller, anxious to sell, tells a cooperating agent during a showing that the agent will be given a commercial lawnmower if he brings in an acceptable offer by the end of the week. All of the following are plausible in this scenario except that the agent should:

    A. legally receive the lawnmower from his broker
    B. report the incident to the listing broker
    C. realize it is a violation of the law to accept the lawnmower
    D. accept the lawnmower because he or she is providing a desired service

65. Regarding real property, which of the following statements is true?

    A. Air rights can be granted separately by deed.
    B. Trade fixtures attached to the building are always the landlord's property.
    C. Emblements are considered as fixtures since they are attached to the land.
    D. Furniture is assumed to be part of the property in a sale.

66. What is the square footage of a room measuring 20 feet by 30 feet?

    A. 500 square feet

    B. 600 square feet

    C. 600 square feet

    D. 840 square feet

67. Rita Lee, a salesperson for XYZ Realty, is required by contract to attend meetings, dress in uniform, and prospect for four hours per day. She receives a biweekly paycheck, less withholdings for taxes and S.S. Rita's relationship with the firm is that of

    A. an independent contractor

    B. an employee

    C. a subagent

    D. a consultant

68. When offering property for cooperation through the MLS, the listing broker is assuring all of the following except

    A. cooperating brokers will be compensated upon completion of the sale

    B. any offer will be accepted as it is written

    C. the seller has the authority to see

    D. the information in the database is deemed to be accurate

69. You are a licensed real estate agent and a realtor, meaning that you are bound to a standard of ethics higher than that of a non-realtor. You find a conflict between the NAR code of ethics and state law. You should

    A. follow the code of ethics so that you do not lose your NAR designation

    B. follow the state law even though it is unethical

    C. ignore the state law because it is unethical

    D. contact the NAR and inform them that they must change their code because part of it is illegal in your state

70. Which fee does not have to be listed in a lender's advertisement when the actual note interest rate is mentioned?

    A. appraisal fee
    B. required down payment
    C. number of payments over loan term
    D. monthly payment amount

71. A doctor calls and states he is prequalified to buy a $325,000 home. He is not familiar with your area and asks where he should live. You reply, "The Meadows Estates, that's where several professionals like yourself live." This is an example of

    A. steering
    B. blockbusting
    C. reverse discrimination
    D. doing your job

72. Kelly Lambert owns an apartment building that was constructed in 1980. According to federal law, which of the following must be attached to the leases Kelly prepares for prospective tenants?

    A. A report of the building's radon level
    B. A lead-based paint disclosure statement
    C. Any known instances of groundwater contamination in the building's water supply
    D. None of the above

73. Broker Penney has finalized the negotiation on his listing at 1000 Main Street. He received earnest money of $5000 for the deal. What must he do with the earnest money?

    A. Put the check in his company's escrow account

B. Put the check in the deal file and turn it over to the closing agency when it closes

C. Put the check in his company's operating account

D. Give the check to the buyer's lender as proof of deposit

74. A salesperson is about to change companies. Should he contact all of his buyer clients and advise them that he will still represent them at his new firm?

A. No, because the listing is with the broker

B. Yes, because a listing is a personal service agreement and stays with the salesperson

C. Yes, because the salesperson is the one the client looks to for representation

D. No, because his new agency will require a 90-day probationary period

75. A landlord not offering as many properties to a family with children that were offered to a single prospect is an example of

A. channeling prospects

B. supportive marketing

C. less favorable treatment

D. malice before the fact

76. For a real estate agency relationship to be enforceable, which of the following is not required?

A. The principal has the power to do what is being assigned.

B. The principal must attain a credit report of the agent, which is updated monthly.

C. The agent must be authorized by a written agreement.

D. The agent must be a real estate licensee.

77. The Quirks put their house on the market, the Schneiders made a written purchase offer, and the Quirks accepted the offer in writing. When is the contract valid?

    A. three days after the Quirks written acceptance
    B. as soon as the signatures are notarized
    C. when it is placed in the public records
    D. when the Schneiders are notified of the acceptance

78. The broker's responsibility at the closing is to

    A. verify and receive the brokerage fee
    B. explain the clauses found in the deed
    C. assist the bank's attorney with the document sign-offs
    D. interpret the terms and conditions contained in the loan documents

79. Agent Carol has just returned from a closing for a property that sold for $250,000. The property was listed by Northern Realty. Carol received 2.5 percent of the total sale price commission for the transaction from the closing agent. Carol has a 55/45 split with her company. How much commission will Carol receive?

    A. $5,000
    B. $3,750
    C. $2,812
    D. $3,438

80. Escrow monies can be defined as and include

    A. promissory notes
    B. A,C, and D
    C. Security deposits
    D. Earnest money

81. Which is not an example of a buyer agency agreement?

A. A dual agency

B. An open buyer's agency

C. An exclusive-agency buyer agency

D. An exclusive buyer agency

82. Which of the following would terminate a listing agreement?

A. The death of the broker

B. The retirement of the salesperson

C. The expiration of the salesperson's license

D. Salesperson procuring his or her broker's license

83. A salesperson negotiates a sale and obtains a written contract signed by all parties. The sale closes but the seller refuses to pay the broker a commission. The broker is not willing to sue the seller for the commission because the seller is his sister-in-law. The salesperson may

A. sue the broker only

B. sue the seller

C. force the broker to sue the seller

D. place a lien against the seller's property for the amount of the commission

84. Keith Sturges wants to buy Dave Flanders' house, but Dave does not want to turn over the title until he receives the purchase price. They could use either a lease option or a land contract. Keith would prefer a lease option because

A. it will allow him to move in immediately.

B. he will be free to change his mind about buying.

C. Dave will be obligated to sell to him.

D. he will not know the eventual sale price.

85. Within the agency agreement is a provision that binds the buyer to paying the broker's fee if, within a stated number of days, the

buyer purchases a property that was shown to the buyer during the agency period. This clause is called the

A. unlimited coverage clause
B. automatic renewal clause
C. limitation of liability clause
D. broker protection clause

86. The buyer has been held to be in default on a contract of sale. If the buyer and seller did not initially agree on liquidated damages, the seller could do which of the following?

A. require the buyer to set aside satisfactory monies in escrow
B. require the buyer to find a substitute purchaser
C. have the buyer incarcerated
D. sue the buyer for compensatory damages

87. One effect of a clause in a sales agreement that states that "time is of the essence" might be that

A. the seller can take care of matters only upon request of the agent
B. all parties must attend to those details called for in the agreement in a timely manner
C. the agent must see that the contract has been fulfilled prior to closing
D. the buyer must deal with the details of the contract as they occur

88. The legal remedy in many sales contracts which allows the non-defaulting party to force the sale is

A. specific performance
B. vendor's lien
C. bilateral promises
D. punitive damages

89. The lender charges two discount points to the buyer. How much does this increase the buyer's closing costs on his $270,000 home if his LTV is 80 percent?

     A. $4,320
     B. $5,400
     C. $4,000
     D. $2,000

90. A buyer, Pepe Lopez, offers in writing to pay $275,333 for a property. Mr. Lopez makes a down payment of 25 percent and finances the balance by obtaining a 30-year conventional loan. The factor for the PI payments is $7.34 per thousand. The lender opens an escrow account for payment of the annual property taxes of $3,000 and the property insurance premium of $600, collecting 1/12 of these amounts with the monthly PI payment. What are the monthly PITI payments for this borrower?

     A. $1,515.71
     B. $2,498.00
     C. $2,798.00
     D. $1,815.71

91. If the buyer's agent splits his commission 50/50 with his broker, and the seller's agent receives 60 percent of his broker's 50 percent share, how much does the buyer's broker receive if the listing broker's fee is 6 percent of the $250,000 sales price of the house?

     A. $7,500
     B. $6,900
     C. $1,875
     D. $3,750

92. If a lender agrees to make a loan based on a 90 percent LTV, what is the amount of a loan for a property appraised for $135,000 and a sale price of $137,800?

    A. $124,020
    B. $105,920
    C. $121,500
    D. $126,000

93. If a seller's agent shares his commission with a buyer's agent,

    A. the seller's agent may deduct that amount from the total he pays his agent.
    B. the seller's agent may advise the seller of the cooperation.
    C. the buyer's agent does not have to disclose this to the buyer.
    D. this is not necessarily an indication of agency representation.

94. Which of the following terms best describes the parties of a P&S contract?

    A. vendor-vendee
    B. mortgagee-mortgagor
    C. grantor-grantee
    D. lessor-lessee

95. Property taxes are paid annually in November for the calendar year. The closing is held on August 15 and the property taxes of $6,500 are prorated to the date of closing. What entries are made on the settlement statement?

    A. charge seller and credit buyer $4,062.00
    B. charge buyer and credit seller $2,437.50
    C. charge seller and credit buyer $1,354.16
    D. charge buyer and credit seller $1,354.16

96. A property is sold for $75,600 in certified check. If transfer taxes are $1.83 per $1,000 of value, how much transfer tax is due?

    A. $138.60
    B. $152.50
    C. $1,525.00
    D. $1,384.20

97. If a homeowner has a first mortgage loan balance of $63,250, a second mortgage balance of $12,000, and unpaid taxes of $4,015, how much equity does the homeowner have in his or her $100,000 home?

    A. $25,000
    B. $24,750
    C. $100,000
    D. $20,735

98. What is the square footage of a family room measuring 20 feet by 23 feet?

    A. 232
    B. 640
    C. 460
    D. 500

99. A house sold for $164,000 and was assessed at 90 percent. If property taxes are $4.30 per $100 of value, what are the annual taxes?

    A. $7,546.80
    B. $4,300.00
    C. $6,346.80
    D. $3,526.00

100. A borrower must pay $2,800 for points on a $140,000 loan. How many points is the lender charging for this loan?

    A. 2

    B. 2.5

    C. 4.5

    D. 4

Answer Key for Practice Exam #1

1. C, $149,139.04

    Explained: $149,570.75 × 0.075 /12 = $934.82 month interest

        $1150.00- $934.82 = $215.18 principal

        $149,570.75 - $215.18 = $149,355.57

        $149,355.57 × 0.075 /12 = $933.47 month interest

        $1150.00- $933.47 = $216.53

        $149,355.57 - $216.53 = $149,139.04

2. D, acceleration clause

3. B, the source of their funds is primarily from checking accounts

4. B, notice of a deficiency judgment

5. C, $76.96

    Explained: Annual premium is $184,694 = $184,694 × .005 = $923.47

        Per month equals- $923.47 /12 = $76.96

6. D, $26,970

    Explained: Gross monthly income is $60,000 /12 = $5,000.

        33 percent of $5,000 = $1,650 for PITI.

        Subtracting monthly property taxes and H.O. Insurance equals $1,650 - $200.00 - $33.33 = $1,416.67.

        At $6.65 per $1,000, $1,416.67 will pay for $213.03, or $213,030 borrowed for their mortgage.

        $1416.67 /6.65 = $213.03.

If they buy a home for $240,000, the buyers will need
$240,000 - $213,030 = $26,970 as a down payment.

7. C, PMI insures conventional mortgages, and MIP insures
    FHA loans

8. A, recorded

9. D, the indebtedness of the borrower

10. A, a subordination clause

11. C, general warranty deed

12. B, either freely or on qualification of the buyer, depending
    on the date of the loan

13. B, ranches are built on a cement slab and do not have a
    true basement

14. B, I, II, and III (all); all 3 stipulations are true for FHA loans

15. A, $288,800; a ¼ section equals 160 acres; $1805/acre × 160 =
    $288,800

16. C, $984.38

    Explained: interest on new loans is collected in advance at the
    closing until the first of next month; $250,000 × 0.90 = $225,000
    $225,000 × 0.075 /360 days in year × 21 days = $984.38
    *(Author's note- Recognize that in typical scenarios, the borrower will
    ALSO be required to pay a monthly mortgage insurance payment/fee,
    for all loans over 80 percent LTV.)*

17. C, mortgagor

18. A, it provides the road map for the closing

19. C, no propane or charcoal grills

20. D, see that a buyer and seller know all settlement costs

21. A, the settlement location must be at an attorney or bank office

22. D, non-judicial power of sale

23. B, law of intestate succession

24. A, the summary of a title search

25. D, percentage lease

26. B, Yes, because the right to smoke is not protected by law

27. A, the buyer's final inspection of the property to check its condition
28. C, testator
29. D, neither party need give the other any notice of termination
30. C, general agent
31. A, subtracting yearly operating expenses from effective gross income
32. D, a valid tenancy at will
33. D, a buyer broker agreement
34. B, lead-paint information booklet
35. A, client
36. D, seeking interested buyers
37. A, in case of an emergency
38. B, $250,000
    Explained: $20,000 / .08 = $250,000
39. D, cost to reproduce – depreciation + value of land = value
40. A, leasehold
41. A, race
42. C, replacement cost of existing homeowner's recent improvements
43. A, loss of value due to any cause
44. C, the sale price of a nearby similar property
45. B, decrease
46. B, gross rent multiplier
47. C, recent sale prices of nearby houses
48. A, seller's market
49. B, $10,200
    Explained: $170,000 × 1.20 = $204,000 /1,000 = 204 × 50 = $10,200
50. A, highest and best use
51. A, adjusted
52. A, conformity
53. B, a metes and bounds survey
54. B, proprietary lease

55. D, 4,178 feet

   Explained: (25 acres × 43,560 square feet/acre) /1,089 front feet = 1,000 feet deep

   (1,000 × 2 sides) + (1,089 × 2 sides) = 4,178 lineal feet

56. C, ownership in severalty

57. A, unsecured judgment

58. D, an appurtenant easement

59. C, fee simple determinable

60. C, 43,560 square feet

61. A, limitation of feasible building sites due to land contours

62. C, married couples

63. D, situs

64. C, contract for deed

65. B, refusing to make a mortgage loan to a minority individual because of a poor credit history

66. D, both A & B; devices and fixtures within a house/structure are not dictated by a land use covenant

67. A, a legal description

68. B, age of property

69. C, a man with two children

70. D, an RE licensee could be liable if he or she should have known about a condition, even if the seller neglected to disclose it

71. A, the owner of a nine-unit apartment building renting to men only

72. B, committed to fraud

73. A, puffing

74. C, $1,375.20

   Explained: $125,000 × 0.020 = $2,500 × 0.55 = $1,375.20

75. D, a 34-year-old man

76. B, when written permission to do so has been obtained from both parties

77. C, counteroffer

78. B, a net listing
79. C, a transaction broker
80. A, the owner of a 20-unit residential apartment building renting only to black men
81. B, explain to the owner that his refusal to sign because of the buyer's race violates federal laws
82. C, a revision
83. A, sue the buyer for compensatory damages
84. A, certain contracts, including those real-estate related, must be in writing to be enforceable
85. C, Yes, either party may withdraw an offer or counteroffer at any time prior to its acceptance
86. A, verify and receive the brokerage fee
87. D, all parties must attend to those details called for in the agreement in a timely manner
88. D, a violation of the Sherman Anti-Trust Act
89. A, $462,000

    Explained: $99,000 × .95 = $94,050 net income
    $99,000 × 0.25 = $24,750 operating expenses
    $94,050 - $24,750 = $69,300
    $69,300 / 0.15 = $462,000

90. D, when the Brown's are notified of the acceptance either verbally or in writing
91. D, $155,000;

    Explained: a loan is based upon many underwriting factors, including the LTV percent. The most restrictive (lowest) factor will be the key factor. Based solely on LTV percent, amount qualified = $180,000 × 0.90 = $162,000. This is higher than the underwriter's decision of $155,000.

92. D, $8,400

    Explained: $350,000 × 0.80 = $280,000 loan amount
    $280,000 × 0.03 = $8,400 = the cost of points

93. A, $3,600

    Explained: $10,500 + $1,500 = $12,000 × 0.30 = $3,600

94. C, 40,139

    Explained: (425 feet × 425 feet) / 9 (conversion factor) = 40,139 square yards

95. D, $7,000

    Explained: $9,000 /12 = $750/month

    $750 /30 = $25.00 /day for taxes

    9 full months = 9 × $750 = $6,750

    10 days in October = 10 × $25/day = $250

    $250 + $6,750 = $7,000

96. D, agreeing to set standard co-broker commission rates

97. A, $10,000 deduction from the value of House B; per the info and comps given, the value of a garage is listed here to be $10,000

98. D, $128,250

    Explained: $135,000 × .95 = $128,250 (LTV is based on the lesser of the appraised value and the sales price)

99. C, $255,000

    Explained: ($3,060 /1.5) × (100 /0.80) = $255,000

100. D, 736

    Explained: 32 × 23 = 736 (length × width = area)

Answer Key for Practice Exam #2

1. D, $613.25

    Explained: A year's interest on the present debt would be $7,358.96 ($86,576 × 0.085). A month's interest is then $613.25.

2. A, $152,885.25

    Explained: 153 × 7.00 = $1,071.00 PI

    $153,000 × 0.075 / 12 = $956.25 interest

    $1071.00 - $956.25 = $114.75 principal

    $153,000 - $114.75 = $152,885.25 remaining balance

3. D, none of the above

4. D, blanket loan

5. B, the indebtedness of the borrower

6. A, loan balance increases

7. C, trust deed

8. D, $99,722.23

   Explained: $100,000 × .075 / 12 = $625

   $902.77 - $625.00 = $277.77

   $100,000 - $277.77 = $99,722.23

9. D, notice of a deficiency judgment

10. D, computerized loan origination

11. C, either freely or on the credit worthiness of the buyer, depending on the date of the loan

12. B, $750

   Explained: security deposit will transfer to new owner- $500 + ½ one month's rent ($250) = $750 total

13. C, an FHA 203b loan

14. A, hypothecation

15. D, in arrears

16. D, a flood zone

17. C, non-judicial zone

18. C, $3,810

   Explained: $5400 / 360 days = $15.00 per day × 254 days = $3,810 debit to the seller. Count, via the "statutory method," the # of days from Jan. 1 thru Sept. 14 (254)

19. D, no smoking on premises

20. B, one-to-four family residential mortgage loans

21. D, the buyer's financial situation

22. A, the buyer's final inspection of the property before closing to check its condition

23. C, closing

24. B, mortgagor

25. A, a report of the building's radon level
26. D, a sublet
27. A, condominium owners can mortgage their units individually
28. C, dedication
29. B, a settlement location
30. A, need do nothing and may remain until the end of their leases
31. D, assigned parking spaces
32. D, people with children
33. C, net lease
34. D, authorize the manager to make personal deals resulting in outside compensation by suppliers
35. D, $10,000 (the penalties for subsequent violations can be as much as $100,000)
36. D, percentage lease
37. C, Yes, because the right to smoke is not protected by law
38. C, 20 years
    Explained: 1/3 of 30 = 10 years of depreciation
    $$30 - 10 = 20 \text{ years}$$
39. C, the sale price of a nearby similar property
40. A, improvements beyond those of other homes in the area
41. A, loss of value due to any cause
42. D, $4,675
    Explained: $85,000 × 1.10 = $93,500
    $$\$93,500 / 1,000 = \$93.50 \times 50 = \$4,675$$
43. C, client
44. B, bring court action
45. B, 18
    Explained: Capitalization rate for annual rate of ROI is computed by dividing a property's annual net income by the property value.
    $$\$152,000 / \$850,000 = .18 = 18 \text{ percent cap rate}$$
46. A, the owner of the property is unknown
47. B, market data approach

48. D, cost to reproduce – depreciation + value of land = value

49. A, plottage value

50. D, annual NOI generated

51. A, properties currently for sale in the same market area

52. A, eminent domain

53. A, value is enhanced because of the principle of conformity

54. D, unless another form of ownership is described in the deed, co-owners who are not spouses of each other are presumed to be tenants in common

55. B, parcels owned separately and areas owned in common for use by parcel owners

56. A, plat

57. A, fee simple determinable

58. C, the income approach to value

59. A, a survey

60. D, 35 feet; the most restrictive limit applies when there is a conflict in legal development language

61. C, an easement in gross

62. A, radon gas

63. A, alluvion

64. D, agent may accept the lawnmower because he is providing a desired service

65. A, air rights can be granted separately by deed

66. C, 600 square feet
Explained: 20 × 30 = 600

67. B, an employee

68. B, any offer will be accepted as written

69. B, follow the state law even though it is unethical

70. A, appraisal fee

71. A, steering

72. D, none of the above

73. A, put the check in his company's escrow account

74. A, No, because the listing is with the broker

75. C, less favorable treatment

76. B, the principal must attain a credit report of the agent which is updated monthly

77. D, when the Scheiders are notified of the acceptance

78. A, verify and receive the brokerage fee

79. D, $3,438

    Explained: $250,000 × 0.025 = $6,250 × 0.55 = $3,437.50 (rounded off)

80. B, answers A, C, and D

81. A, a dual agency

82. A, the death of the broker

83. A, sue the seller

84. B, he will be free to change his mind about buying

85. D, broker protection clause

86. D, sue the buyer for compensatory damages

87. B, all parties must attend to those details called for in the agreement in a timely manner

88. A, specific performance

89. A, $4,320

    Explained: $270,000 × .80 = $216,000 loan amount

    $216,000 × 2 percent = $4,320

90. D, $1,815.71

    Explained: $275,533 × 0.75 = $206,500 loan

    $206,500 × 7.34 /1,000 = $1,515.71 principal and interest

    $3,000 + $600 /12 = $300 for taxes and insurance

    $300 + $1,515.71 PI = $1,815.71 PITI

91. A, $7,500

    Explained: $250,000 × 0.06 = $15,000

    $15,000 × 0.50 = $7,500 total buyer broker share

92. C, $121,500

Explained: the loan is always based on the lesser of the purchase price and the appraised value; $135,000 × 0.90 = $121,500

93. D, this is not necessarily an indication of agency representation

94. A, mortgagee-mortgagor

95. A, charge seller and credit buyer $4,062.00

Explained: $6,500 / 12 = $541.67 per month × 7.5 months = $4,062.50 (round)

96. A, $138.60

Explained: $75,600 / 1000 = $75.6

$75.60 × $1.83 = $138.60

97. B, $24,750

Explained: $100,000 - $63,250 - $12,000 = $24,750; taxes are considered an expense (to be prorated at closing), but not considered a debt

98. C, 460

Explained: 23 × 20 = 460

99. C, $6,346.80

Explained: $164,000 × 0.90 = $147,600

$147,600 × .0430 = $6,346.80

100. A, 2

Explained: $2,800 / $140,000 = .02 = 2.0 percent (2 points)

CASE STUDY:
PRE-EXAM AND
COURSE OPTIONS

Rita L.
Real Estate Sales Agent, 2+ years

It has just been two years that I have been working as a sales agent, and in this amount of time and dealings I have had to use maybe 25 percent of what I had to learn in the license exam. However, foreclosures and short sales were not really taught in the pre-exam course. Currently in our office, nearly half of the listings we are involved with will be either foreclosure sales or short sales due to the general housing crisis.

For me, the hardest part of the exam was the financing section (mortgages, etc.). Not just the math, but the terms themselves and the programs all sound alike with the different acronyms such as Fannie Mae, Freddie Mac, FHA, and VA.

I believe in Massachusetts, it is now required to take the pre-exam prep course, though there are different course options. One can take it spread out over seven or eight weeks or they can get it done all in a week or even a weekend. A few friends and I decided to do the quick, one-week course.

For the exam itself, you have three hours to complete it. I was done in one and a half hours. It was an electronic, multiple-choice exam. They do not tell you your score — just pass or fail.

I was extremely nervous, because I had not taken a test for over 15 years. I studied my notes and organized and typed them out so I could make sense of them in my own way. Then, I went over the notes with two of the friends with whom I took the classes. Two of us passed, but two of us did not.

Every two years, we are required to take 12 hours of continuing education, or your license will be suspended or revoked.

CASE STUDY: THE EXAM & NICHE REAL ESTATE

Suzanne S.
Real Estate Sales Agent, 20+ years

I first worked as a sales agent for about twenty years, and then I got my broker's license, which I have had now for thirteen years. Still, with all this time and deals, there is about one-third of the material from the exam which I have never used. I think a lot of that has to do with the brokerage that you work for, and what niche of real estate you are involved in. For me, I wish they had more questions on commercial real estate, as that is the focus of my business.

The hardest part of the exam, and this was quite a while ago, was the True or False section. Though that might sound like an "easy" part of the test, the way the questions are worded are fairly confusing. If a statement is not 100 percent true and correct, then that statement is False. Many test-takers get hung up on that.

When I took the exam, there were not that many pre-exam prep courses or other avenues around. Courses were not mandatory, and I did not take one. I did the best I could with the help of a reference book and some other literature, and I ended up passing the exam on the first try.

Chapter 8

Decreasing Anxiety and Maintaining Positive Attitude

*I*t is true that some of the material on the license exam is difficult subject matter, but it is something that you can master in time. Although it may not be easy, it is critical that you believe that you can and will pass the exam. Imagine yourself getting the passing grade.

Many taking the exam have not taken a significant exam in 5, 10, or even 35 years. That fact brings with it a certain amount of understandable anxiety. One of the keys to passing the exam is to simply practice taking tests. Be sure to practice with the two practice tests provided in this book. (Do not look at the answers midway.)

Practical Advice on Being and Staying Positive:

1. Eight-year old children take exams every week, and they get through them and survive. Many excel. So can you.

2. Do not single out the real estate license exam as the first test you have taken in the last five years. There is something in your life, be it a business or work task or personal obstacle that you have had to overcome and pass in recent months. In an obscure way, much of life is a test or exam, to some extent. You have been passing tests on a regular basis.

3. Real estate license exam preparation has come a long way in the last 15 years. In additional to this book and other publications, there are online courses, local classroom courses, DVD's, CD's, and other tools that can help you prepare for the exam. Use whichever of these tools will suit your needs and personality. All of these exam prep tools *will* help you pass the exam — most likely on the first try! If you have a smartphone, there are many applications available that can help you study for this particular exam, anywhere, anytime.

4. Do not dwell on some of the statistics regarding the likelihood of passing the exam. Many of the people that fail the exam do not take the exam material seriously enough or do not spend enough time studying for it. The fact that you are reading this book and taking the time to prepare sets you apart from many others.

5. During the test, try not to get frazzled by one or two tough questions. Do not spend too much time on any one question; this can be a killer. Remember that most complete exams are roughly 150 questions. Typically a 70 percent is a passing grade. Getting hung up on a couple questions will hurt your chances, because you will have less time on other questions that you likely know

the answer to. Skip the hard questions and if you have time before the period ends, go back and make your best educated guess.

6. The seven days leading up to the exam are key. Study the material enough every day or night to feel comfortable. But remember that it is okay to feel like you do not know everything on the exam. On a similar note, do not pull an "all-nighter" before exam day. This has been proven by many researchers to be a detriment to your exam success because you will not be mentally sharp without a good night of sleep.

7. Remain confident. Self-confidence is the key to success in many aspects of life, including taking exams. Trust your knowledge and abilities. You have studied all the material, now you just have to answer some questions about all you have learned. Relax, feel confident, and do your best.

Words of Wisdom

1. There are no set rules regarding how to become a successful agent. Some agents enjoy prospecting by phone and others are great at chatting up people in the supermarket line. You might meet your clients while on vacation or out in public. Find an angle to build your business that suits your personality and style and use it to charge forward toward success.

2. Make sure that everyone you know (your "sphere of influence") knows that you are now a real estate agent. Call them on the phone, send them a postcard, tell them in person, pass out your cards. If you are tenacious enough about it your sphere will eventually see you as a real estate expert — and turn to you with their real estate questions and needs.

3. Starting a career in real estate does not guarantee immediate monetary gratification. Real estate can be lucrative but it does take dedication and often quite a bit of time to achieve a steady stream of income. It is important to remain positive while building your business.

    It is helpful to think of your business as a garden. Your sphere of influence and prospecting efforts provide the seeds for future business. Realize that not everything is going to sprout at once and some seeds may never grow. But by tending to it with care and intention, the payoff will help your business flourish. And by properly tending to the needs of the clients in your garden of real estate, you sow the seeds for future business.

4. New agents in real estate need a good amount of direction in their business and someone to ask lots and lots of questions. Do not assume you know everything just because you passed the real estate exam, and do not answer questions that are above your experience or knowledge base. It is okay, in fact imperative, to say, "I do not know!" or, "Can you help me?"

    Remember, more respect is given to agents who ask for help than those who cause damage by giving out misinformation. Make sure you join a company where there is a broker or a mentor that you can access for even the simplest questions and who is available to give additional training on building your business if you feel you require it.

5. Never underestimate the power of the referral. My clients all know that I do a great job for them, but sometimes they need to

be reminded that I can also do a great job for their friends and family. Be proactive about asking for business from past, present and future clientele with regular phone calls, postcards and personal visits. Too many agents forget to harness this powerful pool of potential business. Do not lose touch with those who can spread the word about what an amazing real estate agent you are!

6. Remember whom it is you are working for when you are representing a client in a real estate transaction. Too often, an agent's own interests, like getting paid, can interfere with those of their clients. Your client is paying you to represent their interests, not your own. If a contract falls apart because you are looking out for the best interests of your client, it was never meant to be in the first place. Do not get hung up on the paycheck, move along and find them a better deal!

7. Pursuing a career in real estate goes hand in hand with dealing with the intricacies of life. Realize that in the course of your real estate career, almost anything can happen and more! There are plenty of situations that I have dealt with in real estate transactions that I never imagined could occur. Consult with your broker right away if you think you have a problem and keep a good list of responsible lenders, lawyers, accountants, and other service people that you can quickly refer to your clients. Use these resources, your training, your knowledge, and your compassion to help your clients through stormy transaction waters.

8. Make sure to take as much continuing education as possible. No matter what your state's minimum requirement is, take as many classes as you possibly can on the widest variety of topics available. Real estate school taught you the law, not the strategies that are available to your clients when actually dealing with real estate transactions. There are so many approaches available to clients when buying or selling real estate. A great agent

will educate their clients with the most current and poignant information by first educating themselves.

9. Have you ever heard the saying, "you cannot be all things to all people?" Realize that not all clients are going to work best with you and your personality. In addition, some clients could require a skill set for a transaction that you may not possess. Do not set yourself up for failure by agreeing to represent clients that you do not think you can successfully work with. Instead, refer these potential clients to another agent in your office that may be better suited to meet their needs.

10. Remember that your real estate career should not be all work and no play. Balance is important in any endeavor in life and depriving yourself of personal time will only create a lackluster attitude toward your business. Put time aside for yourself and do things that make you feel good, whether it is hiking up a mountain, going to the spa, or volunteering and giving back to the community.

CASE STUDY: DEALING WITH EMOTIONS BEFORE THE EXAM

Neil W.
Career coach, 5+ years

I am a professional career coach, counselor, and trainer. I assist people by helping them to understand their strengths and motivations and by creating and supporting goals that can help them move forward.

I think a positive attitude is something that you own. If you wonder how to get a more positive attitude or you feel like you have lost yours, find and read an inspiring book about how someone who faced tremendous challenges overcame them to do great things. You might even choose one that tells the tale of someone who had great success in real estate.

About 50 percent of the outcome of your examination will be determined by your mental and emotional state prior to and during the exam. Once a person feels that he or she has prepared for the exam as much as possible, the rest of the preparation involves attitude.

Lessening nervousness prior to an exam is critical. You need to prepare well, and you also need to practice. We all learned back in school that success starts with understanding and learning the material. All of this should lessen your nervousness.

It is your goal to pass the exam on the first attempt. However, should you need a second try, be aware that you now have the familiarity of the real estate exam that you did not before. This should help you feel more confident if you need that second attempt.

Maintaining a positive attitude is very important. In addition to everything else we've discussed, we can't ignore the obvious impacts of health, rest, and nutrition. We all know that we feel better about ourselves when we feel good and healthy. Stress management exercises such as slow breathing and physical exercise can help with maintaining a positive attitude. We also know that when we're tired, we're not our best, so make sure that you are getting enough sleep. Finally, food and nutrition can play a big part, too. So try to eat a healthy, balanced diet — especially on the day of the exam.

CASE STUDY: DEVELOPING A POSITIVE ATTITUDE

Edye M.
Clinical Psychologist, 5+ years

I am a clinical psychologist, with a master's degree in Counseling/Psychology from Lesley College Graduate School, and a Psy.D. (Doctorate in Psychology) from the Massachusetts School of Professional Psychology.

There are a variety of ways that I work with people to assist them in developing and keeping a positive attitude. I often begin by helping my client explore his or her perceptions of self-efficacy (their deep-seated belief in their capacity to perform effectively).

If we find doubts and insecurities, we attempt to understand these negative mind states, and reframe them as old, outdated cognitive framework. These are often belief systems from times in our lives that we did not perform at our best. Studies show that if there exists a sincere interest in a topic or field, and the person is willing to practice, work hard, and apply his or herself, he or she can excel. In order to work hard to master your sincere interest, motivation is key.

Positive attitudes are reinforced by feedback loops. If the person develops a self-disciplined approach to learning, studying, and practicing with "The Complete Guide to Passing Your Real Estate License Exam," they remain on task and gain a sense of consistency.

Test-takers can form a relaxing, yet alert, mental image of themselves, in which they remind themselves of their ability to have a positive outcome — and of passing the exam. They can use this mental image to counter feelings and thoughts of anxiety or doubt about one's readiness. In addition, the person can review their prior successes in exam taking, even if it is merely the practice exams from the book. These recollections of success and mastery of small tasks should all be brought to mind when nervousness enters.

People who fail (in exams or other tasks) put up many psychological defenses that help them avoid what feels like a negative experience for as long as possible. However, these people can have a second chance. They will need to use "self-talk" and "mental imagery" to cope with the negativity. They may wish to give up when they are triggered to re-experience failure. If they are willing to seek help to deal with their recent failure, they, too, can make their dreams of passing come true. However, passing on the first try avoids many of the obstacles that will need to be overcome by those taking it a second or third time.

The top three ways to maintain a positive attitude prior to the exam are:

1. Pay attention and stay interested in the material.

2. Remind yourself of why you are motivated. Imagine yourself having passed the exam and how it will feel to begin to put your knowledge to work.

3. Be mindful of the thoughts and feelings that bubble up in your mind prior to the exam. Self-observe and self-monitor thoughts and feelings about the exam and give your mind the evidence of why it should remain positive. Then, if you find your attitude weakening by fear or doubt, use self-talk to set it straight.

Conclusion

 ost likely, you are now a week or two away from taking your state's real estate salesperson license exam. By this point, you should have reviewed all of the following aspects of real estate:

- Real estate finance/mortgages
- Real estate law
- Real estate principles
- Real estate contracts and deeds
- Appraisals

In addition, you should have fully reviewed the various suggestions regarding test-taking procedures in addition to advice on decreasing anxiety and building your self-confidence for before and during the examination.

Do not forget to practice all of the math review problems; this is a good refresher for most of us who do not use math and geometry knowledge on a regular basis.

Most importantly, complete (in their entirety) both 100-question national practice tests. Grade yourself, and see how you do. Go back and spend more time on the questions and areas of real estate that you do not do so well on.

As far as the state-specific questions and by-laws go, it is key for you to approach your state or another source to determine what needs to be known in addition to the general national coursework.

To approach professional organizations with your questions, go to the NAR directory at **www.realtor.org/directories**. If you are already speaking with a real estate brokerage firm about working for them, the broker will be able to help you with this and give you the state-specific information and guide. If not, it may be wise to go online.

For relatively low cost ($25- $30), certain exam preparation companies will allow you to take practice exams that focus exclusively on your state. Many of these online companies keep all the questions and information up-to-date, and they will allow for immediate grading and scoring to see how you do. They will also provide you with the correct answers. It would be wise to print out the answers (along with their questions), and spend some time studying these as well as the information presented in this book.

For a state-by-state list of exam guidelines, see Appendix B at the end of this book. For a state-by-state list of real estate commissions, see Appendix C.

Remember, you *can* pass the exam — and on your first try! Have confidence in yourself and in the material you have learned from this book.

Good luck!

- A -

Abandonment: Voluntarily surrendering property that is either owned or leased without naming a successor as owner or tenant. An abandoned property tends to revert to the party holding a prior interest, such as a lender. Abandonment does not remove any obligations the person surrendering the property may have had, unless the entity owed those obligations agrees to waive them. In simple terms, abandonment means, "I am leaving, and I give up any rights to the property or its value, but I may still be liable for debts owed."

Abatement: Abatement refers to a reduction of some kind. For instance, if the rent is decreased, that reduction constitutes an abatement. Abatement is also sometimes referred to as free rent or early occupancy.

Abnormal sale: A sale that does not represent a market transaction. If, for example, a house sells for $100,000 on a street where similar houses sell for $200,000, then the first home would be considered an abnormal sale. An appraiser may choose to disregard abnormal sales when selecting similar properties to compare values.

Absentee owner: An owner who does not reside in or personally manage a property. He may engage a property manager to oversee his rental properties.

Absorption rate: The speed and amount of time at which rentable space, in square feet, is filled, or an estimate of the rate at which homes for sale will be purchased. For example, if a particular geographic area has 2,000 homes for sale and 200 are purchased each month, the area has an absorption rate of 10 percent (2,000 / 200).

Abstract of title: A summary of the history of a title to a particular parcel of real estate. It consists of a summary of the original grant and all subsequent conveyances and encumbrances effecting the property, and a certification by the abstractor that the history is complete and accurate.

Abut: To meet, join, or border; the line where separate properties meet. A property can also abut a road, an easement, or other physical landmarks.

Acceleration clause: A clause in a contract that gives the lender the right to demand immediate payment of the balance of the loan; for example, if the borrower defaults on the loan. Other provisions could also trigger acceleration, depending on the terms of the original contract.

For example, a loan agreement could contain an acceleration clause requiring immediate and full payment of the entire loan balance if a payment is more than 60 days overdue.

Acceptance: Agreeing to accept an offer. If one party offers to buy a property at a specific price and under specific terms, and the owner agrees to those terms, then his or her acceptance means the sales contract is complete.

Accessory building: A building that is used for another purpose besides the principal building on a lot. For example, a garage or outbuilding can be an accessory building. Typically does not refer to a separate building used for commercial purposes.

Accord and satisfaction: The settlement of an obligation. An accord is an agreement made by a creditor to accept something different from — or less than — what was originally promised. Once the creditor accepts an accord, the obligation of the debtor is removed. Typically an accord and satisfaction occurs when the two parties are in dispute.

Accrued depreciation: The amount of depreciation expense that has been claimed to the present. Also referred to as accumulated depreciation.

Accrued items, passive: On a closing statement, items of expense that are incurred but not yet payable, such as interest on a mortgage loan or taxes on real property.

Accrued items, active: Expenses prepaid within the current business year, which must be imputed to the new business year. A rent prepayment entitles the company to use its rented facilities during the new business year.

Acknowledgment: A formal declaration made before a duly authorized officer, usually a notary public, by a person who has signed a document. Documents requiring acknowledgement must be witnessed by an authorized officer like a notary public to become legal and enforceable.

Acquisition appraisal: An appraisal to determine market value for a property acquired for public use by a government agency, usually through condemnation or negotiation. The purpose of an acquisition appraisal is to determine the amount the property owner will be compensated.

Acquisition cost: The purchase price, including all fees, that will be necessary to obtain a property; the total cost of the property to the buyer.

Acre: The standard of measurement for property. An acre is calculated in square feet or square yards. One acre equals 4,840 square yards or 43,560 square feet.

Acreage zoning: Zoning requirements that require plans for large building lots in an effort to reduce residential or commercial density. Acreage zoning is sometimes called large-lot zoning or "snob zoning."

Act of God: An act of nature beyond human control, including floods, hurricanes, lightning, and earthquakes. A contract can include an Act of God provision that relieves both parties of obligation where a natural disaster has destroyed or damaged the property.

Actual cash value: Insurance term for the monetary value of an improvement. Actual cash value is determined by subtracting wear and tear from replacement cost.

Actual damages (and special damages): Damages that are a direct result of a wrong; recognizable by a court of law. If a doorway to a property is destroyed, actual damages are confined to the cost of repairing or replacing the doorway; special damages could be the loss of income or business due to the lack of a suitable entry to the property.

Ad valorem: A Latin phrase which means "according to value;" refers to a tax that is imposed on a property's value, typically based on the local government's evaluation of the property.

ADC loan: A loan that covers the Acquisition, Development, and Construction of a development

project. Its purpose is to allow the developer to purchase the land, put in streets and utility services, and construct buildings or houses.

Addendum: An addition or update for an existing contract between parties; allows a revision to a contract without creating an entirely new contract; only enforceable if both parties agree and sign.

Addition: Construction that increases a building's size or significantly adds to it. Finishing previously unfinished space is not considered an addition, but is instead considered an improvement.

Adjudication: A court decision.

Adjustable Rate Mortgage (ARM): A home loan with an interest rate that is adjusted periodically to reflect changes in a specific financial resource; typically based on changes in mortgage loan interest rates, but changes can also be tied to government indexes or financial market indexes. Unlike a fixed-rate loan, the borrower's interest rate (and monthly payments) can change periodically based on the terms of the loan.

Adjustment date: The date at which the interest rate is adjusted for an Adjustable Rate Mortgage (ARM).

Adjustment period: The amount of time between adjustments for the interest rate in an Adjustable Rate Mortgage (ARM).

Advance fee: A fee paid before services are rendered. For example, a real estate broker may require an advance fee to cover advertising expenses associated with marketing the property.

Adverse financial change condition: Provisions in a loan agreement allowing the lender to cancel the agreement if the borrower suffers a major financial setback such as the loss of a job.

Adverse possession: The actual, open, notorious, hostile, and continuous possession of another's land under a claim of title. Possession for a statutory period may be a means of acquiring title. Permission from the owner given in a lease would not constitute

adverse possession because the possession is not hostile. For example, a person can gain title to land by living on the land for 20 years if the legal owner is unknown.

Adviser: A broker or investment banker who represents an owner in a transaction and is paid a retainer and/or a performance fee once a financing or sales transaction has closed.

Aesthetic value: Value of a property based on its appearance; for example, a lakefront property with a view of the lake may result in a higher sales price than comparable properties which do not afford the same view.

Affidavit of title: A written statement, made under oath by a seller or grantor of real property and acknowledged by a notary public, in which the grantor (1) identifies himself or herself and indicates marital status, (2) certifies that since the examination of the title, on the date of the contracts, no defects have occurred in the title, and (3) certifies that he or she is in possession of the property (if applicable).

Affirmation: A declaration as to the truth of a statement. An affirmation is used in place of an oath; for example, when a person objects to swearing an oath for religious or personal reasons.

Affordability index: A measurement of housing affordability compiled by the NAR. The intent of the affordability index is to measure the ability of area residents to buy homes in that area.

Affordable housing: A term frequently used to describe public and private efforts to help low-income individuals purchase homes. Typical programs include below-market interest rates, easier credit terms, or minimal down payments.

Agency: The relationship between a principal and an agent wherein the agent is authorized to represent the principal in certain transactions.

Agency disclosure: A requirement in most states that agents who act for both buyers or sellers must disclose who they are working for in the transaction. For example, a real estate agent working for the seller must provide an agency disclosure agreement notifying potential buyers that she is working on behalf of the sellers and not the buyer.

Agent: One who acts or has the power to act for another. A fiduciary relationship is created under the law of agency when a property owner, as the principal, executes a listing agreement or management contract authorizing a licensed real estate broker to be his or her agent.

Agreement of sale: A legal document the buyer and seller must approve and sign that details the price and terms in the transaction.

Alienation: The act of transferring property to another. Alienation may be voluntary, such as by gift or sale, or involuntary, as through eminent domain or adverse possession.

Alienation clause: The clause in a mortgage or deed of trust that states that the balance of the secured debt becomes immediately due and payable at the lender's option if the property is sold by the borrower. In effect, this clause prevents the borrower from assigning the debt without the lender's approval.

Amenities: Benefits derived from property ownership that are non-monetary. For example, a home in a prestigious neighborhood has an enhanced amenity of ownership. Amenities can also be features that increase a property's desirability, like custom fixtures or professional-grade appliances.

Americans with Disabilities Act (ADA): Addresses rights of individuals with disabilities in employment and public accommodations. Designed to eliminate discrimination against individuals with disabilities by requiring equal access to jobs, public accommodations, government services, public transportation, and telecommunications. Includes the design of buildings intended to serve the public.

Amortization: The usual process of paying a loan's interest and principal via scheduled monthly payments. Simply put, amortization is the gradual paying off of a debt by making periodic installment payments.

Amortization schedule: A chart or table which shows the percentage of each payment that will be applied toward principal and interest over the life of the mortgage and how the loan balance decreases until it reaches zero.

Amortization term: The number of months it will take to amortize (pay off) the loan.

Anchor tenant: The business or individual who is serving as the primary draw to a commercial property. For example, a large department store located at the end of a shopping center may be considered the anchor tenant of the center.

Annexation: The process whereby a city expands its boundaries to include a specific geographic area. Most states require a public vote be held within the city and the area to be annexed in order to determine public approval. Annexation can also refer to the process where personal property becomes attached to real property.

Annual debt service: The required annual principal and interest payments for a loan. If a loan requires principal payments of $300 and interest payments of $50 per month, then the annual debt service of the loan is $4,200 ($350 × 12).

Annual Percentage Rate (APR): The effective rate of interest for a loan per year; this disclosure is required by the Truth in Lending Law. The annual percentage rate is generally higher than the advertised interest rate.

Apartment building: A dwelling unit within a multi-family structure, usually provided as rental housing. Apartment buildings are usually multi-family dwellings with individual living units but a common entranceway or hallway.

Application: The form a borrower must complete to apply for services like a mortgage loan or to rent a dwelling; often includes information like income, savings, assets, debts, and references.

Application fee: A fee some lenders charge that may include fees for items such as property appraisal or a credit report (unless those fees are included elsewhere).

Appointments: Furnishings, fixtures, or equipment found in a home or other building. The items can increase or decrease the usability and/or value of the property.

Apportionment: Prorating property expenses, like taxes and insurance, between the buyer and the seller of a property. Typically used to divide yearly costs between the two parties. For example, if a property is purchased on July 1, the seller may pay 50 percent of the tax liability for that year, and the buyer will be responsible for the other 50 percent.

Appraisal: The estimate of the value of a property on a particular date given by a professional appraiser, usually presented in a written document.

Appraisal report: The written report presented by an appraiser regarding the value of a property; should include a description and summary of the method(s) used to calculate the value of the property.

Appraised value: The dollar amount a professional appraiser assigns to the value of a property in an appraisal report.

Appreciation: An increase in the value of a home or property. Appreciation can be due to inflation, physical additions or changes, changes to market values, and other causes.

Appropriation: To set aside land for public use. For example, a developer of a new subdivision may be required to apportion land for a new school to gain approval to begin the project.

Appurtenance: A right, privilege, or improvement belonging to and passing with the land. An appurtenance is something outside the property itself but is considered a part of the property that adds to its greater enjoyment, like the right to cross another party's land.

(Easements and rights-of-way are considered to be appurtenances.)

Appurtenant easement: An easement that is annexed to the ownership of one parcel and allows the owner the use of the neighbor's land.

Arbitration: Settling disputes through a neutral third party. Arbitration is typically an alternative to filing suit in a court of law. Many real estate sales contracts contain a provision requiring both parties to submit their disputes to arbitration, as a result, both parties have waived their right to filing suit in a public court.

Architecture: The manner in which a building is constructed, including the floor plan, style, appearance, materials used, and building technologies used.

Area: A two-dimensional space. Can refer to a floor area or the area of a lot. For example, a room that measures ten feet by ten feet has an area of 100 square feet (10 × 10 = 100).

ARM index: A number that is publicly published and used as the basis for interest rate adjustments on an ARM.

Arm's length transaction: A transaction among parties where each party acts in his or her own best interests. For example, typically a transaction between a husband and a wife would not be considered arm's length.

Arrears: At the end of a term. For example, interest on a mortgage loan is usually paid in arrears, meaning at the end of a month or other period. Arrears is also sometimes used to signify a default or late payment. If a homeowner has not made mortgage payments for two months, his mortgage can be considered to be in arrears.

Artesian well: A shaft that reaches water that rises because of natural underground pressure.

"As is" condition: A phrase in a purchase or lease contract in which the buyer accepts the existing condition of the premises as well as the presence of any physical defects. "As is" sales provide no guarantees to the buyer. For example, if a property owner sells a home "as is,"

the buyer cannot demand repairs to nonworking appliances.

Asbestos: A mineral once used in insulation and other materials (such as flooring tiles and siding) that can cause respiratory diseases.

Asbestos Containing Materials (ACM): Products or materials made with asbestos. Use of ACMs has been prohibited since the early 1980s, but some older dwellings still may contain ACMs.

As-built drawings: Architectural drawings showing the precise method of construction, location of equipment, and utilities. As-built drawings reflect any changes to the original plans.

Asking price: The list price an owner would like to receive. The asking price is not necessarily the owner's bottom-line price. Asking price can also be described as "advertised price."

Assessed value: The value placed on a home, determined by a tax assessor to calculate a tax base.

Assessor: A public officer who estimates the value of a property for the purpose of taxation.

Asset: A property or item of value.

Asset management: The various tasks and areas involved in managing real estate assets from the time of initial investment until the time it is sold.

Assignment: The transfer of rights and responsibilities from one party to another. The original party remains liable for debt should the second party default, however. A lease is an example of an assignment, since it gives another individual the right to use the leased space. While the tenant may pay rent, the owner is still responsible for making any loan payments.

Assignment of lease: Transfer of rights to use a leased property from one leasing party to another. For example, a college student who does not need an apartment during the summer months may assign the lease to another party for that time period.

Assignment of rents: A contract that assigns rents from the tenant of a property to the mortgage lender in case of a default. Some lenders require an assignment of rents.

Assignor: The person who transfers the rights and interests of a property to another.

Associate broker: A licensed broker whose license is held by another broker. An associate broker qualifies to be a real estate broker but still works for and is supervised by another broker. Associate brokers are sometimes called broker-associates, broker-salespersons, or affiliate brokers.

Association of unit owners: Unit owners of a condominium who act as a group for administering the property. Condominium Owners' Associations are considered an association of unit owners.

Assumable mortgage: A mortgage that is capable of being transferred to a different borrower.

Assumption: The act of assuming the mortgage of a seller.

Assumption clause: A contractual provision that enables the buyer to take responsibility for the mortgage loan from the seller.

Assumption fee: A fee charged to the buyer assuming an existing loan for processing new documents and agreements.

Attachment: The act of taking a person's property into legal custody by writ or other judicial order to hold it available for application to that person's debt to a creditor; the legal seizure of property to force payment of a debt. For example, a landlord may attach a tenant's personal property to force payment of back rent.

Attest: To witness by observation and signature; a third party, who has witnessed the signing of a document by its principles, will attest to the signing.

Attic: Accessible space between the ceiling of the top floor and the structure's roof. Inaccessible space is considered to be a structural cavity and not an attic.

Attorney-in-fact: Person who is authorized to act for another person under a power of attorney. A son who has power of attorney to sell a father's property is considered to be the attorney-in-fact.

Attorney's opinion of title: An abstract of title that an attorney has examined and has certified to be, in his or her opinion, an accurate statement of the facts concerning the property ownership. In short, the attorney has judged the title to a particular party to be good.

Attornment: A tenant's formal agreement to be a tenant of a new landlord. For example, if a previous landlord defaults and the property is foreclosed upon, the new owner may ask all tenants to sign a letter of attornment indicating they recognize the new landlord.

Auction: To sell land or personal property by inviting bidders. The property is sold to the highest bidder. Bids can be written or verbal, public or private. Many states require that foreclosed properties be auctioned.

Auctioneer: Person who conducts an auction; usually requires licensing, especially where real estate auctions are concerned.

Authorization to sell: A listing contract giving an agent the right to find a buyer for a property. The agent is not permitted to enter into an agreement for sale; the agent is allowed to market the property for sale and is entitled to compensation for finding a buyer.

Automated underwriting: Computer systems that permit lenders to expedite the loan approval process and reduce lending costs. Fannie Mae and Freddie Mac each have their own standard automatic underwriting software and loan guidelines.

Automatic extension: A clause in a listing agreement stating that the agreement will continue automatically for a specific period of time after its expiration date. In many states the use of this clause is discouraged or prohibited.

Average occupancy: The average rate of each of the previous 12 months that a property was occupied. A property occupied for 11 of the past 12 months is considered to have an average occupancy of 92 percent (11 / 12).

- B -

Backup offer: An offer to buy or lease real estate that becomes effective if a prior contract falls through. For example, a buyer may make a backup offer on a property already under contract to another party in the hopes that the other party will be unable to purchase the property.

Balance: The amount remaining to be paid toward an obligation. For example, a homeowner who has paid down $25,000 of a $100,000 mortgage has a principal balance of $75,000. Balance also refers to the appraisal principle that states the greatest value in a property will occur when the type and size of the improvements are proportional to each other as well as the land.

Balance sheet: A statement that lists an individual's assets, liabilities, and net worth.

Balloon loan: A type of mortgage in which the monthly payments are not large enough to repay the loan by the end of the term, and the final payment is a large payment that covers the remainder of the obligation. A balloon loan may call for monthly payments of $1,000 per month for 5 years, with a final payment of $100,000.

Balloon payment: A final payment of a mortgage loan that is considerably larger than the required periodic payments because the loan amount was not fully amortized.

Bankruptcy: The financial inability to pay debts when they are due. The debtor seeks relief through court actions that may modify or erase his or her debts.

Bargain and sale deed: A deed that carries with it no warranties against liens or other encumbrances but that does imply that the grantor has the right to convey title. The grantor may add warranties to the deed at his or her discretion. A bargain and sale deed is one in which the grantor of the deed implies to have an interest in the property but offers no warranties of clear title.

Base loan amount: The amount which forms the basis for the loan payments.

Base principal balance: The original loan amount once adjustments for subsequent fundings and principal payments have been made without including accrued interest or other unpaid debts.

Basis point: A term for 1/100 of one percentage point. Typically used by the financial markets. For example, if interest rates decrease from 5.25 percent to 5.15 percent, the reduction is 10 basis points (5.25 − 5.15).

Below grade: Any structure or part of a structure that is below the surface of the ground that surrounds it.

Bench mark: A permanently affixed mark that establishes exact elevation; surveyors use benchmarks to measure site elevations or as starting points for surveys.

Beneficiary: A beneficiary is a person who receives or is entitled to receive the benefits resulting from certain acts. A beneficiary can be a person for whom a trust operates or in whose behalf the income from a trust estate is drawn. The term beneficiary also refers to a lender in a deed of trust loan transaction.

Bequeath: To specify by will the recipient of personal property; does not apply to real estate. (To *devise* is to specify the recipient of real estate.)

Betterment: An improvement to real estate. If a property owner constructs a building on a lot, the building is considered a betterment to the property.

Bill of sale: A written legal document that transfers the ownership of personal property to another party. A bill of sale does not convey title of real estate — it is only used for transferring ownership of personal property.

Binder: An agreement that may accompany an earnest money deposit for the purchase of real property as evidence of the purchaser's good faith and intent to complete the transaction. A binder is not a contract; it signifies intent to join a contract.

Biweekly mortgage: A mortgage repayment plan that requires payments every two weeks to help repay the loan over a shorter amount of time. The payments are exactly half of what a monthly payment would be, but at the end of the year the borrower will have made 26 payments, or the equivalent of 13 monthly payments, causing the loan to be paid off more quickly.

Blighted areas: A section of a city or locality where a majority of the structures are dilapidated or in poor condition.

Blueprint: A detailed, working set of plans used as the guide for construction for a building or structure.

Board of REALTORS®: Group of real estate license holders who are members of the state and National Association of REALTORS®.

Bona fide: In good faith, without fraud. A notarized contract is considered to be a bona fide contract, since a third-party has verified the identities of the signers.

Book value: The value of a property based on its purchase amount, plus upgrades or other additions, with depreciation subtracted. Book value is typically used by corporations to show the value of properties they own.

Boundary: A property line; describes the outer edge of a property.

Branch office: A secondary place of business apart from the principal or main office from which real estate business is conducted. A branch office usually must be run by a licensed real estate broker working on behalf of the broker.

Breach of contract: Violation of any terms or conditions in a contract without legal excuse; for example, failure to make a payment when it is due is considered a breach of contract.

Bridge loan: Mortgage financing between the end of one loan and the beginning of another loan, or a short-term loan for individuals or companies who are still seeking

more permanent financing; frequently used during a property's construction phase; sometimes referred to as a gap loan or a swing loan.

Broker: A person who serves as a go-between between a buyer and seller, typically for a commission.

Brokerage: The business of being a broker; usually refers to the company or organization run by a broker.

Brownfield: A site whose former use involved hazardous materials. Examples are shut down military bases, abandoned gas stations, or shut down manufacturing facilities.

Brownstone: A three-to-five story row house with common walls for adjoining properties.

Budget mortgage: A mortgage involving payments totaling more than interest and principal; typically includes additions for property taxes, insurance, or other fees that, if not paid, could result in foreclosure. A budget mortgage is commonly used in VA, FHA, and conventional residential mortgages. Additional funds are held by the lender in an escrow account until payment is required.

Buffer zone: A strip of land, usually used as a park or designated for a similar use; separating land dedicated to one use from land dedicated to another use. For example, separating residential properties from commercial properties.

Build out: Improvements to a property that have been made according to a tenant's specifications.

Build to suit: A way of leasing property, usually for commercial purposes, in which the developer or landlord builds to a tenant's specifications. The landowner pays for the construction to the specifications of the tenant, and the tenant then leases the land and building from the landowner, who retains ownership. Build to suit is frequently used by tenants who wish to occupy a building of a certain type but do not wish to own the building.

Buildable acres: The portion of land that can be built upon after

allowances for roads, setbacks, anticipated open spaces, and unsuitable areas have been made.

Building code: The laws set forth by the local government regarding end use of a given piece of property. These laws code may dictate the design, materials used, and/or types of improvements that will be allowed. New construction or improvements must meet building code; adherence to requirements is determined by building inspectors.

Building line: Lines a specified distance from the sides of a lot that denote where a building cannot be placed. Building lines are often called setbacks, because a building must be "set back" a specified distance from the property line.

Building permit: Written permission for the construction, alteration, or demolition of an improvement; shows compliance with building codes and zoning ordinances.

Building restrictions: Provisions and specifications in building codes that affect the placement, size, and appearance of a building. Building restrictions include building lines, the allowable height of a structure, and other provisions.

Building standards: Specific elements of construction an owner or developer chooses to use throughout a building. Building standards offered to a tenant of a leased office; for example, might include the types of doors, ceilings, light fixtures, carpet, and other features.

Bulk sale: The sale of a group or collection of real estate assets, usually different properties in different locations. A bulk sale requires the buyer to accept all properties.

Business day: A standard day for conducting business; excludes weekends and holidays.

Buy back agreement: A provision in a contract where the seller agrees to repurchase the property at a stated price if a specified event occurs. For example, a builder could be required to buy back a retail property at a specific price if certain sales thresholds are not met.

Buydown: A financing technique used to reduce the monthly payments for the first few years of a loan. Funds in the form of discount points are given to the lender by the builder or seller to buy down or lower the effective interest rate paid by the buyer, thus reducing the monthly payments for a set time.

Buydown mortgage: A type of home loan in which the lender receives a higher payment in order to convince them to reduce the interest rate during the initial years of the mortgage.

Buyer's agent: A residential real estate salesperson who represents the prospective purchaser in a transaction. The buyer's agent owes the buyer/principal the common-law or statutory agency duties. Similar to a buyer's broker.

Buyer's broker: A residential real estate broker who represents prospective buyers exclusively. As the buyer's agent, the broker owes the buyer/principal the common-law or statutory agency duties. Similar to a buyer's agent.

Buyers' market: A condition where buyers have a wide choice of properties and may negotiate lower prices. Buyer's markets occur when there are more houses for sale than there are buyers. Buyers' markets can be caused by factors like overbuilding, an economic downturn, or a decrease in the local population.

Buyer's remorse: The nervousness some home buyers may feel after signing a sales contract or closing on the purchase of a house.

- C -

Cancellation clause: A contract provision that allows the termination of obligation if certain conditions or events occur. For example, a cancellation clause in a lease can allow the landlord to break the lease if he or she sells the property.

Cap: A limit on how much the monthly payment or interest rate is allowed to increase in an adjustable rate mortgage. Designed to protect the borrower from large increases in the interest rate which would naturally result in large increases to the monthly payment amount.

Capital: Money used to purchase long-term assets. In real estate terms, capital is cash — or the ability to turn an asset into cash. A person who does not have sufficient capital does not have enough cash (or liquid assets that can be turned into cash).

Capital appreciation: An increase in the value of a property after it has been adjusted for capital improvements and partial sales. Capital appreciation refers to the value of a property; a capital gain is realized when the property is actually sold.

Capital gain: The amount of excess when the net proceeds from the sale of an asset are higher than its book value. If a buyer purchases a property for $200,000 and sells it after three years for $300,000, he or she has experienced a capital gain of $100,000.

Capital improvements: Expenses that prolong the life of a property or add improvements to it. Buying a lawn mower is not considered a capital improvement, but constructing a building on a lot is.

Carryback financing: A type of funding in which a seller agrees to hold back a note for a specified portion of the sales price. For example, a buyer with no down payment funds available may arrange for 80 percent financing from a primary lender, with the seller offering to loan him the other 20 percent as carryback financing. The carryback financing in this case is the junior or secondary lien.

Cash flow: The net income from an investment determined by deducting all operating and fixed expenses from the gross income. If expenses exceed income, a negative cash flow results.

Cash out: To completely liquidate an asset. Also refers to a mortgage refinance where a borrower takes cash out of the equity of the property. For example, a borrower owing $100,000 on a property valued at $200,000 who takes a new mortgage of $150,000 has taken $50,000 cash out of the property.

Cashier's check: A check the bank draws on its own resources instead of a depositor's account. A cashier's check is preferred (and frequently required) in real estate transactions, because the bank guarantees payment.

Cash-out refinance: The act of refinancing a mortgage for an amount that is higher than the original amount for the purpose of using the remaining cash for personal use.

Caveat emptor: A Latin phrase meaning "Let the buyer beware." The buyer is responsible for inspecting the property or item and is assumed to be buying at his or her own risk.

Certificate of completion: A document issued by an architect or engineer stating that a property meets all specifications listed on the original plans and blueprints. Many construction contracts specify that final payment must be made when a certificate of completion has been signed.

Certificate of insurance: A document issued by an insurance company to verify coverage. Most lending institutions require a certificate of insurance proving the borrower is carrying adequate insurance to cover the subject property.

Certificate of Occupancy (CO): A written document issued by a local government or building agency that states that a home or building is habitable after meeting all building codes. Indicates the building is in compliance with health and building requirements.

Certificate of sale: The document generally given to the purchaser at a tax foreclosure sale. A certificate of sale does not convey title; normally, it is an instrument certifying that the holder received title to the property after the redemption period passed and that the holder paid the property taxes for that interim period.

Certificate of title: A statement of opinion on the status of the title to a parcel of real property based on an examination of specified public records; typically given by an attorney after a title search.

Certified check: A check the bank draws on a customer's account on which the bank has noted its certification. A cashier's check is preferred (and frequently required) in real estate transactions, because the bank guarantees payment.

Chain of title: The history of conveyances, from some accepted starting point, whereby the present holder of real property derives title. The chain of title is used to prepare an attorney's opinion of title as to whether the owner has a marketable or insurable interest in the property (in other words, a clear title.)

Chattel: Personal property. Chattel is anything owned and tangible other than real estate. Furniture, cars, jewelry, and clothing are all examples of chattel.

Circulation factor: The interior space of a structure that is required for internal office circulation and is not included in the net square footage.

Class "A": A rating usually assigned to properties that will generate the maximum rent per square foot, due to superior quality and/or location.

Class "B": A rating usually assigned to a property that most potential tenants would find desirable but lacks certain attributes that would result in maximum rent per square foot.

Class "C": A rating usually assigned to a property that is physically acceptable but offers few amenities; as a result the rent per square foot will be low.

Clear title: A property title that is free of liens, defects, or other legal encumbrances.

Clearance letter: A letter from a licensed termite inspector showing the results of a termite inspection. Many loans, including FHA and VA loans, require a clearance letter before approving a mortgage.

Closing: The final act of procuring a loan and title in which documents are signed between the buyer and seller and/or their respective representation, and all money and consideration changes hands.

Closing costs: Expenses related to the sale of real estate including the loan, title, and appraisal fees; does not include the price of the property itself.

Closing statement: Detailed cash accounting of a real estate transaction showing all cash received, all charges and credits made, and all cash paid out as a result of the transaction; often, this is presented via a "HUD-1 Settlement Statement."

Cloud on title: Refers to any document, claim, unreleased lien, or encumbrance that may impair the title to real property or make the title doubtful. A cloud on title is usually revealed by a title search and removed by either a quitclaim deed or suit to quiet title; in some instance, however, the clouds cannot be removed quickly.

Cluster housing: A subdivision technique where dwellings are grouped close together with a common area left for recreation. In effect, residents have extremely small yards but can enjoy the large common spaces.

Co-borrower: Another individual who is jointly responsible for the loan and is on the title to the property. A co-signer typically is not on the title to the property.

Code of ethics: A written system of standards for ethical conduct. For example, all REALTORS® are required to follow a code of ethics that defines professional behavior.

Collateral: The property for which a borrower has obtained a loan, thereby assuming the risk of losing the property if the loan is not repaid according to the terms of the loan agreement.

Collection: The effort on the part of a lender, due to a borrower's defaulting on a loan, which involves mailing and recording certain documents in the event that the foreclosure procedure must be implemented.

Commercial leasehold insurance: Insurance to cover the payment of rent in the event the insured tenant cannot pay. Some commercial lenders require commercial leasehold insurance in shopping centers.

Commercial mortgage: A loan used to purchase a piece of commercial property or building.

Commercial mortgage broker: A broker specialized in commercial mortgage applications.

Commercial mortgage lender: A lender specialized in funding commercial mortgage loans.

Commercial property: Property designed for use by retail, wholesale, office, hotel, or other service businesses. Commercial properties are typically not long-term residential structures.

Commingling: The illegal act by a real estate broker or agent where the agent places client or customer funds into an account with his or her own funds. By law, brokers are required to maintain a separate trust or escrow account for other parties' funds held temporarily by the broker. For example, earnest money provided with an offer must be deposited in a separate account.

Commission: Payment to a broker for services rendered, such as in the sale or purchase of real property;

usually a percentage of the selling price of the property.

Commitment: The agreement of a lender to make a loan with given terms for a specific period.

Commitment fee: The fee a lender charges for the guarantee of specified loan terms, to be honored at some point in the future. The commitment fee is required to lock in specific terms on a loan at the time of application.

Common area assessments: Sometimes called Homeowners' Association Fees. Charges paid to the Homeowners' Association by the individual unit owners, in a condominium or Planned Unit Development (PUD), that are usually used to maintain the property and common areas.

Common Area Maintenance (CAM): Charges (over and above rent) to tenants for expenses to maintain hallways, restrooms, parking lots, playgrounds, and other common areas.

Common areas: The portions of a building, land, and amenities, owned or managed by a Planned Unit Development (PUD) or condominium's homeowners' association, that are used by all of the unit owners who share in the common expense of operation and maintenance.

Common law: The body of law based on custom, usage, and court decisions. Common law prevails unless superseded by another law.

Common (or Party) wall: A wall separating two units in a condominium, duplex, or other multi-unit property.

Community property: Property that is acquired by a married couple during the course of their marriage and is considered in many states to be owned jointly, unless certain circumstances are present.

Comparable sales: Also called Comps or Comparables. The recent selling prices of similar properties in the area that are used to help determine the market value of a property, with the assumption that the subject property will sell at a similar price to other similar properties.

Comparables: Properties used in an appraisal report that are substantially equivalent to the subject property.

Comparative unit method: An appraisal technique used to establish specific units of measurement for appraising specific types of property. For example, parking garages are typically compared on a per parking space basis; land is compared per acre or square foot.

Competent party: Persons legally capable of entering a contract. Persons who are under age, mentally insane, or under the influence are not competent parties.

Competitive Market Analysis (CMA): A comparison of the prices of recently sold homes similar to a listing seller's home in terms of location, style, and amenities. Also known as a comparative market analysis.

Completion bond: A legal instrument that guarantees the completion of a project according to specifications.

Compound interest: The amount of interest paid on the principal balance of a mortgage in addition to accrued interest.

Concessions: Cash, or the equivalent, that the landlord pays or allows in the form of rental abatement, additional tenant finish allowance, moving expenses, or other costs expended in order to persuade a tenant to sign a lease.

Condemnation: A government agency's act of taking private property, without the owner's consent, for public use through the power of eminent domain.

Conditional commitment: A lender's agreement to make a loan providing the borrower meets certain conditions.

Conditional sale: A contract to sell a property which states that the seller will retain the title until all contractual conditions have been fulfilled.

Condominium: A type of ownership in which all of the unit owners own the property, common areas, and buildings jointly, and have sole ownership in the unit to which they hold the title.

Condominium conversion: Changing an existing rental property's ownership to the condominium form of ownership.

Condominium hotel: A condominium project that involves registration desks, short-term occupancy, food and telephone services, daily cleaning services, and is generally operated as a commercial hotel even though the units are individually owned (also called a "condotel").

Condominium owners' association: An organization of all unit owners that oversees the common elements and enforces the bylaws.

Conforming loan: A mortgage that meets the conditions to be purchased by Fannie Mae or Freddie Mac.

Construction documents: The drawings and specifications an architect and/or engineer provides to describe construction requirements for a project.

Construction loan: A short-term loan to finance the cost of construction, usually dispensed in stages throughout the construction project. Most construction loans provide for periodic payouts as stages of construction completion are reached.

Construction to permanent loan: A construction loan that can be converted to a longer-term traditional mortgage after construction is complete. Some construction loans are not convertible, requiring the borrower to obtain separate permanent financing; construction to permanent loans contain provisions allowing the conversion of a construction loan into a conventional mortgage.

Consultant: An individual or company that provides the services to institutional investors, such as defining real estate investment policies, making recommendations to advisors or managers, analyzing existing real estate portfolios, monitoring and reporting on portfolio performance, and/or reviewing specified investment opportunities.

Consumer Price Index (CPI): A measurement of inflation, relating to the change in the prices of goods and services that are regularly purchased by a specific population during a certain period of time.

Contiguous space: Refers to several suites or spaces on a floor (or connected floors) in a given building that can be combined and rented to a single tenant.

Contingency: A provision or provisions in a contract that must be met for the contract to be considered enforceable. For example, a buyer may offer a contract that is contingent upon the buyer's obtaining suitable financing; if financing is not obtained, the buyer may back out of the agreement without penalty.

Contour map: A map that displays the topography of the site. The map contains contour lines showing various elevations on the site.

Contract: A legally enforceable promise or set of promises that must be performed and for which, if a breach of the promise occurs, the law provides a remedy. A contract may be either unilateral, by which only one party is bound to act, or bilateral, by which all parties to the instrument are legally bound to act as prescribed.

Contract for deed: An agreement to sell real estate by installment. The buyer may use, occupy, and enjoy the land, but no deed is given until all or a specified part of the sale price has been paid, usually in installments (monthly payments).

Contract for sale: A legal document the buyer and seller must approve and sign that details the price and terms of the transaction.

Contractor: A person or company who contracts to supply goods or services, generally in connection with the development of a property.

Controlled business arrangement: An arrangement where a package of services (such as a real estate firm, title insurance company, mortgage broker and home inspection company), is offered to consumers.

Conventional loan: A long-term loan from a nongovernmental lender that a borrower obtains for the purchase of a home. VA and FHA loans are not considered conventional loans. Fixed rate, fixed term mortgages are typically considered conventional loans.

Conversion: Changing property to a different use or form of ownership. For example, an apartment building can be converted to condominiums, or a large residence can be converted to a multi-tenant apartment building.

Conveyance: A term used to refer to any document that transfers title to real property. The term is also used in describing the act of transferring; also known as "closing."

Cooling-off period: A grace period provided by law that allows a party to back out of a contract legally within a specified period of time. The Truth in Lending Act requires a cooling-off period in transactions involving a personal residence.

Cooperative: Also called a co-op. Cooperatives are a type of ownership by multiple residents of a multi-unit housing complex, in which they all own shares in the cooperative corporation that owns the property and have the right to occupy a particular apartment or unit.

Co-ownership: Title ownership held by two or more persons.

Corporation: A legal entity properly registered with the secretary of state. A corporation can have limited liability, perpetual life, freely transferable shares, and centralized management.

Co-signer: A second individual or party who also signs a promissory note or loan agreement, thereby taking responsibility for the debt in the event that the primary borrower cannot pay. A co-signer typically does not appear on the title or deed.

Cost approach appraisal: The process of estimating the value of a property by adding the appraiser's estimate of the reproduction, replacement, or cost of the building to the estimated land value, less depreciation.

The cost approach bases the value of a property on the cost of replacing it, not on the value of other homes in the area or on its ability to generate income.

Cost approach land value: The estimated value of the basic interest in the land if it were available for development to its highest and best use.

Cost of living index: An indicator of the current price level for goods and services related to a base year. Reflects the increase or decrease in the cost of certain commodities and services.

Counteroffer: A new offer made in response to an offer received. It has the effect of rejecting the original offer, which cannot be accepted thereafter unless revived by the offerer.

Courier fee: The fee that is charged at closing for the delivery of documents between all parties concerned in a real estate transaction.

Courtesy to brokers: The practice of sharing commissions between listing and cooperating brokers.

Covenant: A written agreement between two or more parties in which a party or parties pledge to perform or not perform specified acts with regard to property; usually found in such real estate documents as deeds, mortgages, leases, and contracts for deed.

Covenant not to compete: A clause in an agreement where a party promises not to sell or produce the same goods and services within a specified geographic area of the other party. Also known as a non-compete clause or covenant.

Creative financing: Any financing arrangement other than a traditional mortgage from a third-party lending institution. Creative financing can include loans from the seller, balloon payment loans, wraparound mortgages, and land contracts.

Credit: An agreement in which a borrower promises to repay the lender at a later date and receives something of value in exchange.

Credit history: An individual's record which details his or her current and past financial obligations and performance.

Credit rating: The degree of creditworthiness a person is assigned based on his credit history and current financial status.

Credit report: An individual's record detailing an individual's credit, employment, and residence history used to determine the individual's creditworthiness.

Credit score: Sometimes called a Credit Risk Score (or a FICO score). A credit score is the number listed on a consumer credit report that represents a statistical summary of the information.

Creditor: A party to whom other parties owe money.

Curb appeal: The attractiveness of a house or property as viewed from the street.

- D -

Damages: The amount recoverable by a person who has been injured in any manner, including physical harm, property damage, or violated rights, through the act or default of another. For example, a landlord whose apartment has been damaged by a tenant will seek monetary damages.

Debt: Any amount one party owes to another party; an obligation to pay.

Debt service: The amount of money that is necessary to meet all interest and principal payments on a loan during a specific period.

Debt-to-equity ratio: The relationship between the level of debt and the level of equity in a property. For example, a property with a mortgage of $100,000 and equity of $25,000 has a debt-to-equity ratio of 4:1.

Debt-to-income ratio: The percentage of a borrower's monthly payment on long-term debts divided by his gross monthly income.

Declaration of restrictions:
The set of restrictions filed by a subdivision or a condominium listing rules residents must follow.

Decree: An order by a person in authority; usually from a court or government agency.

Deed: A legal document that conveys property ownership to the buyer. The seller delivers a deed to the buyer after the transaction (including the exchange of funds) has been completed.

Deed in lieu of foreclosure: The act of giving a property back to the lender without undergoing foreclosure. While the end result is the same — the lender regains possession of the property — the expense and repercussions of the foreclosure proceedings is avoided.

Deed in trust: An instrument that grants a trustee under a land trust full power to sell, mortgage, and subdivide a parcel of real estate. The beneficiary controls the trustee's use of these powers under the provisions of the trust agreement. A provision that allows a lender to foreclose on a property in the event that the borrower defaults on the loan.

Deed of trust: An instrument used in some states instead of a mortgage. Legal title to the property is vested in one or more trustees to secure the repayment of a loan. The deed of trust allows the lender to regain possession in case of default.

Deed restrictions: Clauses in a deed limiting the future uses of the property. Deed restrictions may impose a vast variety of limitations and conditions; for example, they may limit the density of buildings, dictate the types of structures that can be erected, or prevent buildings from being used for specific purposes or even from being used at all.

Default: The state that occurs when a borrower fails to fulfill a duty or take care of an obligation, such as making monthly mortgage payments. Not fulfilling conditions of a contract causes the party to be in default.

Defendant: The party sued in an action at law. If one party sues another, the party bringing suit (filing the complaint) is the plaintiff; the party who has been brought suit against is the defendant.

Deferred maintenance: A lack of normal upkeep. Deferred maintenance is an appraisal term used to note items like broken windows, missing shingles, peeling paint, broken guttering, and other property defects that have not been addressed by the owner.

Deferred payment method: The system of making payments at a later date. For example, on a graduated payment mortgage the principal payments and some interest payments are deferred for the first two to five years.

Deficiency judgment: A personal judgment levied against the borrower when a foreclosure sale does not produce sufficient funds to pay the mortgage debt in full.

Delayed exchange: A transaction where a property is traded for the promise to provide a replacement in kind property in the near future. By delaying the exchange, the party involved can defer taxable gains on the original property.

Delinquency: A state that occurs when the borrower fails to make mortgage payments on time, eventually resulting in foreclosure if payments are chronically late.

Delinquent mortgage: A mortgage in which the borrower is behind on payments.

Delivery: Transfer of the possession of an item (including real estate) to another person.

Demand loan: A loan that may be called by the lender at any time; the lender can require repayment of the entire loan balance at any time, for any reason.

Demising wall: A separation between two tenants, or between a tenant and a hallway or corridor. The demising wall creates a boundary between two apartments, for example.

Density: The intensity of land use. For example, if a subdivision has 20 homes in a 20-acre area, the density is one dwelling unit per acre.

Density zoning: Zoning ordinances that restrict the maximum average number of houses per acre that may be built within a particular area, generally in a subdivision.

Department of Housing and Urban Development (HUD): Government agency that implements and oversees federal housing and community development programs including the FHA. Attempts to assure decent, safe, and sanitary housing, and investigates complaints of discrimination in housing.

Deposit: Funds that the buyer provides when offering to purchase or rent property; also referred to as earnest money.

Depreciation: In appraisal, a loss of value in property due to any cause, including physical deterioration, functional obsolescence, and external obsolescence. In real estate investment, an expense deduction for tax purposes taken over the period of ownership of income property.

Description: Formal depiction of the dimensions and locations of a property; serves as the legal location for deed, mortgage, and lease purposes.

Designated agent: A licensee who is authorized by a broker to act as an agent for a specific principal in a transaction.

Design-build: An approach in which a single individual or business is responsible for both the design and construction of a project.

Developer: One who attempts to put land to its most profitable use through the construction of improvements. A person creating a subdivision is a developer.

Development loan: Monies borrowed to buy land, prepare the site, and construct buildings or dwellings; also referred to as a construction loan.

Devise: The gift of real property by will. The donor (giver) is the devisor and the recipient is the devisee.

Direct sales comparisons approach: An appraisal approach where value is estimated by analyzing sales prices of similar properties recently sold; also referred to as a market comparison approach.

Disbursement: Paying out money, such as when a loan is originated or when a business or investment is concluded. Monies given to the borrower at closing are disbursements.

Discharge in bankruptcy: The release of a bankrupt party from the obligation to repay debts that were proved in a bankruptcy proceeding.

Disclaimer: A statement where responsibility is rejected, or to give up ownership of property.

Disclosure: A written statement, presented to a potential buyer, that lists information relevant to a piece of property, whether positive or negative.

Discount broker: A broker who provides service for a lower commission than what is typical in the market. Many discount brokers also charge flat fees rather than on a percentage basis.

Discount point: A unit of measurement used to describe various loan charges; one point equals one percent of the amount of the loan. For example, $2,000 equals one discount point on a $200,000 loan. Typically, discount points are fees that a lender charges to provide a lower interest rate.

Doing Business As (DBA): Used to identify a trade name or a fictitious business name. A company using the designation DBA is not attempting to mislead or defraud customers.

Domicile: The place in which an individual makes his or her primary residence.

Down payment: The difference between the purchase price and the portion that the mortgage lender financed. A down payment typically refers to the amount of cash a borrower puts down on the house.

Dry closing: A closing that is complete except for disbursing funds and delivering documents.

The parties in the closing have fulfilled their duties, and the escrow must complete the closing.

Dry mortgage: A mortgage that carries no personal liability for the borrower; the lender may take the property pledged as collateral for the loan, but may have no recourse to other assets of the borrower. Also called a non-recourse loan.

Dual agency: An individual or company representing both parties to a transaction. Dual agencies are unethical unless both parties agree, and are illegal in many states.

Due diligence: The activities of a prospective purchaser or mortgagor of real property for the purpose of confirming that the property is as represented by the seller and is not subject to environmental or other problems. A person performing due diligence is making a reasonable effort to perform under a contract, to provide accurate and complete information, and/or is examining a property to detect the presence of contaminants or defects.

Due on sale clause: A provision in the mortgage that states that the entire balance of the note is immediately due and payable if the mortgagor transfers (sells) the property.

Duplex: Two dwellings under the same roof.

Duress: Unlawful constraint or action exercised upon a person whereby the person is forced to perform an act against his or her will; a compulsion to do something because of a threat. This kind of contract is voidable.

Dwelling: A place of residence.

- E -

Earnest money: Money deposited by a buyer under the terms of a contract, to be forfeited if the buyer defaults but applied to the purchase price if the sale is closed.

Easement: The right given to a non-ownership party to use a certain part of the property for specified purposes, such as servicing power lines or cable lines.

Economic life: The number of years during which an improvement will add value to the land.

Economic obsolescence: Losses of value from causes outside the property itself. Also referred to as environmental obsolescence and external obsolescence. For example, the value of a home could drop if a large apartment building is constructed on the next lot.

Effective gross income: The potential gross income of an income property, minus a vacancy and collection allowance.

Effective age: An estimate of the physical condition of a building presented by an appraiser.

Effective date: The date on which the sale of securities can commence once a registration statement becomes effective.

Efficiency unit: A small dwelling, usually consisting of a single room, within a multi-family structure. In many cases kitchen or bath facilities are not complete. For example, an efficiency apartment may have a microwave and sink, but no stove or refrigerator.

Egress: Access from land to a public road or other means of exit.

Elevation drawing: A non-perspective drawing of a property from the front, rear, or side that indicates how the planned or existing structure is situated.

Eminent domain: The power of the government to pay the fair market value for a property, appropriating it for public use.

Employee: Someone who works for an employer and has employee status. The employer is obligated to withhold income taxes and Social Security taxes from the compensation of employees. An independent contractor is not an employee.

Employment contract: A document indicating formal employment between employer and employee or between principal and agent. In the real estate business, an employment contract generally takes the form of a listing agreement or management agreement.

Empty nester: Couples whose children have established separate households.

Encroachment: A building or some portion of it — a wall or fence, for instance — that extends beyond the land of the owner and illegally intrudes on some land of an adjoining owner; any improvement or upgrade that illegally intrudes onto another party's property.

Encumbrance: Anything — such as a mortgage, tax, judgment lien, easement, restriction on the use of the land, or an outstanding dower right — that may diminish the value or enjoyment of a property.

Endorsement: The act of signing one's name, as the payee, on the back of a check or note; offering support or credibility to a statement.

Entitlement: To be owed something under the law; the portion of a VA loan that protects the lender if the veteran defaults.

Entity: A person or corporation that is recognized by law.

Environmental audit: A study of the property to determine whether there are any hazards.

Environmental Impact Statement: Legally required documents that must accompany major project proposals where there will likely be an impact on the surrounding environment.

Environmental Protection Agency (EPA): The agency of the United States government that enforces federal pollution laws and implements pollution prevention programs.

Equity: The value of a property after existing liabilities have been deducted; the value of a property over and above all liens against it. A property worth $400,000 with loans totaling $300,000 against it has an equity of $100,000.

Equity buildup: The gradual increase in equity due to the gradual payoff of the loan principal through monthly payments.

Equity mortgage: A line of credit offered against the equity in a home. The equity is secured by a second mortgage on the home; also called a home equity loan.

Equity of redemption: The right of an owner to reclaim property before a foreclosure sale. If the owner can raise enough funds to pay principal, interest, and taxes on the property, he can reclaim the property before a foreclosure sale, even though foreclosure proceedings may be under way.

Errors and Omissions Insurance: A type of policy that insures against the mistakes of a builder or architect.

Escalation clause: The clause in a lease that provides for the rent to be increased to account for increases in the expenses the landlord must pay.

Escalator clause: A provision in a lease that requires the tenant to pay more rent based on an increase in costs.

Escape clause: A provision in a contract that allows one or more of the parties to cancel all or part of the contract if certain events do not occur. For example, a buyer who cannot get approval for financing can cancel the contract if an appropriate escape clause is included in the contract for sale.

Escrow: The closing of a transaction through a third party called an escrow agent who receives certain funds and documents to be delivered upon the performance of certain conditions outlined in the escrow instructions. A valuable item, money or documents deposited with a third party for delivery upon the fulfillment of a condition.

Escrow account: Also referred to as an Impound Account. An account established by a mortgage lender or servicing company for the purpose of holding funds for the payment of items, such as homeowners insurance and property taxes.

Escrow agent: A neutral third party who makes sure that all conditions of a real estate transaction have been met before any funds are transferred or property is recorded.

Escrow agreement: A written agreement between an escrow agent and the contractual parties which defines the basic obligations of each party, the money (or other valuables) to be deposited in escrow, and how the escrow agent is to dispose of the money on deposit.

Escrow contract: An agreement between a buyer, seller, and escrow holder setting forth rights and responsibilities of each. An escrow contract is entered into when earnest money is deposited in a broker's escrow account.

Escrow disbursements: The dispensing of escrow funds for the payment of real estate taxes, hazard insurance, mortgage insurance, and other property expenses as they are due.

Estate: The total assets, including property, of an individual after he has died.

Estate in land: The degree, quantity, nature, and extent of interest a person has in real property.

Estimated closing costs: An estimation of the expenses relating to the sale of real estate.

Et al.: Abbreviation that means "and others."

Et ux.: Abbreviation that means "and wife."

Et vir.: Abbreviation that means "and husband."

Ethics: The system of moral principles and rules that become standards for professional conduct.

Eviction: The legal removal of an occupant from a piece of property.

Evidence of title: Proof of ownership of property; commonly a certificate of title, an abstract of title with lawyer's opinion, title insurance, or a Torrens registration certificate.

Examination of title: A title company's inspection and report of public records and other documents for the purpose of determining the chain of ownership of a property.

Exception: An item not covered by an insurance policy.

Exchange: A transaction in which all or part of the consideration is the transfer of like-kind property (such as real estate for real estate).

Exclusive agency listing: A listing contract under which the owner appoints a real estate broker as his or her exclusive agent for a designated period of time to sell the property, on the owner's stated terms, for a commission. The owner reserves the right to sell without paying anyone a commission if he or she sells to a prospect that has not been introduced or claimed by the broker.

Execute: To sign a contract; to perform a contract fully.

Executed contract: An agreement in which all parties involved have fulfilled their duties.

Executor: The individual who is named in a will to administer an estate. "Executrix" is the feminine form.

Exhibit: A document presented as supporting data for principal document. For example, a contract may have a legal description of the property attached.

Expansion option: A provision in a lease granting a tenant the option to lease additional adjacent space after a specified period of time; common in commercial leases.

Experian: One of the three primary credit-reporting bureaus.

Express agreement: An oral or written contract in which the parties state the contract's terms and express their intentions in words.

Extended coverage: Insurance that covers specific incidences normally not covered by standard homeowners policies. For example, a homeowner who lives next to a baseball field may obtain extended coverage to insure against window damage from balls.

Extender clause: A condition providing for a listing agreement to be automatically renewable until the parties agree to terminate it. Rarely used at present.

Extension: An agreement between two parties to extend the time period specified in a contract. Both parties must agree.

- F -

Fair Credit Reporting Act (FCRA): The federal legislation that governs the processes credit reporting agencies must follow.

Fair Housing Act: The federal law that prohibits discrimination in housing based on race, color, religion, sex, handicap, familial status, and national origin.

Fair market value: The highest price that a buyer would be willing to pay, and the lowest price a seller would be willing to accept.

False advertising: Describing property in a misleading fashion.

Fannie Mae: Federal National Mortgage Association. A quasi-government agency established to purchase any kind of mortgage loans in the secondary mortgage market from the primary lenders.

Fannie Mae Community Home Buyers Program: A community lending model based on borrower income in which mortgage insurers and Fannie Mae offer flexible underwriting guidelines to increase the buying power for a low or moderate-income family and to decrease the total amount of cash needed to purchase a home.

USDA Rural Development: An agency within the U.S. Department of Agriculture that provides credit to farmers and other rural residents.

Feasibility study: A determination of the likelihood that a proposed development will fulfill the objectives of a particular investor. Typically evaluates expenses, income, and most advantageous use and design.

Federal Deposit Insurance Corporation (FDIC): An independent federal agency that insures the deposits in commercial banks.

Federal Emergency Management Agency (FEMA): Among other duties, offers flood insurance to property owners in designated flood plains.

Federal Home Loan Mortgage Corporation (FHLMC): A government agency, also known as Freddie Mac; buys mortgages from lending institutions, combines them with other loans, and sells shares to investors.

Federal Housing Administration (FHA): A government agency that administers many loan programs, loan guarantee programs, and loan insurance programs designed to make housing more available.

Federal National Mortgage Association (FNMA): A government agency, also known as Fannie Mae; the nation's largest supplier of home mortgage funds. The company buys mortgages from lenders and resells them as securities on the secondary mortgage market.

Federal Reserve System: The country's central banking system, which is responsible for the nation's monetary policy by regulating the supply of money and interest rates.

Federal tax lien: A debt attached against a property for unpaid federal taxes. Typically used by the Internal Revenue Service to attach property for payment of an owner's unpaid income taxes.

Fee appraiser: A professional who furnishes appraisal services for a fee, usually to investors who are considering purchasing property. Also called an independent fee appraiser or a review appraiser.

Fee for service: Arrangement where a consumer asks a licensee to perform specific real estate services for a set fee.

Fee simple: The highest interest in real estate recognized by the law; the holder is entitled to all rights to the property.

Feudal system: A system of ownership usually associated with pre-colonial England, in which the king or other sovereign is the source of all rights. The right to possess real property was granted by the sovereign to an individual as a life estate only. Upon the death of the individual, title passed back to the sovereign, not to the decedent's heirs.

FHA loan: A loan insured by the Federal Housing Administration and made by an approved lender in accordance with the FHA's regulations.

Fiduciary relationship: A relationship of trust and confidence, as between trustee and beneficiary, attorney and client, or principal and agent.

Filled land: An area where the grade (level) has been raised by depositing dirt, gravel, or rock. The seller in most cases has the responsibility to disclose filled land to potential buyers.

Finance charge: The amount of interest to be paid on a loan or credit card balance.

Financial institution: A company in the business of making loans, investments, or obtaining deposits.

Financial statement: A document that shows income and expenses for an accounting period, including assets, liabilities, and equity as of a specific point in time.

Financing gap: The difference between the selling price of a property and the funds available to the potential homebuyer to purchase the home. A potential buyer who can arrange $80,000 in financing for a home with a sales price of $100,000 is facing a $20,000 financing gap.

Fire insurance: A form of property insurance covering losses due to fire; often includes additional coverage against smoke or water damage due to a fire.

Fire wall: A wall constructed of fire-resistant materials designed to retard the spread of fire.

Firm commitment: A written agreement a lender makes to loan money for the purchase of property.

First mortgage: The main mortgage on a property; a mortgage that has priority as a lien before all other mortgages. In the case of foreclosure, the first mortgage will be satisfied before other mortgages.

Fiscal year: A continuous 12-month period used for financial reporting; many companies use a fiscal year from January 1 through December 31.

Fixed costs: Expenses that remain the same despite the level of sales or production.

Fixed expenses: Expenses that remain the same regardless of occupancy. Interest expense is typically considered fixed, while electricity costs are considered to be variable because they typically change from month to month.

Fixed rate: An interest rate that does not change over the life of the loan.

Fixed rate mortgage: A mortgage with an interest rate that does not change over the length of the mortgage.

Fixture: An item of personal property that has been converted to real property by being permanently affixed.

Flag lot: A method of subdividing land into individual parcels so that compliance with local subdivision regulations can be avoided.

:An apartment on one level. A 3-room flat is an apartment that has three rooms on one floor.

Flex space: A building that provides a flexible configuration of office or showroom space combined with, for example, manufacturing, laboratory, warehouse, or distribution.

Flexible payment mortgage: A mortgage with payments that are allowed to vary but should be

sufficient to allow amortization (payoff) over the mortgage term. Adjustable rate mortgages are flexible payment mortgages.

Flip: Purchase and immediately resell property at a quick profit.

Flood certification: The process of analyzing whether a property is located in a known flood zone.

Flood insurance: A policy that is required in designated flood zones to protect against loss due to flood damage.

Flood prone area: An area having a 1 percent annual chance of flooding.

Floor plan: The arrangement of rooms in a building or dwelling.

Flue: Chamber in a fireplace that directs smoke and soot through the chimney to the outside.

Footing: A concrete support under a foundation that rests in solid ground and is wider than the structure supported. Footings distribute the weight of the structure over the ground.

For Sale By Owner (FSBO):
A method of selling property in
which the property owner serves
as the selling agent and directly
handles the sales process with the
buyer or buyer's agent.

Forbearance: Restraint in taking
legal action to remedy a default
or other breach of contract in the
hope that the default will be cured
if additional time is granted.

Force majeure: An external force
that is not controlled by the
contractual parties and prevents
them from complying with the
provisions of the contract.

Foreclosure: A legal procedure
whereby property used as security
for a debt is sold to satisfy the debt
in the event of default in payment
of the mortgage note or default
of other terms in the mortgage
document. The foreclosure
procedure brings the rights of
all parties to a conclusion and
passes the title in the mortgaged
property to either the holder of
the mortgage or a third party
who may purchase the realty
at the foreclosure sale, free of
all encumbrances affecting the
property subsequent to
the mortgage.

Forfeiture: The loss of money or
anything of value because of failure
to perform a contract.

Forgery: The illegal act of
counterfeiting documents or
making false signatures.

Foundation drain tile: A pipe,
usually made of clay, placed next to
a foundation to assist water runoff.

Foundation wall: The masonry or
concrete walls below ground level
that serve as the main support for
a structure. Foundation walls also
form the sides of a basement area.

Franchise: An arrangement
between a franchisor and a
franchisee through which the
franchisee uses the company
name of the franchisor and is
provided specified services in
exchange for a fee. Real estate
brokerages may operate as
franchises of a national company.

Fraud: Deception intended to
cause a person to give up property
or a lawful right.

Free and clear title: Title to a property without encumbrances. Generally used to refer to a title free of mortgage debt. Also known as a clear title or a marketable title.

Free-standing building: A structure that is not attached to another structure. A detached garage is considered a free-standing building.

Front end ratio: The measurement a lender uses to compare a borrower's monthly housing expense to gross monthly income.

Front footage: The measurement of a parcel of land by the number of feet of street or road frontage.

Front money: The amount of cash a developer or buyer must have on hand to purchase land and pay other initial expenses before actually developing a project.

Frontage: The portion of a lot along a lake, river, street, or highway.

Full disclosure: A requirement to reveal all information pertinent to a transaction. For example, a broker is required under full disclosure to give the buyer all known facts about the physical condition of a property.

Full recourse: A loan on which the responsibility of a loan is transferred to an endorser or guarantor in the event of default by the borrower.

Functional obsolescence: A loss of value to an improvement to real estate arising from functional problems, often caused by age or poor design. For example, a bedroom that can only be entered by walking through another bedroom would be considered functional obsolescence.

Funding fee: A fee paid to secure some types of mortgage protection, like the fee paid to the Department of Veterans Affairs for the Veteran's Administration to guarantee a VA loan.

- G -

Gambrel roof: A roof with two slopes on two sides; the lower slope is steeper than the upper sections.

Gap in title: A break in the chain of title; when the records do not reflect a transfer to a particular grantor. Can occur if a grantor fails to record a deed, or when records are otherwise incomplete.

Garden apartment: A housing complex where some or all tenants have access to a lawn area.

Garnishment: A legal process where creditors are repaid for outstanding obligations by attaching a portion of the borrower's paycheck. Garnishments typically can only occur after a judgment occurs.

Gazebo: A small, partially enclosed roof structure in a park, garden, or lawn.

General contractor: The main individual or business responsible for (and contracted to perform) the construction of an entire building or project rather than individual duties.

General (or Master) plan: A long-range governmental program to regulate the use and development of property in an orderly fashion; intended to create orderly community growth.

General real estate tax: A tax which is made up of the taxes levied on the real estate by government agencies and municipalities.

General warranty deed: A deed in which the grantor fully warrants good clear title to the premises. Used in most real estate deed transfers, a general warranty deed offers the greatest protection of any deed.

Gift: Money a buyer has received from a relative or other source.

Gift letter: A letter provided to a lender or government agency acknowledging that money to be used, usually for a down payment, is a gift from a relative or friend and carries no obligation for repayment.

Government National Mortgage Association: A government agency, also known as Ginnie Mae, that plays an important role in the secondary mortgage market. It sells mortgage-backed securities that are backed by pools of FHA and VA loans.

Good Faith Estimate (GFE): A lender's or broker's estimate that shows all costs associated with obtaining a home loan including loan processing, title, and inspection fees.

Government loan: A mortgage that is insured or guaranteed by the FHA, the Department of Veterans Affairs (VA), or the Rural Housing Service (RHS).

Government National Mortgage Association (GNMA): A government-owned corporation under the U.S. Department of Housing and Urban Development (HUD) which performs the same role as Fannie Mae and Freddie Mac in providing funds to lenders for making home loans, but only purchases loans that are backed by the federal government; also known as Ginnie Mae.

Government survey method: The system of land description that applies to most of the land in the United States, particularly the western half.

Grace period: A defined time period in which a borrower may make a loan payment after its due date without incurring a penalty.

Grade: The elevation of a hill, road, sidewalk, or slope showing its inclination from level ground. Usually expressed as a percentage of level distance; a 10 percent grade rises 10 feet in each 100 feet of level distance.

Grandfather clause: A term used to describe the concept that a previously permissible condition is still permissible despite changes in law or requirements. A structure built prior to building codes may not have to be upgraded; it is considered to be grandfathered in.

Granny flats: A small room rented within in a residence that is zoned single-family; also sometimes called "in-law apartments."

Grant: The term used to indicate a transfer of property. A person can grant property to another person in a deed.

Grant deed: A type of deed where the grantor affirms that they have not previously conveyed the property to another person, and the property is not encumbered except as already noted on the deed. Grant deeds are common in California.

Gratuitous agent An agent who receives no compensation for his or her services.

GRI: Stands for Graduate, REALTOR® Institute. Denotes a person who has completed prescribed courses in law, finance, investment, appraisal, and salesmanship.

Gross area: The total floor area of a building, usually measured from the outside walls.

Gross building area: The sum of areas at all floor levels, including the basement, mezzanine, and penthouses included in the principal outside faces of the exterior walls without allowing for architectural setbacks or projections.

Gross income: The total income of a household before taxes or expenses have been subtracted.

Gross income multiplier: A figure used as a multiplier of the gross annual income of a property to produce an estimate of the property's value.

Gross leasable area: The amount of floor space that is designed for tenants' occupancy and exclusive use.

Gross Rent Multiplier (GRM): The figure used as a multiplier of the gross monthly income of a property to produce an estimate of the property's value.

Ground lease: A lease of land only, on which the tenant usually owns a building or is required to build as specified in the lease. Such leases are usually long-term net leases; the tenant's rights and obligations continue until the lease expires or is terminated through default.

Groundwater: Water under the surface of the earth.

Guaranteed sale program: A service offered by some brokers in which they agree to pay the owner of a listed property a predetermined price if the property is not sold within a specified period of time. Because the sale is guaranteed, the owner is free to enter into a contract to purchase another home.

Guarantor: The party who makes a guaranty.

Guaranty: An agreement in which the guarantor promises to satisfy the debt or obligations of another, if and when the debtor fails to do so.

Guardian: An individual appointed by the court to oversee and administer the personal affairs and property of an individual incapable of those duties; for example, an orphaned child.

- H -

Habitable room: A room used for living purposes; bathrooms and hallways are not considered habitable rooms. Normally habitable rooms are the only rooms counted towards the number of rooms in a house.

Handicap: A physical or mental impairment that limits one or more life activities as defined by the Fair Housing Act. Also referred to as a disability.

Hard cost: The expenses attributed to constructing property improvements.

Hard money mortgage: A mortgage given to a borrower in exchange for cash rather than a mortgage secured by real estate. Pledging equity in a property against a loan is considered a hard money mortgage.

Hazard insurance: Also known as homeowners insurance or fire insurance. A policy that provides coverage for damage from forces such as fire and wind.

Hearing: A formal procedure with issues of fact or law to be tried and settled. Similar to a trial and can result in a final order.

Height: The height of a building is the distance from the curb or grade level, whichever is higher, to the highest level of a flat root or to the average height of a pitched roof.

Heirs and assigns: Heirs are recipients of an inheritance from a deceased owner; assigns are successors in interest to a property. Usually found in deeds and wills. To will property to heirs and assigns means the person receiving the property can then sell it or will it to his or her own heirs.

Hiatus: A gap in the chain of title; a space existing between adjoining parcels of land due to a faulty legal description.

High rise: In a suburban district, any building taller than six stories. In a business district, any building taller than 25 stories.

High water mark: The line on the shore that marks the level of a medium tide; denotes the boundary of property between a parcel of land and a public waterway.

Highest and best use: The most reasonable, expected, legal use of a piece of vacant land or improved property that is physically possible, supported appropriately, financially feasible, and that results in the highest value.

Highway: A road that serves continuing traffic and is the primary route between communities.

Historic structure: A building that is officially recognized for historic significance and has special tax status.

Hold harmless clause: A clause in a contract where one party agrees to protect the other party from claims and lawsuits; for example, a landlord of a commercial property may include a hold harmless clause that indemnifies them from actions taken by customers of the tenant.

Holdover tenant: A tenant who retains possession of the leased premises after the lease has expired.

Holdbacks: A portion of a loan funding that is not dispersed until an additional condition is met, such as the completion of construction.

Holding company: A company that owns or controls another company or companies.

Holding escrow: An arrangement where an escrow agent holds the final title documents to a title for deed.

Holiday: Legally recognized or widely recognized days when state and federal offices and banks and lending institutions typically are not open for business.

Home Equity Conversion Mortgage (HECM): Also referred to as a Reverse Annuity Mortgage. A type of mortgage in which the lender makes payments to the owner, thereby enabling older homeowners to convert equity in their homes into cash in the form of monthly payments.

Home equity line: An open-ended amount of credit based on the equity a homeowner has accumulated.

Home equity loan: A loan (sometimes called a line of credit) under which a property owner uses his or her residence as collateral and can then draw funds up to a prearranged amount against the property.

Home Inspector: A certified professional who determines the structural soundness and operating systems of a property.

Home ownership: Living in a structure owned by the resident.

Home price: The price that a buyer and seller agree upon, generally based on the home's appraised market value.

Homeowners Association (HOA): A group that governs a community, condominium building, or neighborhood and enforces the covenants, conditions, and restrictions set by the developer.

Homeowners association dues: The monthly payments that are paid to the homeowners' association for maintenance and communal expenses.

Homeowners insurance policy: A standardized package insurance policy that covers a residential real estate owner against financial loss from fire, theft, public liability, and other common risks.

Homeowners warranty: A type of policy homebuyers often purchase to cover repairs, such as heating or air conditioning, should they stop working within the coverage period.

Homestead: Land that is owned and occupied as the family home. In many states a portion of the area or value of this land is protected or exempt from judgments for debts.

Hostile possession: Possession of real property by one person that is adverse to the possession of the title owner. Hostile possession does not recognize the title of the true owner.

House rules: Rules of conduct adopted by the board of a condominium owners association; designed to create harmonious living among owners and occupants.

Housing Expense Ratio (HER): The percentage of gross income that is devoted to housing costs each month.

Housing for the elderly: A project specifically designed for persons 55 and older that provides accommodations and common use space.

Housing starts: An estimate of the number of dwelling units on which construction has begun or will begin during a specific period.

HUD median income: The average income for families in a particular area, which is estimated by HUD.

HUD-1 Settlement Statement: Also known as the closing statement or settlement sheet. An itemized listing of the funds paid at closing.

Hundred percent location: A term that refers to a location in the downtown business district of a city or town that commands the highest land value. Typically reflects the highest rental prices and the highest traffic and pedestrian flow.

HVAC: Heating, Ventilating, and Air Conditioning.

- I -

Illiquidity: Inadequate cash on hand to meet operations. Real estate is generally considered illiquid because it is difficult to convert it quickly to cash.

Impact fees: An expense charged to private developers by the city as a condition for granting permission for a specific project. The purpose of the fee is to defray the cost of extending public services, like water or sewer lines, to the development.

Implied agency: Based on the actions of the parties which imply that they have mutually consented to an agency relationship, an implied agency relationship is formed.

Implied listing: An agreement under which the agreement of the parties is demonstrated by their acts and conduct.

Implied warranty of habitability: A theory in landlord/tenant law in which the landlord renting residential property implies that the property is habitable and fit for its intended use.

Impounds: The part of the monthly mortgage payment that is reserved in an account to pay for hazard insurance, property taxes, and private mortgage insurance.

Improved land: Land that has some improvements, or land that has been partially or fully developed for use. A lot with a well installed is considered to be improved land, even though it is not yet suitable for habitation.

Improvement: Any structure, either privately or publicly owned, erected on a site to enhance the value of the property; for example, building a fence, driveway, curb, sidewalk, street, or sewer.

Improvements: The upgrades or changes made to a building to improve its value or usefulness.

In-house sale: A sale in which the listing broker is the only broker in the transaction. The listing broker may have found the buyer or another salesperson working for the broker found by the buyer.

Income approach: The process of estimating the value of an income-producing property through capitalization of the annual net income expected to be produced by the property during its remaining useful life.

Income property: A particular property that is used to generate income but is not occupied by the owner.

Income statement: A historical financial report indicating the sources and amounts of revenues, amounts of expenses, and profits or losses. Can be prepared on an accrual or a cash basis.

Incorporate: To form a corporation under state regulations.

Incorporation by reference: A method of including the terms of other documents into another document simply by referencing those documents.

Incurable obsolescence: A defect that either cannot be cured or is not financially practical to cure. If curing a structural problem will cost more than the property is worth, the problem is considered an incurable obsolescence.

Indemnify: To protect another person against loss or damage.

Indenture: A written agreement made between two or more persons who have different interests; a deed in which both parties bind themselves to reciprocal obligations.

Independent contractor: Someone who is retained to perform a certain act but who is subject to the control and direction of another only as to the end result and not as to the way in which the act is performed. Unlike an employee, an independent contractor pays for all expenses and Social Security and income taxes and receives no employee benefits. Most real estate salespeople are independent contractors.

Index: A financial table that lenders use for calculating interest rates on ARMs.

Index loan: A long term loan in which the payment terms may be adjusted based on changes in a specified index.

Indicated value: The worth of a subject property as shown in the three basic approaches to value: recent sales of comparable properties, cost less accrued depreciation plus land value, and capitalization of annual net operating income.

Indirect costs: Expenses of development other than the costs of direct material and labor that are related directly to the construction of improvements.

Indirect lighting: Light that is reflected from the ceiling or other object external to the fixture.

Indoor air quality: The presence (or lack of) pollutants in a building, such as tobacco smoke, carbon monoxide, radon, or asbestos.

Industrial park: An area designed and zoned for manufacturing and associated businesses and activities.

Inflation: The gradual reduction of the purchasing power of the dollar, usually related directly to the increases in the money supply by the federal government; the rate at which consumer prices increase each year.

Informed consent: Consent to a certain act that is given after a full and fair disclosure of all facts needed to make a conscious choice.

Infrastructure: The basic public works of a city or subdivision, including roads, bridges, sewer systems, water systems, and public utilities.

Initial interest rate: The original interest rate on an ARM, which is sometimes subject to a variety of adjustments throughout the mortgage.

Initial rate duration: The date specified by most ARMs at which the initial rate expires.

Injunction: A legal action where a court issues a writ that forbids a party from committing an act or compels a party to perform an act.

Inner city: An urban area that is generally recognized as a central residential or commercial part of a city.

Innocent misrepresentation: A misstatement of fact made without the intent to deceive.

Innocent purchaser: A party who is not responsible for cleanup of contaminated property. Applies to a party who knew nothing about the contamination and had an investigation performed before the purchase.

Inquiry notice: Notice the law presumes a reasonable person would obtain by inquiring into a property.

Inside lot: A lot surrounded on each side by other lots, with road frontage on one side; a corner lot has road frontage on two sides.

Inspection fee: The fee that a licensed property inspector charges for determining the current physical condition of the property.

Inspection report: A written report of the property's condition presented by a licensed inspection professional.

Installment contract: A contract for the sale of real estate whereby the purchase price is paid in periodic installments by the purchaser, who is in possession of the property even though title is retained by the seller until a future date, which may be not until final payment. Also called a "contract for deed" or "articles of agreement for warranty deed."

Installment note: A promissory note providing for payment of principal in two or more stated amounts, at different times.

Institutional lender: Financial intermediaries who invest in loans and other securities on behalf of investors or depositors; loans made by institutional lenders are regulated by law.

Instrument: A written legal document created to establish the rights and liabilities of the parties to it.

Insulation: Materials used to slow the transfer of heat or cold through walls and ceilings, reducing energy costs, and maintaining a consistent temperature.

Insulation disclosure: The requirement that real estate brokers, builders, and sellers of new houses must disclose the type, thickness, and R-value of insulation in the house.

Insurable title: A title that can be insured by a title insurance company.

Insurance binder: A temporary insurance policy that is implemented while a permanent policy is drawn up or obtained.

Insured mortgage: A mortgage that is guaranteed by the FHA or by private mortgage insurance (PMI).

Interest: A charge made by a lender for the use of money; the cost for the use of money.

Interest in property: A legal share of ownership in a property.

Interest only loan: A mortgage for which the borrower pays only the interest that accrues on the loan balance each month.

Interest rate: The percentage that is charged for a loan.

Interest rate buy down plans: A plan in which a seller uses funds from the sale of the home to buy down the interest rate and reduce the buyer's monthly payments.

Interim financing: Also known as Bridge or Swing Loans. Short-term financing a seller uses to bridge the gap between the sale of one house and the purchase of another.

International Building Code (IBC): The standard building codes and regulations adopted by the United States since 2000.

Interstate Land Sales Full Disclosure Act: A federal law that regulates the sale of certain real estate in interstate commerce.

Interval ownership: Time share ownership where the owner acquires title to a specific unit for a certain week or weeks per year.

Intrinsic value: An appraisal term referring to the value created by a person's personal preferences for a particular type of property.

Inventory: The entire space of a certain proscribed market without concern for its availability or condition.

Investment property: A piece of real estate that generates some form of income.

Investment structures: Approaches to investing that include unleveraged acquisitions, leveraged acquisitions, traditional debt, participating debt, convertible debt, triple-net leases, and joint ventures.

Involuntary conversion: Condemnation or sudden destruction by nature. A property can be involuntarily converted through eminent domain, or can be destroyed by a natural disaster.

Involuntary lien: A lien placed on property without the consent of the property owner; a mechanics lien is an example of an involuntary lien.

Ironclad agreement: An agreement that cannot be broken by any of the parties involved.

Irrevocable consent: An agreement that cannot be withdrawn or revoked.

- J -

Joint and several liability: A phrase meaning that each of the individual owners is personally responsible for the total damages.

Joint liability: The condition in which responsibility rests with two or more people for fulfilling the terms of a home loan or other financial debt.

Joint tenancy: A form of ownership in which two or more people have equal shares in a piece of property, and rights pass to the surviving owner(s) in the event of death.

Judgment lien: The claim on a property of a debtor resulting from a judgment.

Judicial foreclosure: The usual foreclosure proceeding some states use, which is handled in a civil lawsuit.

Jumbo loan: A type of mortgage that exceeds the required limits set by Fannie Mae and Freddie Mac. Jumbo loans must be maintained in the lender's portfolio or be sold to private investors.

Junior lien: An obligation, such as a second mortgage, that is subordinate in right or lien priority to an existing lien on the same realty.

Junior mortgage: A loan that is a lower priority, behind and after the primary loan.

Jurisdiction: Area of authority for a specific government agency or entity.

Just compensation: The amount that is fair to both the owner and the government when property is appropriated for public use through Eminent Domain.

- K -

Key lot: A lot that has added value because of its strategic location, especially when it is needed for the highest and best use of contiguous property. A key lot is also a lot that adjoins the rear property line of a corner lot and fronts on a secondary street.

Key tenant: A major office building tenant that leases several floors, or a major department store in a shopping center.

Kickers: Payment required by a mortgage in addition to normal principal and interest.

Kitchenette: A space less than 60 square feet that is used for cooking and preparing food.

Knockdown: Pre-manufactured construction materials delivered to the building site unassembled; can be quickly assembled and installed.

- L -

Land banker: Developer who improves raw land for construction purposes and who maintains an inventory of improved lots for future purposes.

Land contract: An installment contract for sale with the buyer receiving equitable title (a right to possession) and the seller retaining legal title. Similar to a contract for deed.

Land description: Legal description of a particular piece of real estate.

Land grant: Grant of public lands by the government, usually for roads, railroads, or agricultural colleges.

Land leaseback: Only the ground is covered by the lease. Structures built on the land revert to the original owner at the termination of the lease.

Land trust: A trust originated by the owner of real property in which real estate is the only asset.

Land use map: A map that shows the types and intensities of different land uses in a particular area.

Landlocked: A lot that has no access to a public road or highway except through an adjacent lot.

Landlord: A person or company who rents property to another person; a landlord is the lessor.

Landlords warrant: The warrant a landlord obtains to take a tenant's personal property to sell at a public sale to compel payment of the rent or other stipulation in the lease.

Landmark: A fixed object serving as a boundary mark for a tract of land. A landmark is also considered to be a monument.

Landscaping: Shrubs, bushes, trees, and other plants surrounding a structure.

Late charge: The fee that is imposed by a lender when the borrower has not made a payment when it was due.

Late payment: The payment made to the lender after the due date has passed.

Latent defect: A hidden structural defect that could not be discovered by ordinary inspection and that threatens the property's soundness or the safety of its inhabitants. Some states impose on sellers and licensees a duty to inspect for and disclose latent defects.

Leaching cesspool: A cesspool that is not watertight and permits liquids to pass into the surrounding soil.

Lead poisoning: Serious illness caused by high concentrations of lead in the body.

Lease: A written or oral contract between a landlord (the lessor) and a tenant (the lessee) that transfers the right to exclusive possession and use of the landlord's real property to the lessee for a specified period of time and for a stated consideration (rent). By state law leases for longer than a certain period of time (generally one year) must be in writing to be enforceable.

Lease option: A financing option that provides for homebuyers to lease a home with an option to buy, with part of the rental payments being applied toward the down payment.

Lease purchase: The purchase of real property, the consummation of which is preceded by a lease, usually long-term. Typically used for tax or financing purposes.

Lease purchase: A lease that gives the tenant the right to purchase the property at an agreed-upon price under certain conditions.

Leasehold improvements: Fixtures attached to real estate that are purchased or installed by the tenant. When the lease expires, the tenant is generally allowed to remove those improvements, provided the removal does not damage the property.

Leasehold state: A way of holding a property title in which the mortgagor does not actually own the property but has a long-term lease on it.

Legal age: The standard of maturity upon which a party is held legally responsible for that party's acts. The legal age for real estate transactions is 18.

Legal description: A description of a specific parcel of real estate complete enough for an independent surveyor to locate and identify it.

Legal notice: Notification of others using the method required by law. For example, a deed recorded in the local courthouse is a legal notice of ownership.

Legatee: A person who receives property by will.

Lessee: A person to whom property is rented under a lease.

Lessor: A person who rents property to another under a lease.

Let: To rent property to a tenant.

Levy: To assess; to seize or collect. To levy a tax is to assess a property and set the rate of taxation. To levy an execution is to seize the property of a person to satisfy an obligation.

Liabilities: A borrower's debts and financial obligations, whether long or short-term.

Liability insurance: A type of policy that protects owners against negligence, personal injury, or property damage claims.

License: A privilege or right granted to a person by a state to operate as a real estate broker or salesperson; the revocable permission for a temporary use of land, a personal right that cannot be sold.

Lien: A claim put on property, making it security for payment of a debt, judgment, mortgage, or taxes.

Lien statement: A statement of the unpaid balance of a promissory note secured by a lien on property, plus the status of interest payments, maturity date, and any claims that may be asserted. A lien statement is also called an offset statement.

Lien waiver: A waiver of a mechanic's lien rights that is sometimes required before the general contractor can receive money under the payment provisions of a construction loan and contract.

Life care facility: A residential development designed to provide medical and nursing care for senior citizens.

Light industry: Zoning designation referring to industrial use encompassing mostly light manufacturing businesses that do not cause noise, air, or water disturbances or pollution.

Limitations of actions: Time within which legal actions must commence or else those actions will be barred or disallowed. Similar to a statute of limitations.

Limited liability company: A form of ownership treated as a partnership for federal tax purposes with limited liability protection for owners.

Limited power of attorney: A power of attorney that is limited to a specific task or set of tasks; does not confer general authority to act on the behalf of another party.

Limited referral agent: A salesperson with an active real estate license who refers prospective buyers or sellers to a brokerage company in return for a referral fee at closing.

Limited warranty deed: A deed containing warranties covering the time period the grantor holds title.

Line of credit: An amount of credit granted by a financial institution up to a specified amount for a certain period of time to a borrower.

Line of sight easement: A right that restricts the use of land within the easement area in any way that will restrict the view.

Line stakes: Stakes set along boundary lines of a parcel of land.

Lineal foot: A measure of one foot, in a straight line, along the ground.

Liquid asset: A type of asset that can be easily converted into cash.

Liquidated damages: An amount predetermined by the parties to a contract as the total compensation to an injured party should the other party breach the contract.

Listing agreement: An agreement between a property owner and a real estate broker which authorizes the broker to attempt to sell or lease the property at a specified price and terms in return for a commission or other compensation.

Listing broker: The listing broker is the broker in a multiple-listing situation from whose office a listing agreement is initiated. The listing broker and the cooperating broker may be the same person.

Loan application fee: A fee lenders charge to cover expenses relating to reviewing a loan application.

Loan commitment: An agreement by a lender or other financial institution to make or insure a loan for the specified amount and terms.

Loan officer: An official representative of a lending institution who is authorized to act on behalf of the lender within specified limits.

Loan origination fee: A fee charged to the borrower by the lender for making a mortgage loan. The fee is usually computed as a percentage of the loan amount.

Loan servicing: The process a lending institution goes through for all loans it manages. This involves processing payments, sending statements, managing the escrow/impound account, providing collection services on delinquent loans, ensuring that insurance and property taxes are made on the property, handling pay-offs and assumptions, as well as various other services.

Loan-To-Value ratio (LTV): The relationship between the amount of the mortgage loan and the value of the real estate being pledged as collateral.

Location, location, location: A popular statement that emphasizes the location of a property in determining its value; often phrased as, "The three most important considerations in real estate are location, location, location."

Lock box structure: An arrangement in which the payments are sent directly from the tenant or borrower to the trustee.

Lock boxes: A special lock placed at a property for sale containing a key to the property; can only be opened by agents with a key to the lock box.

Lock in: A commitment from a lender to a borrower to guarantee a given interest rate for a limited amount of time.

Lock-in period: The period of time during which the borrower is guaranteed a specified interest rate.

Loft: A building area that is unfinished; open space on the first or second floor typically used for manufacturing or retail operations.

London Interbank Offered Rate (LIBOR): An index used to determine interest rate changes for adjustable rate mortgages. Very popular index for interest only mortgage programs.

Long-term lease: A rental agreement that will last at least three years from initial signing to the date of expiration or renewal.

Lot: An individual parcel of land in a subdivision; one of several contiguous parcels of a larger piece of land.

Lot and block (recorded plat) system: A method of describing real property that identifies a parcel of land by reference to lot and block numbers within a subdivision, as specified on a recorded subdivision plat.

Low documentation loan: A mortgage that requires only a basic verification of income and assets.

Low rise: A building that involves fewer than four stories above the ground level.

- M -

Mortgage Guaranty Insurance Corporation (MGIC): A private mortgage insurer, also known as Maggie Mae, which insures mortgages to other investors by protecting them from credit losses and expediting home ownership with low down-payment loans.

Maintenance fee: The charge to homeowners association members each month for the repair and maintenance of common areas.

Management agreement: A contract between the owner of income property and a management firm or individual property manager that outlines the scope of the manager's authority.

Maps and plats: Surveys of pieces of land showing monuments, boundaries, area, ownership, and other features.

Margin: A constant amount that is added to the value of an index for the purpose of adjusting the interest rate on an adjustable rate mortgage; a percentage that is added to the index and fixed for the mortgage term.

Market conditions: Features of the marketplace including interest rates, employment levels, demographics, vacancy rates, and absorption rates.

Market data approach: An estimate of value obtained by comparing property being appraised with recently sold comparable properties.

Market study: A forecast of the demand for a certain type of real estate project in the future, which includes an estimate of the square footage that could be absorbed and the rents that could be charged.

Market value: The price a property would sell for at a particular time in a competitive market.

Marketable title: Good or clear title, reasonably free from the risk of litigation over possible defects.

Master deed: A deed used by a condominium developer for recording a condominium development. Divides a single property into individually owned units.

Master lease: The primary lease that controls other subsequent leases and may cover more property than all subsequent leases combined.

Maturity: The due date of a loan; the end of the period covered by a contract.

Maturity date: The date at which the total principal balance of a loan is due.

Mechanics lien: A claim created for securing payment priority for the price and value of work performed and materials furnished in constructing, repairing, or improving a building or other structure.

Merged credit report: A report that combines information from the three primary credit-reporting agencies including Equifax, Experian, and TransUnion.

Merger: The fusion of two or more interests, such as businesses or investments.

Mezzanine: An intermediate floor between two main stories of a building, or between the floor and ceiling of a one-story structure.

Mezzanine financing: A financing position somewhere between equity and debt, meaning that there are higher-priority debts above and equity below.

Mid-rise: A building which shows four to eight stories above ground level. In a business district, buildings up to 25 stories may also be considered mid rise buildings.

Mile: 1,760 yards or 5,280 feet.

Minimum lot area: The smallest building lot area allowed in a subdivision.

Minimum property requirements: Under FHA loan requirements, a property must be livable, soundly built, and suitably located as to site and location before the agency will underwrite a residential mortgage loan.

Mixed use: A term referring to space within a building or project which can be used for more than one activity.

Mobile home: A dwelling unit manufactured in a factory and designed to be transported to a site and semi-permanently attached.

Model home: A representative home used as part of a sales campaign to show the design, structure, and appearance of units in a development.

Modular housing: Prefabricated housing manufactured at a location other than the actual lot, and transferred in sections to the lot for final construction.

Month-to-month tenancy: A periodic tenancy under which the tenant rents for one month at a time. In the absence of a rental agreement (oral or written), a tenancy is generally considered to be month-to-month. Some leases with fixed terms automatically convert to a month-to-month tenancy once the original term has expired.

Monthly association dues: A payment due each month to a homeowners' association for expenses relating to maintenance and community operations.

Monument: A fixed natural or artificial object used to establish real estate boundaries for a metes-and-bounds description.

Moratorium: A temporary suspension of payments; a time period during which certain activity is not allowed.

Mortgage: An amount of money that is borrowed to purchase a property, using that property as collateral.

Mortgage acceleration clause: A provision enabling a lender to require that the rest of the loan balance is paid in a lump sum under certain circumstances.

Mortgage banker: A financial institution that provides home loans using its own resources, often selling them to investors such as insurance companies or Fannie Mae.

Mortgage broker: An individual who matches prospective borrowers with lenders that the broker is approved to deal with.

Mortgage Insurance (MI): A policy, required by lenders on some loans, that covers the lender against certain losses that are incurred as a result of a default on a home loan.

Mortgage Insurance Premium (MIP): The amount charged for mortgage insurance, either to a government agency or to a private MI company.

Mortgage interest deduction: The tax write-off that the IRS allows most homeowners to deduct for annual interest payments made on real estate loans.

Mortgage preapproval: A process where a lender specifies that a borrower is financially qualified and creditworthy for a specific type of loan under specific terms and conditions.

Mortgagor: The borrower (person receiving the money) in a mortgage loan transaction.

Mudroom: A small room used as the entrance from a yard or play area. Many mudrooms contain a washer and dryer.

Mudsill: The lowest horizontal component of a structure. This is usually a piece of lumber placed directly above the foundation wall.

Multi-dwelling units: A set of properties that provide separate housing areas for more than one family but only require a single mortgage.

Multiple dwelling: A tenement house; any structure used for the accommodation of two or more households in separate living units; an apartment house.

Multiple listing: An arrangement among a group of real estate brokers who agree in advance to provide information about some or all of their listings to the others, and who agree that commissions on sales of those listings will be split between listing and selling brokers.

Multiple listing clause: A provision in an exclusive listing for the authority and obligation on the part of the listing broker to distribute the listing to other brokers in the multiple-listing organization; often called the Multiple Listing Service.

Multiple Listing Service (MLS): A marketing organization composed of member brokers who agree to share their listing agreements with one another in the hope of procuring ready, willing, and able buyers for their properties more quickly than they could on their own. Most multiple-listing services accept exclusive-right-to-sell or exclusive-agency listings from their member brokers.

Municipal ordinance: Rules, regulations, and codes enacted into law by local governing bodies; typically cover building standards and subdivision requirements.

- N -

Narrative report: An appraisal report presented in descriptive paragraphs, as opposed to an appraisal presented in form, letter, or table format.

National Association of REALTORS®: An organization of REALTORS® devoted to encouraging professionalism in real estate activities.

Negative amortization: An event that occurs when the deferred interest on an ARM is added, and the balance increases instead of decreases.

Negative cash flow: A situation in which a property owner must make an outlay of funds to operate a property; a situation where income does not cover operating expenses.

Negotiation: The process of bargaining to reach an agreement. Successful negotiation results in a contract between parties.

Net after taxes: Net operating income after deducting all charges, including federal and state taxes.

Net assets: The total value of assets minus total liabilities based on market value.

Net income: The monetary sum arrived at after deducting expenses from a business or investment but before deducting depreciation expenses.

Net lease: A lease requiring the tenant to pay not only rent but also costs incurred in maintaining the property, including taxes, insurance, utilities, and repairs.

Net Operating Income (NOI): The pre-tax figure of gross revenue minus operating expenses and an allowance for expected vacancy.

Net sales proceeds: The income from the sale of an asset, or part of an asset, minus brokerage commissions, closing costs, and market expenses.

Net usable acre: The portion of a property that is suitable for building, subtracting for zoning regulations, density requirements, and other building code restrictions.

Net worth: The worth of an individual or company computed on the basis of the difference between all assets and liabilities.

No cash out refinance: Sometimes referred to as a rate and term refinance. A refinancing transaction which is intended only to cover the balance due on the current loan and any costs associated with obtaining the new mortgage.

No cost loan: A loan for which there are no costs associated with the loan that are charged by the lender, but that typically does carry a slightly higher interest rate.

No deal, no commission clause: A clause in a listing contract that stipulates a commission is to be paid only if a contract passes.

No documentation loan: A type of loan application that requires no income or asset verification; usually granted based on strong credit with a large down payment; often referred to as a "no-doc loan."

Nominee: A person designated to act for another as a representative, but only in a limited and specified sense. A nominee corporation, for example, could purchase real estate on behalf of another person when that person wishes to remain anonymous.

Non-compete clause: A provision in a lease agreement that specifies that the tenant's business is the only one that may operate in the property in question, thereby preventing a competitor moving in next door.

Nonconforming loan: Any loan that is too large or does not meet certain qualifications to be purchased by Fannie Mae or Freddie Mac.

Nonconforming use: A use of property that is permitted to continue after a zoning ordinance prohibiting it has been established for the area.

Nondisclosure: The failure to reveal a fact, with or without the intention to conceal it.

Nonrecourse loan: A loan in which the borrower is not held personally liable in the case of default.

Normal wear and tear: Physical depreciation resulting from age and ordinary use of the property. For example, carpeting may have a physical life of five years based on normal wear and tear.

Notary public: An officer who is authorized to take acknowledgements to certain types of contracts, like deeds, contracts, and mortgages, and before whom affidavits may be sworn.

Notice of default: A formal written notification a borrower receives once the borrower is in default, stating that legal action may be taken.

Notice to quit: A notice to a tenant to vacate rented property; can also be used by a tenant who wishes to vacate rented property on a specified date.

Nuisance: A land use whose associated activities are incompatible with surrounding land uses; for example, a land use that creates offensive fumes may be incompatible with a residential neighborhood.

Null and void: That which cannot be legally enforced; having no legal force, effect, or worth.

- O -

Observed condition: An appraisal method used to compare depreciation. The appraiser calculates a total depreciation amount by considering physical deterioration, functional obsolescence, and external obsolescence.

Obsolescence: The loss of value due to factors that are outmoded or less useful; a loss in value due to reduced desirability and usefulness. Obsolescence may be functional or economic.

Occupancy agreement: An agreement to permit the buyer to occupy the property before the close of escrow in consideration of paying the seller a specified amount of rent.

Occupancy permit: A permit issued by the appropriate local governing body to establish that the property is suitable for habitation by meeting certain safety and health standards.

Occupancy rate: The ratio of rented space relative to the amount of space available for rent. An apartment building with 8 out of 10 apartments rented has an occupancy rate of 80 percent.

Off-site management: Property management functions performed away from the premises.

Off-street parking: Parking spaces located on private property.

Offer: A term that describes a specified price or spread to sell whole loans or securities; an expression of willingness to purchase a property at a specified price or of willingness to sell.

Offer and acceptance: Two essential components of a valid contract; a "meeting of the minds;" creates an agreement of sale.

Offer to lease: A document used to create an agreement for the lessor to lease commercial space to a lessee on specified terms and conditions. At closing, the parties sign a formal lease agreement.

Office building: A structure used primarily for the conduct of business relating to administration, clerical services, consulting, and other client services not related to retail sales. Office buildings can hold single or multiple firms.

Office exclusive: A listing that is retained by one real estate office to the exclusion of other brokers; a listing in which the seller refuses to submit the listing to a multiple listing service (MLS).

On or before: A phrase in contracts referring to the time by which a certain act must take place.

On-site management: Property management functions that must be performed on the premises; for example, showing rental units.

One hundred percent commission: A commission arrangement between a real estate broker and a salesperson in which the salesperson receives the full net commission on certain real estate sales; typically occurs after specified quotas have been met or administrative fees have been paid to the broker.

Open-end loan: A loan that is expandable by increments up to a maximum dollar amount, the full loan being secured by the same original mortgage.

Open house: A method of showing a house for sale where the home is left open for inspection by interested parties; typically a salesperson or broker is present.

Open listing: A listing contract under which the broker's commission is contingent on the broker's producing a ready, willing, and able buyer before the property is sold by the seller or another broker.

Open space: A section of land or water that has been dedicated for public or private use or enjoyment.

Operating budget: A reasonable expectation of future income and expenses from property operations.

Operating expense: The regular costs associated with operating and managing a property.

Opinion of title: An opinion from an attorney, generally in certificate form, as to the validity of the title to the property being sold. Also called a "title abstract."

Option ARM loan: A type of mortgage in which the borrower has a variety of payment options each month.

Option listing: Listing with a provision that gives the listing broker the right to purchase the listed property.

Option to renew: A lease provision giving the tenant the right to extend the lease for an additional period of time under set terms.

Oral contract: A verbal contract or unwritten agreement. Unwritten agreements for the sale or use of real estate are generally not enforceable.

Ordinance: Municipal rules governing the use of land.

Orientation: The position of a structure on a site relative to sunlight angles and prevailing winds. A house with a north to south orientation is designed to take advantage of the sun in winter for heating purposes.

Origination fee: A fee that most lenders charge for the purpose of covering the costs associated with arranging the loan.

Out parcel: Individual retail sites located within a shopping center; a tract of land adjacent to a larger tract of which it was originally an integral part.

Outside of closing: Payment of certain closing costs to someone directly, and not through the closing process itself. Noted on settlement statements as POC (paid outside closing).

Outstanding balance: The amount of a loan that remains to be paid. An outstanding balance specifies an obligation.

Over improvement: A land use considered too intensive for the land. Building a $1,000,000 home in a neighborhood with $200,000 homes would be considered an over improvement.

Overage: Amounts to be paid based on gross sales over the base rent in a lease.

Overhang: The part of a roof that extends beyond the exterior wall.

Owner financing: A transaction in which the property seller agrees to finance all or part of the amount of the purchase.

Owner occupant: Property owner who physically occupies the property.

- P -

Pad: The area in a mobile home park allocated for the placement of a mobile home unit; a foundation or site suited for a specific type of improvement.

Paper: A business term referring to a mortgage, note, or contract for deed, usually taken back from the buyer by a seller when real property is sold.

Parapet: The part of the wall of a house that rises above the roof line.

Parcel: A specific portion of a larger tract; a lot.

Parking ratio: A figure, generally expressed as square footage, that compares a building's total rentable square footage to its total number of parking spaces.

Partial payment: An amount paid that is not large enough to cover the normal monthly payment on a mortgage loan or rental agreement.

Partial sale: The act of selling a real estate interest that is smaller than the whole property.

Participating broker: A brokerage company or its sales agent who obtains a buyer for a property that is listed with another brokerage company; the participating broker normally splits the commission with the seller's broker in an agreed upon amount — usually 50 percent.

Parties: Principals in a transaction or judicial proceeding. A buyer and a seller are the principals in a sales contract; a broker is not.

Partition: The division of co-tenants' interests in real property when all the parties do not voluntarily agree to terminate the co-ownership; takes place through court procedures.

Payment bond: A surety bond through which a contractor assures an owner that material and labor provided in the construction of a building will be fully paid for, and that no mechanics' liens will be filed against the owner.

Payoff statement: The document signed by a lender indicating the amount required to pay a loan balance in full and satisfy the debt; used in the settlement process to protect both the seller's and the buyer's interests.

Penthouse: A luxury housing unit located on the top floor of a high rise building.

Per diem interest: Interest that is charged or accrued daily.

Percentage lease: A lease, commonly used for commercial

property, whose rental is based on the tenant's gross sales at the premises; it usually stipulates a base monthly rental plus a percentage of any gross sales above a certain amount.

Percentage rent: The amount of rent that is adjusted based on the percentage of gross sales or revenues the tenant receives.

Percolation test: A test of the soil to determine if it will absorb and drain water adequately to use a septic system for sewage disposal.

Perfecting title: Removing a cloud or claim against a title to real estate.

Performance bond: A bond that contractor posts to guarantee full performance of a contract in which the proceeds will be used for completing the contract or compensating the owner for loss in the event of nonperformance.

Periodic tenancy: A leasehold estate that continues from period to period, such as month-to-month or year-to-year; the tenant has no automatic right to extend the period of tenancy.

Permanent financing: A long-term loan, not a loan used for short-term purposes like a construction loan or bridge loan.

Permissive waste: The failure of lessees or life tenants to maintain and make reasonable repairs to the property under their control. Also referred to as negligent or passive waste.

Personal property: Any items belonging to a person that is not real estate; property that is movable and not fixed to land; also known as chattels.

Personal representative: The title given to the person designated in a will or appointed by the probate court to settle the estate of a deceased person. Frequently referred to as an executor or administrator.

Phase I Audit: An initial evaluation of a property to determine the existence of environmental problems. A Phase I audit is required to support a claim to be an innocent purchaser if environmental problems are later discovered.

Physical deterioration: A reduction in a property's value resulting from a decline in physical condition; can be caused by action of the elements or by ordinary wear and tear.

Physical life: The expected period of time for a real estate investment to exist physically; the actual age or life span over which a structure is considered habitable.

Pier: A column placed under a structure to support its weight.

Piggyback loan: A combination of a construction loan with a permanent loan commitment; one mortgage held by more than one lender, with one lender holding the rights of the others in subordination.

Pipestem lot: A narrow lot, usually rectangular, that provides street or road access in heavily-developed areas. The short side of the lot is the side bordering the road; commonly found where road frontage is at a premium; typical in beachfront or lakefront developments; also referred to as

flag lots, especially when the lot creates an L-shape.

Pitch: The slope of a roof or other surface; thick black substance used for repairing a driveway, street, or roof.

PITI (Principal, Interest, Taxes, Insurance): The items that are included in the monthly payment to the lender for an impounded loan, as well as mortgage insurance.

Planned Unit Development (PUD): A type of ownership where individuals actually own the building or unit they live in, but common areas are owned jointly with the other members of the development or association. Contrasts with condominiums, where an individual actually owns the airspace of his unit, but the buildings and common areas are owned jointly with the others in the development or association.

Planning commission: A group of citizens appointed by local government officials to conduct hearings and recommend amendments to zoning ordinances. Also called a planning board, zoning commission, or zoning board.

Plans and specifications: All the drawings pertaining to a development under consideration, including the building and mechanical and electrical drawings. Includes written instructions to the builder for materials, workmanship, style, colors, and finishes.

Plat: A chart or map of a certain area showing the boundaries of individual lots, streets, and easements.

Plat book: A public record of maps of subdivided land, showing the division of the land into blocks, lots, and parcels; it indicates the dimensions of individual parcels.

Plat map: A map of a town, section, or subdivision indicating the location and boundaries of individual properties.

Plaza: A public square or meeting place usually in the center of an area; for example, the center of a shopping complex.

Plot plan: A diagram showing the proposed or existing use of a specific parcel of land. Typically shows the location, dimensions, parking areas, and landscaping.

Pocket listing: A listing whose entry into the multiple listing service (MLS) is delayed until the last moment so the listing broker will have more time to find a buyer before another salesperson can find a buyer. In effect, the listing is kept "in the pocket of" the listing broker.

Point: A fee a lender charges to provide a lower interest rate, equal to one percent of the amount of the loan; also referred to as a discount point.

Postdated check: A check with a face date later than the actual date on which it was written. A check written on May 25 with a date of June 1 is a postdated check.

Potable water: Water suitable for drinking.

Power of attorney: A written instrument authorizing a person (who becomes the attorney-in-fact) to act as agent for another person to the extent indicated in the instrument.

Preapproval letter: The letter a lender presents which states the amount of money they are willing to lend a potential buyer.

Prequalified loan: An opinion given by a lender that states that based on an examination of a credit report and an interview with a prospective borrower that borrower will qualify for a specific loan. Pre-qualification does not include a formal review of financial documents to ensure the borrower will qualify.

Preliminary report: A title report made before a title insurance policy is issued. A preliminary report is not considered a title abstract; instead, it states a willingness to insure the title upon closing.

Premises: Land and tenements; an estate; the subject matter of a conveyance.

Premium: The cost of an insurance policy; the value of a mortgage or bond in excess of its face amount; the amount over market value paid for some exceptional quality or feature.

Prepaid expenses: The amount of money that is paid before it is due, including taxes, insurance, and/or assessments.

Prepaid fees: The charges that a borrower must pay in advance regarding certain recurring items, such as interest, property taxes, hazard insurance, and PMI, if applicable.

Prepaid interest: The amount of interest that is paid before its due date.

Prepayment: The money that is paid to reduce the principal balance of a loan before the date it is due.

Prepayment penalty: A charge imposed on a borrower who pays off the loan principal early. This penalty compensates the lender for interest and other charges that would otherwise be lost.

Presale: Sale of proposed properties, such as condominiums or newly constructed dwellings, before actual construction begins.

Preservation district: A zoning district established to protect and preserve parkland, wilderness areas, open spaces, beach reserves, scenic areas, historic areas, forestry, and grazing.

Prevailing rate: A term used to describe the average interest rate currently charged by lending institutions on mortgage loans.

Price: The amount of money exchanged for something of value. Price is not value; value is an opinion of worth, whereas price is an actual amount paid that establishes value.

Prime rate: The lowest interest rate reserved for a bank's preferred customers for short term loans.

Principal broker: The licensed broker directly in charge of and responsible for the operations conducted by the brokerage firm.

Principal residence: The place a person lives most of the time.

Principle of conformity: The concept that a property will probably increase in value if its size, age, condition, and style are similar to other properties in the immediate area.

Priority: The order of position or time. The priority of liens is generally determined by the chronological order in which the lien documents are recorded; tax liens, however, have priority even over previously recorded liens.

Private Mortgage Insurance (PMI): Insurance provided by a private carrier that protects a lender against a loss in the event of a foreclosure and deficiency typically required when the loan amount exceeds 80 percent of the home's value.

Pro forma: A statement showing what is expected to occur rather than actual results.

Pro rata: The proportionate amount of expenses per tenant for the property's maintenance and operation.

Probate: A legal process by which a court determines who will inherit a decedent's property and what the estate's assets are.

Processing fee: A fee some lenders charge for gathering the information necessary to process the loan.

Profit and loss statement: A detailed breakdown of the income and expenses of a business, resulting in the operating position (or profit or loss) of a business over a specified period of time.

Progress payments: Payments made as portions of a construction project are completed; construction loan funds disbursed by the lender over the course of the project instead of in one lump sum at the beginning of the project.

Promissory note: A written agreement to repay the specific amount over a certain period of time.

Property: The rights or interests an individual has in land or goods to the exclusion of all other parties; rights gained from the ownership of wealth.

Property manager: Someone who manages real estate for another person for compensation. Duties include collecting rents, maintaining the property, and keeping up all accounting.

Property reports: The mandatory federal and state documents compiled by sub-dividers and developers to provide potential purchasers with facts about a property, prior to their purchase.

Property tax: The tax that must be paid on private property, not on real property like real estate.

Proration: Expenses that are allocated between the seller and the buyer; expenses that are either prepaid or paid in arrears that are divided or distributed between buyer and seller at the closing.

Prospect: A person considered likely to buy.

Public auction: An announced public meeting held at a specified location for the purpose of selling property to repay a mortgage in default.

Public land: Land owned by the federal government available for purchase by a private citizen if the land is no longer needed for government purposes.

Public sale: An auction sale of property with notice to the general public beforehand.

Punch list: An itemized list that documents incomplete or unsatisfactory items after the contractor has declared the space to be mostly complete.

Purchase and Sale (P&S) Agreement: The written contract the buyer and seller both sign defining the terms and conditions under which a property is sold.

Purchasers policy: A title insurance furnished by a seller to a purchaser under a real estate sales contract insuring the property against defects in title. Also called an owners policy.

- Q -

Quadraplex: A four-plex; a dwelling unit containing four separate residential units.

Qualification: Reviewing a borrower's credit and payment capacity before approving a loan.

Qualified acceptance: An acceptance, in law, that amounts to a rejection of an offer and is a counteroffer; an acceptance of an offer upon certain conditions, or a qualification that has the effect of altering or modifying the terms of an offer.

Qualified buyer: An individual or company who is in the market and displays some evidence of being financially able to buy a home or property within a specific price range.

Qualifying ratio: The measurement a lender uses to determine how much they are willing to lend to a potential buyer.

Quitclaim deed: A written document that releases a party from any interest they may have in a property; in real estate terms, a conveyance by which the grantor transfers whatever interest he or she has in the real estate, without warranties or obligations.

- R -

Radon: A naturally occurring gas that is suspected of causing lung cancer.

Rafter: The structural member that supports a roof.

Range of value: The market value of a property, usually stated as an amount between a high and a low limit. For example, real estate brokers often estimate a range of value for a property to help the owner determine the listing price.

Rate lock: The commitment of a lender to a borrower that guarantees a certain interest rate for a specific amount of time.

Raw land: A piece of property that has not been developed and remains in its natural state.

Ready, willing, and able buyer: One who is prepared to buy property on the seller's terms and is ready to take positive steps to consummate the transaction; capable of an action, and disposed to take that action.

Real Estate Settlement Procedures Act (RESPA): The federal law that requires certain disclosures to consumers about mortgage loan settlements. The law also prohibits the payment or receipt of kickbacks and certain

kinds of referral fees. It also requires lenders to notify borrowers regarding closing costs in advance.

Real estate: Land and everything more or less attached to it; ownership below to the center of the earth and above to the heavens; the activities concerned with ownership and transfer of physical property.

Real estate agent: An individual who is licensed to negotiate and transact the real estate sales.

Real estate fundamentals: The factors that drive the value of property.

Real Estate Investment Trust (REIT): Trust ownership of real estate by a group of individuals who purchase certificates of ownership in the trust, which in turn invests the money in real property and distributes the profits back to the investors free of corporate income tax.

Real estate license law: State law enacted to protect the public from fraud, dishonesty, and incompetence in the purchase and sale of real estate.

Real Estate Owned (REO): The real estate that a savings institution owns as a result of foreclosure on borrowers in default; properties that did not sell at foreclosure auction and have reverted to ownership by the lender.

Real estate recovery fund: A fund established in some states from real estate license revenues to cover claims of aggrieved parties who have suffered monetary damage through the actions of a real estate licensee.

Real property: The interests, benefits, and rights inherent in real estate ownership; land and anything else of a permanent nature that is affixed to the land.

Realtist: A member of a national organization known as the National Association of Real Estate Brokers (NAREB).

REALTOR®: A registered trademark term reserved for the sole use of active members of local REALTOR® boards affiliated with the National Association of REALTORS®.

Reasonable time: A fair length of time that may be allowed or required for an act to be completed considering the nature of the act and the surrounding circumstances. Contracts that do not include reasonable time frames for the completion of acts are often challengeable in court.

Recapture clause: A clause in a contract permitting the party who grants an interest or right to take it back under certain conditions. A recapture clause may also be used to give a ground lessee the right to purchase the fee after a set period of time has elapsed.

Recapture rate: A term used in appraisals to describe the rate of recovery of an investment.

Reciprocal easements: Easements and restrictions limiting the use of the land for the benefit of all owners in a subdivision or development; easements that apply to all involved.

Reclamation: Causing a change in land from an unusable or undevelopable state to a developable state; converting wasted natural resources into productive assets. Draining swampland would be considered reclamation.

Reconveyance: An event that occurs when a mortgage debt is retired—the lender conveys the ownership back to the borrower, free of the debt.

Record owner: The owner of record; the owner of the property as shown by an examination of the records; the individual or company having recorded title.

Record title: Title as it appears from an examination of public records; the title on record.

Recording: The act of entering or recording documents affecting or conveying interests in real estate in the recorder's office established in each county. Until it is recorded, a deed or mortgage ordinarily is not effective against subsequent purchasers or mortgagees; the documentation that the registrar's office keeps of the details of properly executed legal documents.

Recording fee: A fee real estate agents charge for moving the sale

of a piece of property into the public record.

Recreational lease: A contract in which the lessor leases recreational facilities to a tenant for rent considerations. Typically offered by developers of large subdivisions that include swimming pools, tennis courts, or other recreational facilities constructed by the developer but for use by the residents.

Rectangular (government) survey system: A system established in 1785 by the federal government, providing for surveying and describing land by reference to principal meridians and base lines.

Redlining: An illegal practice of a lender who refuses to make home loans in certain areas, regardless of the qualifications of prospective borrowers.

Reentry: The legal right of a landlord to possess the property when the term for possession by the tenant has expired.

Referral agency: A brokerage company where licensed salespeople agree to obtain leads only on prospective buyers and sellers; no other real estate services are permitted. The referral agency then receives a fee on sale from the agency referred to.

Refinance: To replace an old loan with a new loan; to pay off one loan with the proceeds from another loan.

Registered land: Land that is registered in the Torrens system.

Registrar: The person who maintains accurate and official records like deeds, mortgages, and other recorded documents.

Regulation: A rule or order prescribed for management or government. Regulations frequently have the force and effect of law.

Regulation Z: A federal legislation under the Truth in Lending Act that requires lenders to advise the borrower in writing of all costs that are associated with the credit portion of a financial transaction.

Rehab (Short for Rehabilitation): Refers to an extensive renovation intended to extend the life of a building or project.

Rehabilitate: To restore a structure to the condition of good repair.

Rehabilitation mortgage: A loan meant to fund the repairing and improving of a resale home or building.

Reinstatement: To bring something back to its prior position. A defaulted loan that is returned to paid-up status is considered a reinstatement.

Reissue rate: A reduced charge by a title insurance company for a new policy if a previous policy on the same property was recently issued.

Release: To free real estate from a mortgage; also known as a release of lien.

Relocation clause: A lease stipulation that allows the landlord to move the tenant to another dwelling within the building.

Relocation company: A company that contracts with other firms to arrange the relocation of an employee from one city to another. Typically handles the sale of a home and the purchase of a new home, along with other moving-related services.

Remaining balance: The amount of the principal on a home loan that has not yet been paid.

Remaining term: The original term of the loan after the number of payments made has been subtracted; the number of payments or time period left on a loan.

Remediation: Corrective action to clean up an environmentally contaminated site or to reduce the contamination to an acceptable level.

Rendering: Drawing or painting showing a perspective view of a prospective development to show how it will look when completed; typically an artistic view rather than a merely technical view of the proposed development or property.

Renegotiation of lease: The review of an existing lease at a specific time to negotiate new lease terms.

Renewal option: A clause in a lease agreement that allows a tenant to extend the term of a lease.

Rent: The fee paid for the occupancy and/or use of any rental property or equipment.

Rent control: Regulations by state or local governments restricting the amount of rent landlords can charge tenants; designed to keep the cost of housing affordable for residents.

Rent escalation: Adjustment of rent by the landlord to cover changes in cost of living or for property maintenance costs.

Rent roll: A list of tenants showing the lease rent and the expiration rate for each tenant.

Rent schedule: A statement of proposed rental rates, determined by the owner or the property manager or both, based on a building's estimated expenses, market supply and demand, and the owner's long-range goals for the property.

Rental agency: A person who is compensated or receives

consideration to act as an intermediary between a landlord and a prospective tenant.

Rental agreement: A written or oral agreement that establishes or modifies the terms and conditions concerning the use and occupancy of a dwelling and its premises.

Rental growth rate: The projected trend of market rental rates over a particular period of analysis.

Repairs: Work performed to restore a property to a former condition without extending its useful life. An improvement is not a repair. Repairs are operating expenses, not capital expenses.

Replacement cost: The projected cost by current standards of constructing a building that is equivalent to the building being appraised.

Replacement reserve fund: Money that is set aside for replacing of common property in a condominium, PUD, or cooperative project.

Reproduction cost: The construction cost at current prices of an exact duplicate of the subject property.

Request for Proposal (RFP): A formal request that invites investment managers to submit information regarding investment strategies, historical investment performance, current investment opportunities, investment management fees, and other pension fund client relationships used by their firm.

Rescission: The practice of one party's canceling or terminating a contract, which has the effect of returning the parties to their original positions before the contract was made.

Reserve account: An account that must be funded by the borrower to protect the lender.

Reserve fund: An account maintained to provide funds for anticipated expenditures to maintain a building. Reserve funds are typically held in escrow.

Residence: The place where one lives, particularly the dwelling where one lives.

Resident manager: Individual who supervises the care of an apartment complex while living in one of the units in the complex.

Resort property: Property that lends itself to vacationers, recreation, or leisure activity because of its natural resources, beauty, or its improvements. Beaches, lakes, golf courses, and ski resorts are all considered resort properties.

Restriction: A limitation placed on the use of property, contained in the deed or other written instrument, or in local ordinances.

Restrictive covenant: A clause in a deed that limits the way the real estate ownership may be used.

Resubdivision: Taking an existing subdivision and dividing it even further into additional lots.

Retainage: Money earned by a contractor but not paid to the contractor until the completion of construction or at other agreed-upon stages or dates.

Retaining wall: A vertical partition used to restrict the movement of soil or water.

Revenue stamp: Stamps affixed to deeds and other documents to indicate the payment of the state's transfer tax.

Reverse mortgage: A type of mortgage designed for persons with substantial equity where the lender makes periodic payments to the borrower; the payments are taken from the equity in the property.

Review appraiser: An appraiser who specializes in appraisal reviews. Typically a review appraiser works for a bank or the government.

Revolving debt: A credit arrangement which enables a customer to borrow against a predetermined line of credit when purchasing goods and services.

Rider: An amendment or attachment to a contract; an addendum.

Right of first refusa:l A lease clause that gives a tenant the first opportunity to buy a property or to lease additional space in a property at the same price and terms as those contained in an offer from a third-party that the owner has expressed a willingness to accept.

Right of way: The right given by one landowner to another to pass over the land, construct a roadway, or use as a pathway, without actually transferring ownership.

Right to rescission: A legal provision that enables borrowers to cancel certain loan types within three days after they sign.

Right to use: The legal right to use or occupy a property.

Roll over risk: The possibility that tenants will not renew their lease.

Roof inspection clause: A clause sometimes inserted in real estate contracts stating that the seller must supply a report of the kind and condition of a structure's roof. If the roof is found to be faulty or in disrepair, it must be repaired at the seller's expense.

Rooming house: A house where bedrooms are furnished to paying guests; can, but does not have to, assume kitchen privileges are granted.

Row house: Single family dwelling units attached to each other by common walls, usually with a common façade.

Rules and regulations: Real estate licensing authority orders that govern licensees' activities; they usually have the same force and effect as statutory law.

Run with the land: An expression indicating a right or restriction that affects all current and future owners of a property; the right "runs with the land."

Rural: An area outside large and moderate-sized cities and their surrounding population concentrations.

R-value: A measure of the heat conductivity of a material; used to designate the insulation quality of building materials.

- S -

Sale and leaseback: A transaction in which an owner sells his or her improved property and, as part of the same transaction, signs a long-term lease to remain in possession of the premises.

Sales associate: Licensed salesperson or broker who works for a broker.

Sales comparison approach: The process of estimating the value of a property by examining and comparing actual sales of comparable properties.

Sales contract: An agreement that both the buyer and seller sign defining the terms of a property sale.

Salesperson: A person who performs real estate activities while employed by or associated with a licensed real estate broker.

Satellite tenant: Tenants in a shopping center or mall other than the anchor tenants.

Scarcity: A lack of supply of some commodity or item; in real estate terms, the scarcity of available properties (supply) tends to lead to an increase in prices if the number of buyers is high (demand).

Schematics: Preliminary architectural drawings and sketches created at the planning stage of a project; basic layouts not containing final details.

Seasoned loan: A loan on which several payments have been received or collected.

Second mortgage: A secondary loan obtained upon a piece of property; a subordinated lien created over a mortgage loan.

Secondary financing: A junior mortgage placed on property to help finance the purchase price. Most government loan programs, like FHA or VA loans, permit secondary financing with certain restrictions.

Section 8 housing: Privately owned rental dwelling units participating in the government's low income rental housing assistance program. The Department of Housing and Urban Development pays a portion of the fair market rent value, with the tenant paying the other portion.

Security deposit: A payment by a tenant, held by the landlord during the lease term, and kept (wholly or partially) on default, or on destruction of the premises by the tenant.

Seller carry back: An arrangement in which the seller provides some or all of the financing to purchase a home.

Seller financing: A debt instrument taken by the seller to provide financing to a buyer.

Seller's market: Economic conditions that favor sellers, due to circumstances like a scarcity of supply or excessive demand.

Selling broker: The licensed real estate broker that finds or brings forth the buyer.

Semi-detached dwelling: A residence that shares one wall with an adjoining building, sometimes called a party wall.

Servicer: An organization that collects principal and interest payments from borrowers and manages borrowers' escrow accounts on behalf of a trustee.

Setback: The amount of space local zoning regulations require between a lot line and a building line; the distance required from a given reference point before a structure can be built.

Settlement: The same as closing; the act of adjusting and prorating the credits and charges to conclude a real estate transaction.

Settlement or closing fees: Fees that the escrow agent receives for carrying out the written instructions in the agreement between borrower and lender and/ or buyer and seller.

Shell lease: A lease in which a tenant leases the unfinished shell of a building and agrees to complete construction.

Short sale: A sale of secured real property that results in less money than is owed the lender. The lender releases its mortgage so the property can be sold free and clear to the new purchaser. By doing so, the lender has cut its losses by agreeing to a short sale instead of initiating the foreclosure process.

Sick building syndrome: A phrase used to describe indoor air quality problems in commercial and industrial problems that lead to headaches, nausea, and skin and eye irritations.

Sight line: A view plane; a direction of view along a specific orientation or plane.

Silent second: An unrecorded second mortgage, typically kept secret from the underlying first mortgage.

Single family residence: A residential structure designed to include one dwelling, or to house one family; a private home.

Site: A plot of land prepared for or underlying a structure or development; the location of a property.

Site analysis: A determination of how suitable a specific parcel of land is for a particular use.

Site development: The implementation of all improvements that are needed for a site before construction may begin.

Site plan: A detailed description and map of the location of improvements to a parcel.

Slab: The flat, exposed surface that is laid over the structural support beams to form the floor of a building.

Slum clearance: The clearing of old decrepit buildings to allow the land to be put to a better and more productive use; frequently referred to as urban renewal.

Small claims court: A court where claims of typically less than $1,000 are adjudicated; provides a relatively inexpensive forum for the disposition of minor controversies or disagreements.

Soft money: Money contributed to a development or investment that is tax deductible; a term used to describe costs that do not physically go into construction, like interest during construction, legal fees, and architectural fees.

Solar heating: A natural system of heating using the energy of the sun to provide heat to the household or to heat water.

Sole proprietorship: Ownership of a business with no formal entity created as a business structure; a business owner with no partners.

Space plan: A chart or map of space requirements for a tenant which include wall/door locations, room sizes, and even furniture layouts.

Spec ("Speculative") home: A single family dwelling constructed in anticipation of finding a buyer. A spec home is built by a contractor in hopes of finding a buyer, and not due to a contract already reached with a buyer to build the home.

Special assessment: A tax or levy customarily imposed against only those specific parcels of real estate that will benefit from a proposed public improvement like a street or sewer.

Special conditions: Specific conditions in a real estate contract that must be satisfied before a contract is considered binding; frequently referred to as a contingency.

Special use permit: A right granted by a zoning authority to conduct certain activities not normally allowed within the zoning district. Also called a conditional use permit.

Special warranty deed: A deed in which the grantor warrants, or guarantees, the title only against defects arising during the period of his or her tenure and ownership of the property and not against defects existing before that time, generally using the language, "by, through, or under the grantor but not otherwise."

Specifications: Detailed instructions provided in conjunction with plans and blueprints for construction. Specifications frequently describe the materials to be used, dimensions, colors, or construction techniques.

Speculation: An investment or other decision whose success depends on an event or change that is not certain to occur. A developer may purchase land for a higher than market price based on his or her speculation that a zoning change will take place that will increase the value of the property.

Spite fence: A fence that is erected of a height or type designed to annoy a neighbor. Some states have statutes restricting the height of a fence to avoid the spite fence situation.

Split level: A home with a one-story wing constructed beside or between the levels of a two-story wing.

Splitting fees: Sharing compensation. In real estate terms, a broker can generally only split a commission with the buyer, seller, or another licensed real estate salesperson.

Spot loan: A loan on a particular property (usually a condominium) by a lender who has not previously financed that particular condominium project. Many lenders are unwilling to lend money for a single unit in a large condominium development unless they receive special fees for legal fees and other services.

Spot zoning: Rezoning a parcel of land where all surrounding parcels are zoned for a different use. Spot zoning is usually disallowed in courts.

Square foot method: The appraisal method of estimating building costs by multiplying

the number of square feet in the improvements being appraised by the cost per square foot for recently constructed similar improvements.

Staging: A temporary scaffolding used to support workers and materials; a slang term used to describe the process of preparing a home for viewing by prospective buyers.

Staking: Identifying the boundaries of a parcel of land by placing stakes or pins in the ground, or by painting marks on stone walls or rocks. Staking shows the boundaries of the property but does not show the existence of possible encroachments.

Standard metropolitan statistical area: A designation given to counties with at least one central city with 50,000 or more residents.

Standards of Practice: The code of ethics created by the National Association of REALTORS® describing the ethical behaviors licensees are expected to follow.

Starts: The term used to indicate the number of residential units begun within a specific period of time.

State certified appraiser: An appraiser certified by a state to conduct residential or general appraisals.

Statute: A law established by an act of legislature.

Statute of limitations: The law pertaining to the period of time within which certain actions must be brought to court.

Stigmatized property: A property that has acquired an undesirable reputation due to an event that occurred on or near it, such as violent crime, gang-related activity, illness, or personal tragedy. Some states restrict the disclosure of information about stigmatized properties.

Straight lease: Otherwise known as a gross lease agreement, which specifies an amount of rent that should be paid regularly during the complete term of the lease. Also referred to as a "flat lease."

Straw man: A person who purchases property that is then conveyed to another in order to conceal the identity of the eventual purchaser.

Street: A fully improved roadway serving local traffic.

Strip center: Any shopping area that is made up of a row of stores but is not large enough to be anchored by a grocery or department store; also known as a strip mall.

Structural alterations: Changes to the supporting members of a building.

Structural defects: Damage to the load-bearing portion of a home that affects the use of the home for dwelling purposes; includes damage from shifting soil not due to earthquake or flood.

Structural density: The ratio of the total ground floor area of a building to the total land area of the lot. The typical density for a general purpose industrial building is approximately one to three zones.

Structure: Any constructed improvement to a site; may include buildings, fences, garages, sheds, or utility buildings.

Studio: An efficiency unit or apartment.

Sub agency: The relationship under which a sales agent attempts to sell a property listed with another agent. Sub agency is common under multiple listing service arrangements.

Sub prime loan: A loan offered to applicants with less than high credit ratings. Sub prime loans typically carry higher interest rates and higher fees.

Subagent: One who is employed by a person already acting as an agent. Typically a reference to a salesperson licensed under a broker (agent) who is employed under the terms of a listing agreement.

Subcontractor: A contractor who has been hired by the general contractor, often specializing in a certain required task for the construction project.

Subdivision: A tract of land divided by the owner, known as the sub-divider, into blocks, building

lots, and streets according to a recorded subdivision plat, which must comply with local ordinances and regulations; the most common type of housing development created by dividing a larger tract of land into individual lots for sale or lease.

Subdivision and development ordinances: Municipal ordinances that establish requirements for subdivisions and development.

Subjective value: The amount a specific person might pay to possess a property. Also referred to as personal value.

Sublease: A lease from a lessee to another lessee. The new lessee becomes a sub lessee or tenant.

Subletting: Leasing a premise by a lessee to a third party for part of the lessee's remaining term. Also known as subleasing.

Subordinate financing: Any loan with a priority lower than loans that were obtained beforehand.

Subordinate loan: A second or third mortgage obtained with the same property being used as collateral.

Subordinated classes: Classes that have the lowest priority of receiving payments from underlying mortgage loans.

Subordination: The act of sharing credit loss risk at varying rates among two or more classes of securities; relegation to a lesser position, usually in respect to a right or security.

Subordination clause: A clause or document that permits a mortgage recorded at a later date to take priority over an existing mortgage.

Subpoena duces tecum: A court order to produce books, records, and other documents.

Subscribe: To place a signature at the end of a document.

Subsidized housing: Apartments, nursing homes, or single family dwellings that receive a government subsidy.

Substantial improvement: Any improvement made to a building at least three years after the building was placed in service;

improvements made over 25 percent of the value of the building over a two-year period.

Sub-surface rights: Ownership rights in a parcel of real estate to the water, minerals, gas, oil, and so forth that lie beneath the surface of the property.

Summary possession: Eviction; the process used by a landlord to regain possession of the leased premises if the tenant has breached the lease or remains after the term of the lease.

Super jumbo mortgage: A term that classifies a loan that is over $650,000 for some lenders, and over $1,000,000 for others.

Superfund: A commonly used name for the federal environmental cleanup law that requires previous owners to clean up waste on a particular site. Existence on the Superfund list imposes strict liability on the parties involved.

Supply and demand: The appraisal principle that follows the interrelationship of the supply of and demand for real estate. As appraising is based on economic concepts, this principle recognizes that real property is subject to the influences of the marketplace just as is any other commodity.

Surcharge: Additional rent charged to tenants who consume utility services in excess of the amounts allowed in the terms of the lease.

Surety: A person who willingly binds himself to the debt or obligation of another party.

Surety bond: An agreement by an insurance or bonding company to be responsible for certain possible defaults, debts, or obligations contracted for by an insured party; in essence, a policy insuring one's personal and/or financial integrity. In the real estate business a surety bond is generally used to ensure that a particular project will be completed at a certain date or that a contract will be performed as stated.

Surface water: Diffused storm water, not a concentrated flow within a stream.

Surrender: The cancellation of a lease by mutual consent of the lessor and the lessee.

Survey: The process by which boundaries are measured and land areas are determined; the on-site measurement of lot lines, dimensions, and position of a house on a lot, including the determination of any existing encroachments or easements.

Survivorship : The right of a joint tenant or joint tenants to maintain ownership rights following the death of another joint tenant.

Sweat equity: A slang expression describing non-cash improvements that an owner adds to a piece of property. Refers to work performed personally by the owner or owners.

- T -

Takeout financing: A commitment to provide permanent financing following construction of a planned project. The takeout commitment is generally based on specific conditions, such as the completion of a certain number of units, or sales of a certain percentage of units. Most construction lenders require takeout financing.

Tangible personal property:
Property that can be seen, touched, and moved without great difficulty; excludes real estate.

Tangible property: Real estate and other valuables that can be seen and touched.

Tax base: The determined value of all property that lies within the jurisdiction of the taxing authority.

Tax certificate: The document issued to a person as a receipt for paying delinquent taxes on a property owned by another, entitling the person to receive a deed to the property if the property is not redeemed within a certain period of time.

Tax deed: An instrument, similar to a certificate of sale, given to a purchaser at a tax sale. See also certificate of sale.

Tax deferred exchange: A transaction where a property is traded for the promise to provide a replacement like-kind property in the near future. By delaying the exchange, the party involved can defer taxable gains on the original

property. Also known as a tax free exchange, or a 1031 exchange.

Tax lien: A charge against property created by operation of law. Tax liens and assessments take priority over all other liens.

Tax map: A document showing the location, dimensions, and other information pertaining to a parcel of land subject to property taxes. Usually kept as a public record at a local tax office or courthouse.

Tax rate: The ratio of a tax assessment to the amount being taxed. The tax rate is established according to assessed valuations.

Tax sale: A court-ordered sale of real property to raise money to cover delinquent taxes.

Teaser rate: A low, short-term interest rate offered on a mortgage in order to convince the potential borrower to apply.

Tenancy at sufferance: Tenancy established when a person who had been a lawful tenant wrongfully remains in possession of property after the expiration of a lease.

Tenancy at will: A license to use or occupy lands and buildings at the will of the owner. The tenant may leave the property at any time, or the owner may require the tenant to leave at any time.

Tenancy in common: A form of co-ownership by which each owner holds an undivided interest in real property as if he or she were the sole owner. Each individual owner has the right to partition. Unlike joint tenants, tenants in common have right of inheritance.

Tenant: One who holds or possesses lands or tenements by any kind of right or title; also called a lessee.

Tenant at will: A person who possesses a piece of real estate with the owner's permission.

Tenant contributions: All costs the tenant is responsible for in excess of normal rent payments; for example, cutting the grass, if required by the lease, is considered a tenant contribution.

Tenant improvement (TI): The upgrades or repairs that are made to the leased premises by or for a tenant.

Tenant Improvement allowance: The specified amount of money that the landlord contributes toward tenant improvements.

Tender: An offer to perform an obligation; to perform under contract; to pay or deliver.

Tenement: Possessions that are permanent and fixed; structures attached to land; older apartment units.

Termination of listing: The cancellation of a broker employment contract.

Termite inspection: An examination of a structure by a qualified person to determine the existence of termite infestation. Most sales contracts as well as an FHA-backed loan will require a termite inspection.

Termite shield: Metal sheeting placed in the exterior walls of a house near ground level to prevent termites from entering the house.

Testimonium: A clause that cites the act and date in a deed or other conveyance. A testimonium could read: "In witness whereof, the parties to these presents have hereunto set their hands and seals this day and year."

Thin market: A real estate market where there are few buyers and sellers and a slow rate of turnover of properties. Also called a limited market.

Third party: A person who is not directly involved in a transaction or contract but may be involved or affected by it.

Time is of the essence: A phrase in a contract that requires the performance of a certain act within a stated period of time.

Time value of money: An economic principle that states that the value of a dollar received today is worth more than the value of a dollar received in the future, since the dollar received in the future cannot be invested or enjoyed at present.

Timeshare: A form of ownership involving purchasing a specific period of time or percentage of interest in a vacation property.

Timeshare Ownership Plan (TSO): A form of timesharing in which a number of individuals hold title to a particular unit as tenants in common, entitling each to use the property at specified times during the year.

Title: The right to or ownership of land; the evidence of ownership of land.

Title company: A business that determines that a property title is clear and that provides title insurance.

Title exam: An analysis of the public records to confirm that the seller is the legal owner and there are no encumbrances on the property.

Title insurance: A policy insuring the owner or mortgagee against loss by reason of defects in the title to a parcel of real estate, other than encumbrances, defects, and matters specifically excluded by the policy.

Title report: A preliminary report indicating the current state of the title. Does not describe the chain of title.

Title search: The process of analyzing all transactions existing in the public record to determine whether any title defects could interfere with the clear transfer of property ownership.

Topography: The nature of the surface of the land; the land's contour.

Total expense ratio: The comparison of monthly debt obligations to gross monthly income.

Total inventory: The total amount of square footage commanded by property within a geographical area.

Total lender fees: Charges which the lender requires for obtaining the loan, aside from other fees associated with the transfer of a property.

Total monthly housing costs: The amount that must be paid each month to cover principal, interest, property taxes, PMI, and/or either hazard insurance or homeowners' association dues.

Townhouse: An attached home that is not considered to be a condominium.

Township: The principal unit of the rectangular (government) survey system. A township is a square with six-mile sides and an area of 36 square miles.

Township lines: All the lines in a rectangular survey system that run east and west, parallel to the base line six miles apart.

Township tiers: Township lines that form strips of land and are designated by consecutive numbers north or south of the base line.

Track record: A developer or builder's reputation for producing on a timely and economical basis; the history of a real estate salesperson or broker's sales performance.

Tract: A parcel of land generally held for subdividing; a subdivision.

Tract house: A dwelling that has a similar style and floor plan to those of other houses in a development.

Trade fixture: Any personal property that is attached to a structure and used in the business but is removable once the lease is terminated.

Transfer of ownership: Any process in which a property changes hands from one owner to another.

Transfer tax: An amount specified by state or local authorities when ownership in a piece of property changes hands.

Tread: The horizontal surface of a stair resting on the riser. The tread is the part of the stairs that is stepped on.

Treasury Index: A measurement that is used to derive interest rate changes for ARMs.

Treble damages: Damages provided for by statute in certain cases; calls for a tripling of the actual damages.

Trespass: Unlawful entry or possession of property.

Triple net lease ("NNN"): A lease that requires the tenant to pay all property expenses on top of the rental payments.

Triplex: A building with three apartment or townhouse units.

Truss: A type of roof construction using a framework of beams or members that support the roof load and leaves wide spans between supports.

Trust account: A separate bank account segregated from a broker's own funds, in which a broker is required to deposit all monies collected for clients. In some states, this is referred to as an escrow account.

Trust deed: An instrument used to create a mortgage lien by which the borrower conveys title to a trustee, who holds it as security for the benefit of the note holder (the lender); also called a deed of trust.

Truth in lending: The federal legislation requiring lenders to disclose the terms and conditions of a mortgage in writing.

Turn key project: A project in which someone other than the owner is responsible for the construction of a building or for tenant improvements; a development in which the developer is responsible for completing the entire project on behalf of the buyer.

Turnover: The rate at which tenants, salespersons, or employees leave; the frequency with which property in a particular area is bought and sold.

- U -

Under contract: The period of time during which a buyer's offer to purchase a property has been accepted, and the buyer is able to finalize financing arrangements without the concern of the seller making a deal with another buyer.

Underfloor ducts: Floor channels that provide for the flexible placement of telephone and electrical lines in commercial and office buildings.

Underground storage tank: A tank below ground level that stores liquids, including fuels, industrial products, or waste.

Under improvement: A structure or development of lower cost than the highest and best use of a site.

Undersigned: The person whose name appears signed at the end of a document; the subscriber.

Underwriting: The process during which lenders analyze the risks a particular borrower presents and set appropriate conditions for the loan.

Underwriting fee: A fee that mortgage lenders charge for verifying the information on the loan application and making a final decision on approving the loan.

Undisclosed agency: A relationship between an agent and a client where the client is unaware that the agent represents the other party in the transaction. Many states require licensed agents to disclose their agency relationships.

Undivided interest: An ownership right to use and possess a property that is shared among co-owners, with no co-owner having exclusive right to any portion of the property.

Unencumbered: A term that refers to property free of liens or other encumbrances.

Unenforceable contract: A contract that has all the elements of a valid contract, yet neither party can sue the other to force performance of it. For example, an unsigned contract is generally unenforceable.

Unethical: Lacking in moral principles, failing to conform to an accepted code of behavior.

Unfair and deceptive practices: A practice is unfair if it is immoral, unethical, oppressive, or if it is intended to deceive or mislead.

Unfinished office space: Space in a building without dividing walls, lighting, ceilings, air conditioning, and other services. Typically a landlord leases unfinished space after providing standard items or by providing a construction allowance amount to the tenant.

Uniform Residential Appraisal Report (URAR): A standard form for reporting the appraisal of a dwelling. The URAR is required by major secondary mortgage purchases and includes checklists and definitions printed on the form.

Uniform Settlement Statement: A special HUD form that itemizes all charges to be paid by a borrower and seller in connection with the settlement (usually a HUD-1 form).

Unimproved land: Land that has received no development, construction, or site preparation.

Unit: A suite of rooms making up a residence for one tenant. A unit generally has a separate entrance.

Unmarketable title: A title that contains substantial defects; may require a quiet title suit to repair.

Unrecorded deed: A deed that transfers right of ownership from one owner to another without being officially documented.

Unsecured loan: A loan that has no collateral or security pledged. An unsecured loan is approved based on the reputation and credit history of the borrower, not on the value of an underlying asset.

Upgrades: Changes in design or improvements to a property after the purchase but before the closing date. The purchaser typically absorbs the cost for upgrades.

Upside down: A slang phrase for a borrower that owes more in debt for a property than the value of the property itself.

Upzoning: Changing zoning classification from lower to higher use.

Urban: Real estate located in an area of high density development; frequently referred to as a city.

Urban renewal: Redeveloping deteriorated sections of a city through demolition and new construction, or through extensive rehabilitation. Many urban renewal projects are government funded or subsidized.

Urban sprawl: A term used to describe low density development in suburban areas adjacent to a major city. Residents of those areas typically commute back into the city for employment or shopping.

Usable square footage: The total area that is included within the exterior walls of the tenant's space.

Use: The particular purpose for which a property is intended to be employed.

Use tax: Tax imposed on the purchaser or importer of tangible personal property.

Useful life: The economic period during which a cash flow is expected; the period to depreciate a building for tax purposes.

Usury: Charging interest at a higher rate than the maximum rate established by state law.

Utilities: Services like water, sewer, electricity, telephone, and gas that are generally required to operate a building or a residence. Also used to describe the charges for utility services.

Utility easement: Use of another's property for the purpose of running electric, water, gas, or sewer lines.

- V -

VA loan: A mortgage loan on approved property made to a qualified veteran by an authorized lender and guaranteed by the Department of Veterans Affairs to limit the lender's possible loss.

Vacancy factor: The percentage of gross revenue that pro forma income statements expect to be lost due to vacancies.

Vacancy rate: The percentage of space that is available to rent.

Vacate: To move out.

Vacation home: A dwelling used occasionally by the owner for recreational or resort purposes. Can be rented to others for a portion of the year.

Valid contract: A contract that complies with all the essentials of a contract and is binding and enforceable on all parties.

Valuable consideration: A type of promised payment upon which a promisee can enforce a claim against an unwilling promisor. Can be in the form of money or time.

Value added: The anticipated increase in property value expected from fixing a condition causing depreciation or from improving a service or condition.

Variable payment plan: Any mortgage repayment schedule that provides for periodic changes in the amount of monthly payments.

Variable rate: The interest rate on a loan that varies over the term of the loan according to a predetermined index; also called **adjustable rate mortgage**.

Variance: Permission obtained from zoning authorities to build a structure or conduct a use that is expressly prohibited by the current zoning laws; an exception from the zoning ordinances.

Vendors lien: A lien belonging to a vendor for unpaid purchase price of land, where the vendor has not taken any other lien or security beyond the personal obligation of the purchaser.

Veneer: Wood or brick exterior that covers a less attractive or less expensive surface.

Vent: A small opening to allow the passage of air.

Verification: Sworn statements before a qualified officer that the contents of an instrument are correct.

Verification of Deposit (VOD): The confirmation statement a borrower's bank may be asked to sign to verify the borrower's account balances and history.

Verification of Employment (VOE): The confirmation statement a borrower's employer may be asked to sign in order to verify the borrower's position and salary.

Vestibule: A small entrance hall to a building or to a room.

Veterans Administration (VA): The federal government agency that assists veterans in purchasing a home without a down payment. In general, a veteran who has served more than 120 days active duty is eligible for a home loan with no down payment.

Villa: A one-story residence often owned as a condominium, and usually built in units of two or four, including an enclosed parking area and a yard.

Violation: An act, deed, or condition contrary to law or to permissible use of real property.

Visual rights: The right to prevent a structure like a billboard from being placed where it would obstruct a scenic view.

Voluntary lien: A lien placed on property with the knowledge and consent of the property owner.

- W -

Wainscoting: Facing of the lower part of an interior wall.

Waiver: The voluntary renunciation, abandonment, or surrender of a claim, right, or privilege.

Walk through: Final inspection of a property just before closing to assure the buyer that the property is vacant and no damage has occurred.

Walkup: An apartment building with several levels and no elevator.

Wall to wall carpeting: Carpeting that fully covers the floor area in a room.

Warehouse: A structure designed for the storage of commercial inventory.

Warehouse fee: A closing cost fee that represents the lender's expense of temporarily holding a borrower's loan before it is sold on the secondary mortgage market.

Warranty: A promise contained in a contract; a promise that certain stated facts are true.

Warranty deed: A deed that contains a covenant that the grantor will protect the grantee against any and all claims.

Waste line: A pipe that carries water from a bathtub, shower, sink, or other fixture, excluding a toilet.

Water rights: Common Law rights held by owners of land adjacent to rivers, lakes, or oceans, including restrictions on those rights and land ownership.

Water table: The upper level at which underground water is normally found in a particular area.

Waterfront property: Real estate abutting a body of water such as a lake, river, canal, or ocean.

Way: A street, alley, or other thoroughfare permanently established for the passage of people or vehicles.

Wear and tear: Physical deterioration of property as the result of use, weathering, and age.

Weep hole: Small holes left in a wall to permit the drainage of surplus water.

Weighted average rental rates: The average ratio of unequal rental rates across two or more buildings in a market.

Wetlands: Land normally saturated with water. Marshes and swamps are wetlands. Wetlands are typically protected from development by environmental law.

Will: A written document, properly witnessed, providing for the transfer of title to property owned by the deceased, called the testator.

Without recourse: Words used in endorsing a note or bill to signify that the holder is not to seek recourse from the debtor in the event of nonpayment. The creditor only has recourse to the property.

Work letter: A detailed addition to a lease defining all improvement work to be done by the landlord, and specifying what work the tenant will perform at his or her own expense.

Workers Compensation Acts: Laws that require an employer to obtain insurance coverage to protect his or her employees who are injured in the course of their employment.

Working drawings: The detailed blueprints for a construction project that comprise the contractual documents which describe the exact manner in which a project is to be built.

Wraparound debt: Mortgage debt in which the face amount of the loan overstates the actual debt; incorporates a special agreement between the parties for payment of debt service on the existing mortgage.

Wraparound mortgage: A loan obtained by a buyer to use for the remaining balance on the seller's first mortgage, as well as an additional amount requested by the seller.

Writ of execution: A court order authorizing an officer of the court to sell property of the defendant to satisfy a judgment.

Write off: A procedure used in accounting when an asset is determined to be uncollectible and is therefore considered to be a loss.

- X Y Z -

X: A mark that can substitute for a signature in some cases, if a person cannot write. Requires the presence and affirmation of a notary.

X bracing: Cross bracing in a partition.

Yard: The open grounds of a property.

Year to year tenancy: A periodic tenancy in which the rent is reserved from year to year.

Yield: The actual return on an investment, usually paid in dividends or interest.

Yield spread: The difference in income derived from a commercial mortgage and from a benchmark value. Also the difference between a mortgage's wholesale rate and retail rate. Mortgage brokers get paid primarily via maintaining a yield spread.

Zero lot line: A form of cluster housing development where individual dwelling units are placed on separately platted lots. Units may be attached to one another, but do not have to be.

Zone condemnation: The demolition and clearance of entire areas to make room for new construction.

Zoning: The act of dividing a city or town into particular areas and applying laws and regulations regarding the architectural design, structure, and intended uses of buildings within those areas.

Zoning ordinance: The regulations and laws that control the use or improvement of land in a particular area or zone.

Pre-Approval Letter

ABC Mortgage Company
Date

RE: Buyer First and Last Name

Dear Buyer First and Last Name,

This will confirm that ABC Mortgage Company has obtained a copy of your credit report and reviewed your loan scenario. We have utilized Desktop Underwriting and are pleased to inform you that you are pre-approved for the following:

Purchase Price: $137,000
Loan Amount: $137,000
Loan Program: USDA

This pre-approval letter is subject to compliance with any and all regulations required by the respective agencies or other investors, subject to continuance of credit standing, income, employment and property appraisal and all additional documentation from the borrower, and is subject to final lender approval.

If you have any questions, please feel free to call me.

Sincerely,
John Doe
NMLS 11111
ABC Mortgage Company
123 Main Street
Anywhere, FL 22222

PH 555.555.5555
FAX 555.555.5555
johndoe@abcmortgagecompany.com

State-by-State Guidelines for the Real Estate Agent Exam

*T*o find the state-by-state guidelines for the real estate agent exam, navigate through **www.tests.com**.

For example, to see the guidelines for Alabama, the link is **www.tests.com/Alabama-Real-Estate-Agent-Exam**.

From this webpage, there is a list of every state's guidelines in the panel on the right-hand side of the page. To find your state, simply click the corresponding link.

Another option is to browse through Mortgage News Daily's website at **www.mortgagenewsdaily.com/real_estate_license**. From this page, there is also a panel on the right-hand side of the page that presents every state.

State Real Estate Commissions & Bureaus

Alabama Real Estate Commission
1201 Carmichael Way
Montgomery, AL 36106
(334) 242-5544
https://arec.alabama.gov

Alaska Real Estate Commission
Robert B. Atwood Building
550 West 7th Avenue #1500
Anchorage, AK 99501
(907) 269-8160
www.commerce.alaska.gov

Arizona Department of Real Estate
2910 N. 44th Street, Suite 100
Phoenix, AZ 85018
(602) 771 7799
www.re.state.az.us

Arkansas Real Estate Commission
612 South Summit Street
Little Rock, AR 72201-4740
(501) 683-8010
www.arec.arkansas.gov

California Bureau of Real Estate
1651 Exposition Blvd.
Sacramento, CA 95815
1 (877) 373-4542
www.dre.ca.gov

Colorado Department of
Regulatory Agencies
Division of Real Estate
1560 Broadway, Suite 925
Denver, CO 80202
(303) 894-2166
www.colorado.gov

Connecticut Department of
Consumer Protection
Real Estate Division
165 Capital Avenue
Hartford, CT 06106-1630
(860) 713-6100
www.ct.gov

Delaware Real Estate Commission
Cannon Building, Suite 203
861 Silver Lake Blvd.
Dover, DE 19904
(302) 744-4500
www.dpr.delaware.gov

Florida Real Estate Commission
Department of Business and
Professional Regulation
1940 North Monroe Street
Tallahassee, FL 32399-1027
(850) 487-1395
www.myfloridalicense.com

Georgia Real Estate Commission
229 Peachtree Street, N.E.
International Tower, Suite 1000
Atlanta, GA 30303-1605
(404) 656-3916
www.grec.state.ga.us

Hawaii Department of Commerce
and Consumer Affairs
Real Estate Branch
King Kalakaua Building

335 Merchant Street, Rm 333
Honolulu, HI 96813
(808) 586-2643
http://cca.hawaii.gov

Idaho Real Estate Commission
575 E. Parkcenter Blvd. Suite 180
Boise, ID 83706
(208) 334-3285
http://irec.idaho.gov

Illinois Department of Financial
and Professional Regulation
Division of Real Estate
320 West Washington Street,
3rd Floor
Springfield, IL 62786
1 (888) 473-4858
www.idfpr.com
Note: For Illinois, there is also a
Chicago office. Visit the website for
more information.

Professional Licensing Agency
Attn: Indiana Real Estate
Commission
402 W Washington Street,
Room W072
Indianapolis, IN 46204
www.in.gov

Professional Licensing Bureau
200 E Grand Ave #350
Des Moines, IA 50309

(515) 281-7393

http://plb.iowa.gov

Kansas Real Estate Commission
Three Townsite Plaza, Ste. 200
120 SE 6th Avenue
Topeka, KS 66603-3511
(785) 296-3411
www.kansas.gov

Kentucky Real Estate Commission
10200 Linn Station Read
Suite 201
Louisville, KY 40223
(502) 429-7250
http://krec.ky.gov

Louisiana Real Estate Commission
P.O. Box 14785
Baton Rouge, LA 70898-4785
(225) 925-1923
www.irec.state.la.us
Note: The physical address differs from the mailing address. Provided here is the mailing address. See the website for more information.

Maine Department of Professional
and Financial Regulation
Office of Professional and
Occupational Registration
35 State House Station
Augusta, Maine 04333-0035
(207) 624-8603
www.maine.gov

Note: The physical address differs from the mailing address. Provided here is the mailing address. See the website for more information.

Real Estate Commission
500 North Calvert Street
Baltimore, MD 21202
(410) 230-6200
www.dllr.state.md.us

Office of Consumer Affairs &
Business Regulation
Ten Park Plaza, Suite 5170
Boston, MA 02116
(617) 973-8700
www.mass.gov

Michigan Department of Licensing
and Regulatory Affairs
P.O. Box 30004
Lansing, MI 48909
(517) 373-1820
www.michigan.gov
Note: The physical address differs from the mailing address. Provided here is the mailing address. See the website for more information.

Minnesota Department of
Commerce
85 7th Place East
St. Paul, MN 55101
(651) 539-1600
http://mn.gov

Mississippi Real Estate Commission
P.O. Box 12685
Jackson, MS 39236
(601) 321-6970
www.mrec.ms.gov
Note: The physical address differs from the mailing address. Provided here is the mailing address. See the website for more information.

Missouri Division of Professional Registration
3605 Missouri Boulevard
P.O. Box 1335
Jefferson City, MO 65102-1335
(573) 751-0293
http://pr.mo.gov

Montana Board of Realty Regulation
301 South Park, 4th Floor
P.O. Box 200513
Helena, MT 59620-0513
(406) 841-2202
http://bsd.dli.mt.gov

Nebraska Real Estate Commission
301 Centennial Mall South
P.O. Box 94667
Lincoln, NE 68509-4667
(402) 471-2004
www.nrec.ne.gov

Department of Business and Industry
Nevada Real Estate Division
2501 E. Sahara Ave, Suite 102
Las Vegas, Nevada 89104
(702) 486-4033
http://red.nv.gov
Note: There is a second office located in Carson City. For more information, visit the website.

NH Real Estate Commission
121 South Fruit Street
Concord, NH 03301-2412
(603) 271-2219
www.nh.gov

NJ Real Estate Commission
P.O. Box 328
Trenton, NJ 08625-0328
(609) 292-7272
www.nj.gov
Note: The physical address differs from the mailing address. Provided here is the mailing address. See the website for more information.

New Mexico Real Estate Commission
5500 San Antonio Dr. NE Suite B
Albuquerque, New Mexico 87109
(505) 222-9820
www.rld.state.nm.us

Department of State
Division of Licensing Services
One Commerce Plaza, 99
Washington Ave
Albany, NY 12231-0001
(518) 474-4429
www.dos.ny.gov

North Carolina Real Estate
Commission
P.O. Box 17100
Raleigh, NC 27619-7100
(919) 875-3700
www.ncrec.gov
Note: The physical address differs from the mailing address. Provided here is the mailing address. See the website for more information.

Real Estate Commission
P.O. Box 727
Bismarck, ND 58502-0727
www.realestatend.org
Note: The physical address differs from the mailing address. Provided here is the mailing address. See the website for more information.

Ohio Department of Commerce
Division of Real Estate and
Professional Licensing
77 South High Street, 20th Floor
Columbus, OH 43215-6133
(614) 466-4100
www.com.ohio.gov

Oklahoma Real Estate
Commission
Denver N Davison Building
1915 N Stiles Ave, Suite 200
Oklahoma City, Oklahoma 73105
(405) 521-3387
www.ok.gov

Oregon Real Estate Agency
530 Center St NE Ste 100
Salem, OR 97301-3740
(503) 378-4170
www.oregon.gov

State Real Estate Commission
P.O. Box 2649
Harrisburg, PA 17105-2649
(717) 783-3658
www.dos.pa.gov
Note: The physical address differs from the mailing address. Provided here is the mailing address. See the website for more information.

Rhode Island Department of
Business Regulation
Division of Commercial Licensing
and Regulation Real Estate
1511 Pontiac Avenue
Cranston, RI 02920
(401) 462-9500
www.dbr.state.ri.us

South Carolina Department of
Labor Licensing and Regulation
Real Estate Commission
P.O. Box 11329
Columbia, SC 29211
(803) 896-4300
www.llronline.com
*Note: The physical address differs
from the mailing address. Provided
here is the mailing address. See the
website for more information.*

South Dakota Real Estate
Commission
221 W. Capital, Suite 101
Pierre, SD 57501
(605) 773-3600
http://dlr.sd.gov

Tennessee Department of
Commerce & Insurance
Real Estate Commission
500 James Robertson Parkway
Davy Crockett Tower
Nashville, TN 37243-0565
(615) 741-2241
www.tn.gov

Texas Real Estate Commission
P.O. Box 12188
Austin, TX 78711-2188
(512) 936-3000
www.trec.state.tx.us

*Note: The physical address differs
from the mailing address. Provided
here is the mailing address. See the
website for more information.*

Utah Division of Real Estate
P.O. Box 146711
Salt Lake City, UT 84114-6711
(801) 530-6747
http://realestate.utah.gov
*Note: The physical address differs
from the mailing address. Provided
here is the mailing address. See the
website for more information.*

Vermont Office of Professional
Regulation
128 State Street
Montpelier, VT 05633-1101
(802) 828-2363
www.sec.state.vt.us

Department of Professional and
Occupational Regulation
9960 Mayland Drive
Suite 400
Richmond, VA 23233-1485
(804) 367-8526
www.dpor.virginia.gov

Washington Real Estate Licensing
Department of Licensing
PO Box 3917
Seattle, WA 98124-3917

(360) 664-6488

www.dol.wa.gov

Note: The physical address differs from the mailing address. Provided here is the mailing address. See the website for more information.

West Virginia
Real Estate Commission
300 Capitol Street, Suite 400
Charleston, WV 25301
(304) 558-3555

www.wvrec.org

State of Wisconson
Department of Safety and
Professional Services
P.O. Box 8935
Madison, WI 53708-8935
(608) 266-2112

http://dsps.wi.gov

Note: The physical address differs from the mailing address. Provided here is the mailing address. See the website for more information.

Real Estate Commission
2617 E. Lincolnway, Suite H
Cheyenne, WY 82002
(307) 777-7141

http://realestate.wyo.gov

Uniform Appraisal Report

Typical Fannie Mae Appraisal Form #1004

Uniform Residential Appraisal Report

File #

The purpose of this summary appraisal report is to provide the lender/client with an accurate, and adequately supported, opinion of the market value of the subject property.

SUBJECT

Property Address		City		State	Zip Code
Borrower	Owner of Public Record			County	

Legal Description

Assessor's Parcel #   Tax Year   R.E. Taxes $

Neighborhood Name   Map Reference   Census Tract

Occupant ☐ Owner ☐ Tenant ☐ Vacant   Special Assessments $ ☐ PUD   HOA $ ☐ per year ☐ per month

Property Rights Appraised ☐ Fee Simple ☐ Leasehold ☐ Other (describe)

Assignment Type ☐ Purchase Transaction ☐ Refinance Transaction ☐ Other (describe)

Lender/Client   Address

Is the subject property currently offered for sale or has it been offered for sale in the twelve months prior to the effective date of this appraisal? ☐ Yes ☐ No

Report data source(s) used, offering price(s), and date(s).

CONTRACT

I ☐ did ☐ did not analyze the contract for sale for the subject purchase transaction. Explain the results of the analysis of the contract for sale or why the analysis was not performed.

Contract Price $ Date of Contract   Is the property seller the owner of public record? ☐ Yes ☐ No   Data Source(s)

Is there any financial assistance (loan charges, sale concessions, gift or downpayment assistance, etc.) to be paid by any party on behalf of the borrower? ☐ Yes ☐ No

If Yes, report the total dollar amount and describe the items to be paid.

NEIGHBORHOOD

Note: Race and the racial composition of the neighborhood are not appraisal factors.

Neighborhood Characteristics			One-Unit Housing Trends			One-Unit Housing		Present Land Use %	
Location ☐ Urban	☐ Suburban	☐ Rural	Property Values ☐ Increasing	☐ Stable	☐ Declining	PRICE	AGE	One-Unit	%
Built-Up ☐ Over 75%	☐ 25–75%	☐ Under 25%	Demand/Supply ☐ Shortage	☐ In Balance	☐ Over Supply	$ (000)	(yrs)	2-4 Unit	%
Growth ☐ Rapid	☐ Stable	☐ Slow	Marketing Time ☐ Under 3 mths	☐ 3–6 mths	☐ Over 6 mths	Low		Multi-Family	%
Neighborhood Boundaries						High		Commercial	%
						Pred.		Other	%

Neighborhood Description

Market Conditions (including support for the above conclusions)

SITE

Dimensions   Area   Shape   View

Specific Zoning Classification   Zoning Description

Zoning Compliance ☐ Legal ☐ Legal Nonconforming (Grandfathered Use) ☐ No Zoning ☐ Illegal (describe)

Is the highest and best use of the subject property as improved (or as proposed per plans and specifications) the present use? ☐ Yes ☐ No   If No, describe

Utilities	Public	Other (describe)		Public	Other (describe)	Off-site Improvements—Type	Public	Private
Electricity	☐	☐	Water	☐	☐	Street	☐	☐
Gas	☐	☐	Sanitary Sewer	☐	☐	Alley	☐	☐

FEMA Special Flood Hazard Area ☐ Yes ☐ No   FEMA Flood Zone   FEMA Map #   FEMA Map Date

Are the utilities and off-site improvements typical for the market area? ☐ Yes ☐ No   If No, describe

Are there any adverse site conditions or external factors (easements, encroachments, environmental conditions, land uses, etc.)? ☐ Yes ☐ No   If Yes, describe

IMPROVEMENTS

General Description	Foundation	Exterior Description materials/condition	Interior materials/condition
Units ☐ One ☐ One with Accessory Unit	☐ Concrete Slab ☐ Crawl Space	Foundation Walls	Floors
# of Stories	☐ Full Basement ☐ Partial Basement	Exterior Walls	Walls
Type ☐ Det. ☐ Att. ☐ S-Det./End Unit	Basement Area sq. ft.	Roof Surface	Trim/Finish
☐ Existing ☐ Proposed ☐ Under Const.	Basement Finish %	Gutters & Downspouts	Bath Floor
Design (Style)	☐ Outside Entry/Exit ☐ Sump Pump	Window Type	Bath Wainscot
Year Built	Evidence of ☐ Infestation	Storm Sash/Insulated	Car Storage ☐ None
Effective Age (Yrs)	☐ Dampness ☐ Settlement	Screens	☐ Driveway # of Cars
Attic ☐ None	Heating ☐ FWA ☐ HWBB ☐ Radiant	Amenities ☐ Woodstove(s) #	Driveway Surface
☐ Drop Stair ☐ Stairs	☐ Other Fuel	☐ Fireplace(s) # ☐ Fence	☐ Garage # of Cars
☐ Floor ☐ Scuttle	Cooling ☐ Central Air Conditioning	☐ Patio/Deck ☐ Porch	☐ Carport # of Cars
☐ Finished ☐ Heated	☐ Individual ☐ Other	☐ Pool ☐ Other	☐ Att. ☐ Det. ☐ Built-in

Appliances ☐ Refrigerator ☐ Range/Oven ☐ Dishwasher ☐ Disposal ☐ Microwave ☐ Washer/Dryer ☐ Other (describe)

Finished area above grade contains: Rooms   Bedrooms   Bath(s)   Square Feet of Gross Living Area Above Grade

Additional features (special energy efficient items, etc.)

Describe the condition of the property (including needed repairs, deterioration, renovations, remodeling, etc.).

Are there any physical deficiencies or adverse conditions that affect the livability, soundness, or structural integrity of the property? ☐ Yes ☐ No   If Yes, describe

Does the property generally conform to the neighborhood (functional utility, style, condition, use, construction, etc.)? ☐ Yes ☐ No   If No, describe

Typical Fannie Mae Appraisal Form #1004

Uniform Residential Appraisal Report

File #

There are ____ comparable properties currently offered for sale in the subject neighborhood ranging in price from $ ____			to $ ____	
There are ____ comparable sales in the subject neighborhood within the past twelve months ranging in sale price from $ ____			to $ ____	

FEATURE	SUBJECT	COMPARABLE SALE #1	COMPARABLE SALE #2	COMPARABLE SALE #3
Address				
Proximity to Subject				
Sale Price	$	$	$	$
Sale Price/Gross Liv. Area	$ sq. ft.	$ sq. ft.	$ sq. ft.	$ sq. ft.
Data Source(s)				
Verification Source(s)				

VALUE ADJUSTMENTS	DESCRIPTION	DESCRIPTION	+(-) $ Adjustment	DESCRIPTION	+(-) $ Adjustment	DESCRIPTION	+(-) $ Adjustment
Sale or Financing Concessions							
Date of Sale/Time							
Location							
Leasehold/Fee Simple							
Site							
View							
Design (Style)							
Quality of Construction							
Actual Age							
Condition							
Above Grade Room Count	Total	Bdrms.	Baths	Total	Bdrms.	Baths	Total	Bdrms.	Baths	Total	Bdrms.	Baths
Gross Living Area	sq. ft.	sq. ft.	sq. ft.	sq. ft.
Basement & Finished Rooms Below Grade							
Functional Utility							
Heating/Cooling							
Energy Efficient Items							
Garage/Carport							
Porch/Patio/Deck							
Net Adjustment (Total)		☐ + ☐ -	$	☐ + ☐ -	$	☐ + ☐ -	$
Adjusted Sale Price of Comparables		Net Adj. % Gross Adj. %	$	Net Adj. % Gross Adj. %	$	Net Adj. % Gross Adj. %	$

I ☐ did ☐ did not research the sale or transfer history of the subject property and comparable sales. If not, explain

My research ☐ did ☐ did not reveal any prior sales or transfers of the subject property for the three years prior to the effective date of this appraisal.
Data source(s)
My research ☐ did ☐ did not reveal any prior sales or transfers of the comparable sales for the year prior to the date of sale of the comparable sale.
Data source(s)
Report the results of the research and analysis of the prior sale or transfer history of the subject property and comparable sales (report additional prior sales on page 3).

ITEM	SUBJECT	COMPARABLE SALE #1	COMPARABLE SALE #2	COMPARABLE SALE #3
Date of Prior Sale/Transfer				
Price of Prior Sale/Transfer				
Data Source(s)				
Effective Date of Data Source(s)				

Analysis of prior sale or transfer history of the subject property and comparable sales

Summary of Sales Comparison Approach

Indicated Value by Sales Comparison Approach $

Indicated Value by: Sales Comparison Approach $	Cost Approach (if developed) $	Income Approach (if developed) $

This appraisal is made ☐ "as is", ☐ subject to completion per plans and specifications on the basis of a hypothetical condition that the improvements have been completed, ☐ subject to the following repairs or alterations on the basis of a hypothetical condition that the repairs or alterations have been completed, or ☐ subject to the following required inspection based on the extraordinary assumption that the condition or deficiency does not require alteration or repair:

Based on a complete visual inspection of the interior and exterior areas of the subject property, defined scope of work, statement of assumptions and limiting conditions, and appraiser's certification, my (our) opinion of the market value, as defined, of the real property that is the subject of this report is
$ ____ , as of ____ , which is the date of inspection and the effective date of this appraisal.

Freddie Mac Form 70 March 2005	Page 2 of 6	Fannie Mae Form 1004 March 2005

Typical Fannie Mae Appraisal Form #1004

Uniform Residential Appraisal Report

File #

A D D I T I O N A L   C O M M E N T S

COST APPROACH TO VALUE (not required by Fannie Mae)

Provide adequate information for the lender/client to replicate the below cost figures and calculations.

Support for the opinion of site value (summary of comparable land sales or other methods for estimating site value)

C O S T   A P P R O A C H

ESTIMATED ☐ REPRODUCTION OR ☐ REPLACEMENT COST NEW	OPINION OF SITE VALUE	= $
Source of cost data	Dwelling Sq. Ft. @ $	=$
Quality rating from cost service Effective date of cost data	Sq. Ft. @ $	=$
Comments on Cost Approach (gross living area calculations, depreciation, etc.)		
	Garage/Carport Sq. Ft. @ $	=$
	Total Estimate of Cost-New	= $
	Less Physical	Functional	External	
	Depreciation	=$( )
	Depreciated Cost of Improvements	=$
	"As-is" Value of Site Improvements	=$
Estimated Remaining Economic Life (HUD and VA only) Years	Indicated Value By Cost Approach	=$

INCOME APPROACH TO VALUE (not required by Fannie Mae)

I N C O M E

Estimated Monthly Market Rent $ X Gross Rent Multiplier   = $ Indicated Value by Income Approach

Summary of Income Approach (including support for market rent and GRM)

PROJECT INFORMATION FOR PUDs (if applicable)

P U D   I N F O R M A T I O N

Is the developer/builder in control of the Homeowners' Association (HOA)? ☐ Yes ☐ No   Unit type(s) ☐ Detached ☐ Attached

Provide the following information for PUDs ONLY if the developer/builder is in control of the HOA and the subject property is an attached dwelling unit.

Legal name of project

Total number of phases   Total number of units   Total number of units sold

Total number of units rented   Total number of units for sale   Data source(s)

Was the project created by the conversion of an existing building(s) into a PUD? ☐ Yes ☐ No If Yes, date of conversion

Does the project contain any multi-dwelling units? ☐ Yes ☐ No Data source(s)

Are the units, common elements, and recreation facilities complete? ☐ Yes ☐ No If No, describe the status of completion.

Are the common elements leased to or by the Homeowners' Association? ☐ Yes ☐ No If Yes, describe the rental terms and options.

Describe common elements and recreational facilities

Freddie Mac Form 70 March 2005	Page 3 of 6	Fannie Mae Form 1004 March 2005

Typical Fannie Mae Appraisal Form #1004

Uniform Residential Appraisal Report   File

This report form is designed to report an appraisal of a one-unit property or a one-unit property with an accessory unit; including a unit in a planned unit development (PUD). This report form is not designed to report an appraisal of a manufactured home or a unit in a condominium or cooperative project.

This appraisal report is subject to the following scope of work, intended use, intended user, definition of market value, statement of assumptions and limiting conditions, and certifications. Modifications, additions, or deletions to the intended use, intended user, definition of market value, or assumptions and limiting conditions are not permitted. The appraiser may expand the scope of work to include any additional research or analysis necessary based on the complexity of this appraisal assignment. Modifications or deletions to the certifications are also not permitted. However, additional certifications that do not constitute material alterations to this appraisal report, such as those required by law or those related to the appraiser's continuing education or membership in an appraisal organization, are permitted.

SCOPE OF WORK: The scope of work for this appraisal is defined by the complexity of this appraisal assignment and the reporting requirements of this appraisal report form, including the following definition of market value, statement of assumptions and limiting conditions, and certifications. The appraiser must, at a minimum: (1) perform a complete visual inspection of the interior and exterior areas of the subject property, (2) inspect the neighborhood, (3) inspect each of the comparable sales from at least the street, (4) research, verify, and analyze data from reliable public and/or private sources, and (5) report his or her analysis, opinions, and conclusions in this appraisal report.

INTENDED USE: The intended use of this appraisal report is for the lender/client to evaluate the property that is the subject of this appraisal for a mortgage finance transaction.

INTENDED USER: The intended user of this appraisal report is the lender/client.

DEFINITION OF MARKET VALUE: The most probable price which a property should bring in a competitive and open market under all conditions requisite to a fair sale, the buyer and seller, each acting prudently, knowledgeably and assuming the price is not affected by undue stimulus. Implicit in this definition is the consummation of a sale as of a specified date and the passing of title from seller to buyer under conditions whereby: (1) buyer and seller are typically motivated; (2) both parties are well informed or well advised, and each acting in what he or she considers his or her own best interest; (3) a reasonable time is allowed for exposure in the open market; (4) payment is made in terms of cash in U. S. dollars or in terms of financial arrangements comparable thereto; and (5) the price represents the normal consideration for the property sold unaffected by special or creative financing or sales concessions* granted by anyone associated with the sale.

*Adjustments to the comparables must be made for special or creative financing or sales concessions. No adjustments are necessary for those costs which are normally paid by sellers as a result of tradition or law in a market area; these costs are readily identifiable since the seller pays these costs in virtually all sales transactions. Special or creative financing adjustments can be made to the comparable property by comparisons to financing terms offered by a third party institutional lender that is not already involved in the property or transaction. Any adjustment should not be calculated on a mechanical dollar for dollar cost of the financing or concession but the dollar amount of any adjustment should approximate the market's reaction to the financing or concessions based on the appraiser's judgment.

STATEMENT OF ASSUMPTIONS AND LIMITING CONDITIONS: The appraiser's certification in this report is subject to the following assumptions and limiting conditions:

1. The appraiser will not be responsible for matters of a legal nature that affect either the property being appraised or the title to it, except for information that he or she became aware of during the research involved in performing this appraisal. The appraiser assumes that the title is good and marketable and will not render any opinions about the title.

2. The appraiser has provided a sketch in this appraisal report to show the approximate dimensions of the improvements. The sketch is included only to assist the reader in visualizing the property and understanding the appraiser's determination of its size.

3. The appraiser has examined the available flood maps that are provided by the Federal Emergency Management Agency (or other data sources) and has noted in this appraisal report whether any portion of the subject site is located in an identified Special Flood Hazard Area. Because the appraiser is not a surveyor, he or she makes no guarantees, express or implied, regarding this determination.

4. The appraiser will not give testimony or appear in court because he or she made an appraisal of the property in question, unless specific arrangements to do so have been made beforehand, or as otherwise required by law.

5. The appraiser has noted in this appraisal report any adverse conditions (such as needed repairs, deterioration, the presence of hazardous wastes, toxic substances, etc.) observed during the inspection of the subject property or that he or she became aware of during the research involved in performing this appraisal. Unless otherwise stated in this appraisal report, the appraiser has no knowledge of any hidden or unapparent physical deficiencies or adverse conditions of the property (such as, but not limited to, needed repairs, deterioration, the presence of hazardous wastes, toxic substances, adverse environmental conditions, etc.) that would make the property less valuable, and has assumed that there are no such conditions and makes no guarantees or warranties, express or implied. The appraiser will not be responsible for any such conditions that do exist or for any engineering or testing that might be required to discover whether such conditions exist. Because the appraiser is not an expert in the field of environmental hazards, this appraisal report must not be considered as an environmental assessment of the property.

6. The appraiser has based his or her appraisal report and valuation conclusion for an appraisal that is subject to satisfactory completion, repairs, or alterations on the assumption that the completion, repairs, or alterations of the subject property will be performed in a professional manner.

Typical Fannie Mae Appraisal Form #1004

Uniform Residential Appraisal Report

File #

APPRAISER'S CERTIFICATION: The Appraiser certifies and agrees that:

1. I have, at a minimum, developed and reported this appraisal in accordance with the scope of work requirements stated in this appraisal report.

2. I performed a complete visual inspection of the interior and exterior areas of the subject property. I reported the condition of the improvements in factual, specific terms. I identified and reported the physical deficiencies that could affect the livability, soundness, or structural integrity of the property.

3. I performed this appraisal in accordance with the requirements of the Uniform Standards of Professional Appraisal Practice that were adopted and promulgated by the Appraisal Standards Board of The Appraisal Foundation and that were in place at the time this appraisal report was prepared.

4. I developed my opinion of the market value of the real property that is the subject of this report based on the sales comparison approach to value. I have adequate comparable market data to develop a reliable sales comparison approach for this appraisal assignment. I further certify that I considered the cost and income approaches to value but did not develop them, unless otherwise indicated in this report.

5. I researched, verified, analyzed, and reported on any current agreement for sale for the subject property, any offering for sale of the subject property in the twelve months prior to the effective date of this appraisal, and the prior sales of the subject property for a minimum of three years prior to the effective date of this appraisal, unless otherwise indicated in this report.

6. I researched, verified, analyzed, and reported on the prior sales of the comparable sales for a minimum of one year prior to the date of sale of the comparable sale, unless otherwise indicated in this report.

7. I selected and used comparable sales that are locationally, physically, and functionally the most similar to the subject property.

8. I have not used comparable sales that were the result of combining a land sale with the contract purchase price of a home that has been built or will be built on the land.

9. I have reported adjustments to the comparable sales that reflect the market's reaction to the differences between the subject property and the comparable sales.

10. I verified, from a disinterested source, all information in this report that was provided by parties who have a financial interest in the sale or financing of the subject property.

11. I have knowledge and experience in appraising this type of property in this market area.

12. I am aware of, and have access to, the necessary and appropriate public and private data sources, such as multiple listing services, tax assessment records, public land records and other such data sources for the area in which the property is located.

13. I obtained the information, estimates, and opinions furnished by other parties and expressed in this appraisal report from reliable sources that I believe to be true and correct.

14. I have taken into consideration the factors that have an impact on value with respect to the subject neighborhood, subject property, and the proximity of the subject property to adverse influences in the development of my opinion of market value. I have noted in this appraisal report any adverse conditions (such as, but not limited to, needed repairs, deterioration, the presence of hazardous wastes, toxic substances, adverse environmental conditions, etc.) observed during the inspection of the subject property or that I became aware of during the research involved in performing this appraisal. I have considered these adverse conditions in my analysis of the property value, and have reported on the effect of the conditions on the value and marketability of the subject property.

15. I have not knowingly withheld any significant information from this appraisal report and, to the best of my knowledge, all statements and information in this appraisal report are true and correct.

16. I stated in this appraisal report my own personal, unbiased, and professional analysis, opinions, and conclusions, which are subject only to the assumptions and limiting conditions in this appraisal report.

17. I have no present or prospective interest in the property that is the subject of this report, and I have no present or prospective personal interest or bias with respect to the participants in the transaction. I did not base, either partially or completely, my analysis and/or opinion of market value in this appraisal report on the race, color, religion, sex, age, marital status, handicap, familial status, or national origin of either the prospective owners or occupants of the subject property or of the present owners or occupants of the properties in the vicinity of the subject property or on any other basis prohibited by law.

18. My employment and/or compensation for performing this appraisal or any future or anticipated appraisals was not conditioned on any agreement or understanding, written or otherwise, that I would report (or present analysis supporting) a predetermined specific value, a predetermined minimum value, a range or direction in value, a value that favors the cause of any party, or the attainment of a specific result or occurrence of a specific subsequent event (such as approval of a pending mortgage loan application).

19. I personally prepared all conclusions and opinions about the real estate that were set forth in this appraisal report. If I relied on significant real property appraisal assistance from any individual or individuals in the performance of this appraisal or the preparation of this appraisal report, I have named such individual(s) and disclosed the specific tasks performed in this appraisal report. I certify that any individual so named is qualified to perform the tasks. I have not authorized anyone to make a change to any item in this appraisal report; therefore, any change made to this appraisal is unauthorized and I will take no responsibility for it.

20. I identified the lender/client in this appraisal report who is the individual, organization, or agent for the organization that ordered and will receive this appraisal report.

Freddie Mac Form 70 March 2005   Page 5 of 6   Fannie Mae Form 1004 March 2005

Typical Fannie Mae Appraisal Form #1004

Uniform Residential Appraisal Report

File #

21. The lender/client may disclose or distribute this appraisal report to: the borrower; another lender at the request of the borrower; the mortgagee or its successors and assigns; mortgage insurers; government sponsored enterprises; other secondary market participants; data collection or reporting services; professional appraisal organizations; any department, agency, or instrumentality of the United States; and any state, the District of Columbia, or other jurisdictions; without having to obtain the appraiser's or supervisory appraiser's (if applicable) consent. Such consent must be obtained before this appraisal report may be disclosed or distributed to any other party (including, but not limited to, the public through advertising, public relations, news, sales, or other media).

22. I am aware that any disclosure or distribution of this appraisal report by me or the lender/client may be subject to certain laws and regulations. Further, I am also subject to the provisions of the Uniform Standards of Professional Appraisal Practice that pertain to disclosure or distribution by me.

23. The borrower, another lender at the request of the borrower, the mortgagee or its successors and assigns, mortgage insurers, government sponsored enterprises, and other secondary market participants may rely on this appraisal report as part of any mortgage finance transaction that involves any one or more of these parties.

24. If this appraisal report was transmitted as an "electronic record" containing my "electronic signature," as those terms are defined in applicable federal and/or state laws (excluding audio and video recordings), or a facsimile transmission of this appraisal report containing a copy or representation of my signature, the appraisal report shall be as effective, enforceable and valid as if a paper version of this appraisal report were delivered containing my original hand written signature.

25. Any intentional or negligent misrepresentation(s) contained in this appraisal report may result in civil liability and/or criminal penalties including, but not limited to, fine or imprisonment or both under the provisions of Title 18, United States Code, Section 1001, et seq., or similar state laws.

SUPERVISORY APPRAISER'S CERTIFICATION: The Supervisory Appraiser certifies and agrees that:

1. I directly supervised the appraiser for this appraisal assignment, have read the appraisal report, and agree with the appraiser's analysis, opinions, statements, conclusions, and the appraiser's certification.

2. I accept full responsibility for the contents of this appraisal report including, but not limited to, the appraiser's analysis, opinions, statements, conclusions, and the appraiser's certification.

3. The appraiser identified in this appraisal report is either a sub-contractor or an employee of the supervisory appraiser (or the appraisal firm), is qualified to perform this appraisal, and is acceptable to perform this appraisal under the applicable state law.

4. This appraisal report complies with the Uniform Standards of Professional Appraisal Practice that were adopted and promulgated by the Appraisal Standards Board of The Appraisal Foundation and that were in place at the time this appraisal report was prepared.

5. If this appraisal report was transmitted as an "electronic record" containing my "electronic signature," as those terms are defined in applicable federal and/or state laws (excluding audio and video recordings), or a facsimile transmission of this appraisal report containing a copy or representation of my signature, the appraisal report shall be as effective, enforceable and valid as if a paper version of this appraisal report were delivered containing my original hand written signature.

APPRAISER

Signature_____
Name _____
Company Name _____
Company Address_____

Telephone Number _____
Email Address_____
Date of Signature and Report_____
Effective Date of Appraisal _____
State Certification #_____
or State License #_____
or Other (describe) _____ State # _____
State _____
Expiration Date of Certification or License _____

ADDRESS OF PROPERTY APPRAISED

_____
_____
APPRAISED VALUE OF SUBJECT PROPERTY $ _____
LENDER/CLIENT
Name _____
Company Name _____
Company Address_____
_____
Email Address_____

SUPERVISORY APPRAISER (ONLY IF REQUIRED)

Signature _____
Name_____
Company Name _____
Company Address_____
_____
Telephone Number _____
Email Address _____
Date of Signature _____
State Certification #_____
or State License # _____
State _____
Expiration Date of Certification or License _____

SUBJECT PROPERTY

☐ Did not inspect subject property
☐ Did inspect exterior of subject property from street
Date of Inspection _____
☐ Did inspect interior and exterior of subject property
Date of Inspection _____

COMPARABLE SALES

☐ Did not inspect exterior of comparable sales from street
☐ Did inspect exterior of comparable sales from street
Date of Inspection _____

Sample Good Faith Estimate

OMB Approval No. 2502-0265

Good Faith Estimate (GFE)

Name of Originator	Borrower
Originator Address	Property Address
Originator Phone Number	
Originator Email	Date of GFE

Purpose

This GFE gives you an estimate of your settlement charges and loan terms if you are approved for this loan. For more information, see HUD's *Special Information Booklet* on settlement charges, your *Truth-in-Lending Disclosures*, and other consumer information at www.hud.gov/respa. If you decide you would like to proceed with this loan, contact us.

Shopping for your loan

Only you can shop for the best loan for you. Compare this GFE with other loan offers, so you can find the best loan. Use the shopping chart on page 3 to compare all the offers you receive.

Important dates

1. The interest rate for this GFE is available through [   ]. After this time, the interest rate, some of your loan Origination Charges, and the monthly payment shown below can change until you lock your interest rate.

2. This estimate for all other settlement charges is available through [   ].

3. After you lock your interest rate, you must go to settlement within [ ] days (your rate lock period) to receive the locked interest rate.

4. You must lock the interest rate at least [ ] days before settlement.

Summary of your loan

Your initial loan amount is	$
Your loan term is	years
Your initial interest rate is	%
Your initial monthly amount owed for principal, interest, and any mortgage insurance is	$ per month
Can your interest rate rise?	☐ No ☐ Yes, it can rise to a maximum of %. The first change will be in
Even if you make payments on time, can your loan balance rise?	☐ No ☐ Yes, it can rise to a maximum of $
Even if you make payments on time, can your monthly amount owed for principal, interest, and any mortgage insurance rise?	☐ No ☐ Yes, the first increase can be in and the monthly amount owed can rise to $. The maximum it can ever rise to is $
Does your loan have a prepayment penalty?	☐ No ☐ Yes, your maximum prepayment penalty is $
Does your loan have a balloon payment?	☐ No ☐ Yes, you have a balloon payment of $ due in years.

Escrow account information

Some lenders require an escrow account to hold funds for paying property taxes or other property-related charges in addition to your monthly amount owed of $ [   ].
Do we require you to have an escrow account for your loan?
☐ No, you do not have an escrow account. You must pay these charges directly when due.
☐ Yes, you have an escrow account. It may or may not cover all of these charges. Ask us.

Summary of your settlement charges

A	Your Adjusted Origination Charges (See page 2)	$
B	Your Charges for All Other Settlement Services (See page 2)	$
A + B	Total Estimated Settlement Charges	$

Understanding your estimated settlement charges

Some of these charges can change at settlement. See the top of page 3 for more information.

Your Adjusted Origination Charges

1. Our origination charge
This charge is for getting this loan for you.

2. Your credit or charge (points) for the specific interest rate chosen

☐ The credit or charge for the interest rate of ⬚ % is included in "Our origination charge." (See item 1 above.)

☐ You receive a credit of $⬚ for this interest rate of ⬚ %. This credit **reduces** your settlement charges.

☐ You pay a charge of $⬚ for this interest rate of ⬚ %. This charge (points) **increases** your total settlement charges.

The tradeoff table on page 3 shows that you can change your total settlement charges by choosing a different interest rate for this loan.

A Your Adjusted Origination Charges — $

Your Charges for All Other Settlement Services

3. Required services that we select
These charges are for services we require to complete your settlement. We will choose the providers of these services.

Service	Charge

4. Title services and lender's title insurance
This charge includes the services of a title or settlement agent, for example, and title insurance to protect the lender, if required.

5. Owner's title insurance
You may purchase an owner's title insurance policy to protect your interest in the property.

6. Required services that you can shop for
These charges are for other services that are required to complete your settlement. We can identify providers of these services or you can shop for them yourself. Our estimates for providing these services are below.

Service	Charge

7. Government recording charges
These charges are for state and local fees to record your loan and title documents.

8. Transfer taxes
These charges are for state and local fees on mortgages and home sales.

9. Initial deposit for your escrow account
This charge is held in an escrow account to pay future recurring charges on your property and includes ☐ all property taxes, ☐ all insurance, and ☐ other ⬚

10. Daily interest charges
This charge is for the daily interest on your loan from the day of your settlement until the first day of the next month or the first day of your normal mortgage payment cycle. This amount is $⬚ per day for ⬚ days (if your settlement is ⬚).

11. Homeowner's insurance
This charge is for the insurance you must buy for the property to protect from a loss, such as fire.

Policy	Charge

B Your Charges for All Other Settlement Services — $

A + B Total Estimated Settlement Charges — $

Good Faith Estimate (HUD-GFE) 2

Instructions

Understanding which charges can change at settlement

This GFE estimates your settlement charges. At your settlement, you will receive a HUD-1, a form that lists your actual costs. Compare the charges on the HUD-1 with the charges on this GFE. Charges can change if you select your own provider and do not use the companies we identify. (See below for details.)

These charges **cannot increase** at settlement:	The total of these charges **can increase up to 10%** at settlement:	These charges **can change** at settlement:
<ul><li>Our origination charge</li><li>Your credit or charge (points) for the specific interest rate chosen (after you lock in your interest rate)</li><li>Your adjusted origination charges (after you lock in your interest rate)</li><li>Transfer taxes</li></ul>	<ul><li>Required services that we select</li><li>Title services and lender's title insurance (if we select them or you use companies we identify)</li><li>Owner's title insurance (if you use companies we identify)</li><li>Required services that you can shop for (if you use companies we identify)</li><li>Government recording charges</li></ul>	<ul><li>Required services that you can shop for (if you do not use companies we identify)</li><li>Title services and lender's title insurance (if you do not use companies we identify)</li><li>Owner's title insurance (if you do not use companies we identify)</li><li>Initial deposit for your escrow account</li><li>Daily interest charges</li><li>Homeowner's insurance</li></ul>

Using the tradeoff table

In this GFE, we offered you this loan with a particular interest rate and estimated settlement charges. However:

- If you want to choose this same loan with **lower settlement charges,** then you will have a **higher interest rate.**
- If you want to choose this same loan with a **lower interest rate,** then you will have **higher settlement charges.**

If you would like to choose an available option, you must ask us for a new GFE.

Loan originators have the option to complete this table. Please ask for additional information if the table is not completed.

	The loan in this GFE	The same loan with lower settlement charges	The same loan with a lower interest rate
Your initial loan amount	$	$	$
Your initial interest rate[1]	%	%	%
Your initial monthly amount owed	$	$	$
Change in the monthly amount owed from this GFE	No change	You will pay $ **more** every month	You will pay $ **less** every month
Change in the amount you will pay at settlement with this interest rate	No change	Your settlement charges will be **reduced** by $	Your settlement charges will **increase** by $
How much your total estimated settlement charges will be	$	$	$

[1] For an adjustable rate loan, the comparisons above are for the initial interest rate before adjustments are made.

Using the shopping chart

Use this chart to compare GFEs from different loan originators. Fill in the information by using a different column for each GFE you receive. By comparing loan offers, you can shop for the best loan.

	This loan	Loan 2	Loan 3	Loan 4
Loan originator name				
Initial loan amount				
Loan term				
Initial interest rate				
Initial monthly amount owed				
Rate lock period				
Can interest rate rise?				
Can loan balance rise?				
Can monthly amount owed rise?				
Prepayment penalty?				
Balloon payment?				
Total Estimated Settlement Charges				

If your loan is sold in the future

Some lenders may sell your loan after settlement. Any fees lenders receive in the future cannot change the loan you receive or the charges you paid at settlement.

 Good Faith Estimate (HUD-GFE) 3

Acronyms

ACM: Asbestos Containing Materials

ADA: Americans with Disabilities Act

APR: Annual Percentage Rate

ARM: Adjustable-Rate Mortgages

AVM: Automated Valuation Model

BPO: Broker Price Opinion

CAM: Common Area Maintenance

CBA: Controlled Business Arrangement

CLO: Computerized Loan Origination

CMA: Comparative/Competitive Market Analysis

CO: Certificate of Occupancy

CPA: Certified Public Accountant

CPI: Consumer Price Index

CTC: Clear to Close

DBA: Doing Business As

DTI: Debt-to-Income Ratio

EPA: Environmental Protection Agency

FCRA: Fair Credit Reporting Act

FDIC: Federal Deposit Insurance Corporation

FEMA: Federal Emergency Management Agency

FHA: Federal Housing Administration (not to be confused with the Federal Housing Authority)

FHLMC: Federal Home Loan Mortgage Corporation

FNMA: Federal National Mortgage Association

FSBO: For Sale By Owner

GFE: Good Faith Estimate

GNMA: Government National Mortgage Association

GRI: Graduate, REALTOR® Institute

GRM: Gross Rent Multiplier

HECM: Home Equity Conversion Mortgage

HELOC: Home Equity Lines of Credit

HER: Housing Expense Ratio

HOA: Homeowners Association

HUD: Department of Housing and Urban Development

HVAC: Heating, Ventilating and Air Conditioning

IBC: International Building Code

LCD: Lowest Common Denominator

LIBOR: London InterBank Offered Rate

LTV: Loan-to-Value Ratio

MGIC: Mortgage Guaranty Insurance Corporation

MI: Mortgage Insurance

MIP: Mortgage Insurance Premium

MLS: Multiple Listing Service

NAR: National Association of REALTORS®

NNN: Net lease, or triple net lease

NOI: Net Operating Income

P&I: Principal and Interest

P&S Agreement: Purchase and Sale Agreement

PITI: Principal, Interest, Taxes, Insurance

PMI: Private Mortgage Insurance

POC: Paid Outside Closing

PUD: Planned Unit Development

REIT: Real Estate Investment Trust

REO: Real Estate Owned

RESPA: Real Estate Settlement Procedures Act

RFP: Request for Proposal

ROI: Return on Investment

TI: Tenant Improvement

TILA: Truth in Lending Act

TSO: Timeshare Ownership Plan

URAR: Uniform Residential Appraisal Report

VA: Department of Veterans Affairs

VOD: Verification of Deposit

VOE: Verification of Employment

Bibliography

"Assessing Civil Penalties for Fair Housing Act Cases." *Legal Information Institute.* Cornell University, 18 Jan. 2013. Web. 29 Jan. 2016.

"US Existing Single-Family Home Median Sales Price: November 2015." YCharts, 2015. Web. 29 Jan. 2016.

Gleason, Laura. "The New Dollar Threshold for Regulation Z Coverage." *Consumer Compliance Outlook.* Federal Reserve System, 2011. Web. 29 Jan. 2016.

http://www.homequitybuilder.info. Brentwood, NH: Ken Lambert Mortgage Enterprises LLC, 2008.

James Peter Regan. *Massachusetts Real Estate Principles and Practices.* Melrose, MA: North Shore Press, 2004. Print.

Real Estate Sales Exam. 2nd ed. New York: Learning Express LLC, 2007. Print.

Zibel, Alan, and Annamaria Andriotis. "Lenders Step Up Financing to Subprime Borrowers." *WSJ.* Dow Jones & Company, 18 Feb. 2015. Web. 29 Jan. 2016.

Index

A

Appraisal process, 142, 8

B

Bilateral, 36, 37, 226, 281

Bill of sale , 53, 85, 269

Breach of contract, 53, 270, 299

Buyer agency, 36, 66, 70, 224, 225

C

Chain of title, 58, 275, 301, 305, 357

Comparative market analysis, 136, 216, 217, 279

Computerized Loan Origination, 393, 111, 207, 236, 7

Controlled Business Arrangement, 393, 110, 281, 7

Credit Unions, 127, 128, 8

D

Debt-to-Income Ratio, 394, 101, 117, 132, 284

Destruction of property, 69, 86, 7

Disposition, 33, 348

E

Encumbrances, 68, 256, 268, 276, 299, 300, 357, 360

Escheat, 33, 59

Equity of redemption, 32, 180, 291

F

Federal Fair Housing Law, 87, 7

Federal Home Loan Mortgage Corporation, 394, 102, 295

Federal Housing Administration, 394, 87, 102, 295, 296

Federal National Mortgage Association, 394, 102, 295, 296

G

Good Faith Estimate, 389, 394, 90, 103, 187, 302, 10

Gross Lease, 62, 212, 213, 351

L

Land contracts, 129, 283, 8

Lease purchase, 62, 315, 316

License law, 79, 338, 7

Loan-To-Value Ratio, 395, 102, 104, 117, 318

Loan process, 116, 7

M

Multiple Listing Service, 395, 67, 70, 87, 323, 327, 333, 352, 6

P

Percentage lease, 62, 185, 213, 231, 237, 330

Planned Unit Development, 395, 105, 218, 278, 332

Private Mortgage Insurance, 395, 104, 106, 308, 311, 335

Q

Quitclaim deed, 55, 182, 276, 337

R

Real Estate Settlement Procedures Act, 395, 90, 107, 338

Regulation Z, 397, 89-91, 341, 7

Right of first refusal, 36, 63, 86

Right of rescission, 90, 92, 7

S

Scarcity, 32, 139, 346, 347

Statute of limitations, 38, 187, 317, 351

Strategies, 19, 23, 69, 70, 247, 343, 2, 5, 6

T

Taxation, 34, 170, 216, 265, 316, 9

Triple net lease, 395, 61, 212, 359

Truth in Lending Act, 396, 89, 282, 341, 7

U

Unilateral, 36, 37, 69, 281

V

Valid contract, 39, 200, 327, 361, 363

Z

Zoning ordinance, 34, 325, 367